The Arising Mountain

An Expedition to The Lord's Coming Summit

Clifford A. Jennings

CubitHound Publishing
Highland, Maryland 20777

Verses marked NASB are taken from the New American Standard Bible®. ©1960, 1962, 1963, 1968, 1971, 1973, 1975, 1977, 1995 by the Lockman Foundation.

Verses marked NIV are taken from The Holy Bible, New International Version®. ©1973, 1978, 1984, 2011 by the International Bible Society. Quotes here are taken from the 1984 version.

Verses marked KJV are taken from the King James Version of the Bible, while those marked ASV are from the Authorized Standard Version of the Bible.

Citations marked ISBE are taken from the International Standard Bible Encyclopedia. James Orr, editor, Grand Rapids, MI: Eerdmans Publishing Company, 1939. Citations marked "Strong's" are taken from The New Strong's Exhaustive Concordance of the Bible, James Strong, editor, Nashville, TN: Thomas Nelson Publishers, 1990; first published 1890.

References to "The Approaching Country" are to the prior (and companion) book by that name, by this author. See Bibliography.

Cover art by Leah Rose Jennings.

All illustrations (with the exception of certain backgrounds or other elements as explained in footnotes) are by the author. Color & higher-resolution versions of all figures are available for download on www.EarthAwaits.com.

The Arising Mountain
An Expedition to the Lord's Coming Summit

Copyright © 2017 by Clifford Allen Jennings
Published by CubitHound Publishing, Highland, MD 20777
www.EarthAwaits.com

ISBN-10   0-9903894-2-1
ISBN-13   978-0-9903894-2-2
Library of Congress Control Number: 2017909472

All rights reserved. No part of this publication may be reproduced, stored in a retrieval system, or transmitted in any form or by any means – electronic, mechanical, digital, photocopy, recording, or any other – except for printed quotations in printed reviews, without prior written permission of the author.

To my mother, Mary Jean Jennings.

Your deep faith formed so much of my spiritual foundation, and your unfailing encouragement has always been a key source of strength. Thank you so much for your role in this endeavor.

Acknowledgments

Many sincere thanks to my wonderful review team: Kathy Himebaugh, Linda Jennings, and Ben Jennings. Your insights have proved, time and again, to be invaluable. Thank you so much.

Contents

Acknowledgments v
Contents vii
List of Figures ix
Preface xi

Chapter 1: Seeing the Mountain 1
The Idea of the Mountain 3
The Great Uplifting 7
The Higher Elevations 15

Chapter 2: Mapping The Sacred 23
A Brief Fly-Over 25
The Priestly-Temple Region 30
The Levitical Region 34
The City Region 39

Chapter 3: Marking the Borders 43
A Needed Datum 45
Ground Zero 49
Orientation 57
Plotting the Grid 62
Probing Further 68

Chapter 4: Lay of the Land 71
The Current Canvas 73
Necessary Distinctions 76
New Contours 84
Capital Landscaping 92

Chapter 5: River and Tree 97
Streams for Bookends 99
Returning Garden 102
Living River 106

Chapter 6: Neighbors and Borders 121
District Review 123
Copious Communities 126
Purposeful Partitions 137
Distinctive Divisions 148

Chapter 7: Royal Thoroughfares 155
Preparing the Way 157

The Implicit Network	159
The Royal Highway	172
A Peek at the Paths	185
Chapter 8: Tiara of Towns	***197***
Further Renewals	199
Jerusalem's Neighbors	208
Temple Neighbors	215
A Threefold Exaltation	231
Chapter 9: Mountain of Joy	***237***
Focus of the World	239
Source of Healing	244
Pinnacle of Creation	254
Selected Bibliography	275
About the Author	277

List of Figures

Figure 1: The Dedicated Region 26
Figure 2: Sacred District Scriptural Diagram 28
Figure 3: Sacred District Dimensions 29
Figure 4: The Priestly-Temple Region 32
Figure 5: The Levitical Region 37
Figure 6: The City Region 41
Figure 7: City Area Comparison 41
Figure 8: Ezekiel's City Centered on Mount Moriah 56
Figure 9: Key North-to-South Distances 63
Figure 10: Sacred District Spatial Arrangement 65
Figure 11: A Topographic Look at the Data 67
Figure 12: Present-Day Sacred District Topology 73
Figure 13: Essential Shape of the Sacred District 88
Figure 14: Terrain Features of Future Jerusalem 93
Figure 15: Primary Sacred District Rivers 105
Figure 16: Temple River Depth vs. Distance 110
Figure 17: Changes in the North Red Sea Area 117
Figure 18: Schematic Model of Millennial Zion 124
Figure 19: Comparing Major City Populations 129
Figure 20: Main Borders of the Sacred District 153
Figure 21: Internal City Highways 160
Figure 22: Sacred District Highway Network 171
Figure 23: Central Mountain Ridge 180
Figure 24: Sacred District and the Kings Highway 182
Figure 25: Sacred District Central Highway 187
Figure 26: Implied Features of Roads and Walls 194
Figure 27: Towers, Gates & Bridges 195
Figure 28: Towers, Gates & Bridges (cont'd) 196
Figure 29: Ancient Sites within the Sacred District 207
Figure 30: Bethany 209
Figure 31: Gibeah 211
Figure 32: Mizpah and Gibeon 216
Figure 33: Gibeon to Geba 223

Figure 34: Geba and Michmash 227
Figure 35: Seneh and Bozez, Looking East 229
Figure 36: The Three Exaltations...234
Figure 37: Key Towns of the Sacred District..........................236
Figure 38: A-Ram / Ramah Area..249
Figure 39: Ramah and the Temple Peak.................................252

Preface

The journey continues!

In our prior adventure[1] into the future we discovered the map of the Holy Land as it will exist in days ahead, according to prophetic guidance found in the Bible. In advance we witnessed future geography and natural phenomena in that region of the world, as real as for any country we might visit today, and as sure as God's many other promises to us through His Word. These prophesied circumstances haven't come about yet. But, as have all God's declarations, they certainly will.

The big separating factor between the Holy Land we might travel to today and the one we will visit in *this* excursion is simply that of *time*. We can know about the Holy Land of the past and present; and we can also know of the vastly different version of it in the future, thanks to God's informing us beforehand.

The time gap between the two is getting smaller and smaller; and the prophesied Country, in all its prophetic wonder, is coming closer to existence each day. No, we can't physically see it yet. But as to realistically comprehending what is about to take place, we today have a huge advantage over our ancient brothers and sisters who first heard the prophets: for us, the time of fulfillment is right at our doorstep.

Signs all around us loudly declare that the King is coming. We approach the long-foretold conclusion of a vast era, seeing world events and conditions rapidly conforming to the patterns and details He described long ago. With unprecedented evidence that increases almost daily, we can, as in no other time, look forward to the coming of "The Anointed," *ha Mashiach,* the Messiah, the Christos, Christ [2]. In a vortex-like culmination of explicit prophecies too numerous to count, global events and God's Word compel us to look toward the coming Day of the *Lord*, the reign of *The Anointed*.

This future setting of His "Millennial[3]" reign is what we will continue to explore here. We are won't try to describe Heavenly or eternal circumstances, but instead realities coming to this very world we were born into. We won't emphasize events leading up to or surrounding the Lord's return, that is, the "birth pains" of this creation prophesied to usher in its final stage. Rather, we

---

[1] The Approaching Country, described in the Bibliography.
[2] Since these titles are linguistically interchangeable, we will use them interchangeably in the text that follows.
[3] The term "Millennium" will be used as short-hand here for the coming reign of Messiah, and it derives from Revelation 20:2-7 where one thousand years is cited as its duration.

will continue looking beyond to what will be "born" after those "birth pains," to the coming kingdom of creation's Creator, *here on this earth*. It will not be the so-called "end times" events in view here, but the astounding – and almost always overlooked – things that come *after* that brief transition.

In our first "expedition" we discovered many details of the future country of Israel, such as how it will be geographically shaped and internally organized. In this next journey though, our charter is more explicit. We will focus tightly upon, and delve more deeply into, a very particular and most special piece of this "Approaching Country."

Here is the future geographic context. Set among the twelve tribal portions of the coming Holy Land will be a unique province belonging personally to the coming King: Jesus, or (in Hebrew) *Yeshua*. A long time ago, He came as the anointed ("messiah," *mashiach*) high priest[4]; but soon He will come as the anointed King, ruling over not only Israel, but the entire world[5]. This King and Prince[6] will be given His own province within Israel, a huge strip of land approaching the size of the surrounding tribal allocations.

All this was carefully examined in our prior journey, which also touched upon our objective here. In the middle of the Prince's Province will reside a *very* special piece of property which the Prince-King and His people will give to God the Father[7]. This precious offering of property, the central core of the holy province that Jesus will personally own, is the subject of our expedition here. This will be the "Sacred District," the most holy area in the coming age[8], and probably the holiest area that has ever existed on this planet.

Like the spies of the Exodus story, we will make a reconnaissance trip to this holiest territory.

Though all this might seem a smaller endeavor than the prior expedition, rest assured that the opposite is the case. For as with Narnia, the further one travels into this prophesied land, the bigger the story gets. But be advised: this adventure is not a fictional one. The things we will witness are as real as anything we might see and touch right now. True, the landscapes and features haven't materialized yet. But thanks to God's informing and invitation, that need not stop us from exploring; we can fully appreciate what He has shared with us.

So, once again, let us embark on something quite different than what is generally discussed in "prophesy conversations," or any other for that matter. Though this Sacred District is generally ignored today by many Christians and Jews, and everyone else, it will become the *most* important place for *every* living

---

[4] E.g., Hebrews 4:14-5:10. The Biblical term *mashiach* first applies to priestly anointing.
[5] E.g., Psalms 2:6; Revelation 12:5, 19:15. The Biblical term *mashiach* has an additional application: *anointing* of a king.
[6] The title "Prince," for Jesus, underscores His being the prophesied Son of David and heir to that king's throne and authority. It also underscores Jesus' being the Son of God. Both senses will be emphasized throughout this study.
[7] Ezekiel 48:8.
[8] Ezekiel 48:20.

person on the earth, in a time soon to come. For it will enfold the Mountain of God Almighty, the joyful focus of the entire Earth. It will comprise the Mountain from which the coming King rules this world in wisdom, firmness and love.

This is the very Mountain that we will, here and now, begin to climb.

Cliff Jennings
Highland, Maryland
February 2017

Chapter 1: Seeing the Mountain

...the Lord shall reign over them in mount Zion from henceforth, even for ever.
Micah 4:7b, KJV

This is what the Lord says: "I will return to Zion and dwell in Jerusalem. Then Jerusalem will be called the City of Truth, and the mountain of the Lord Almighty will be called the Holy Mountain."
Zechariah 8:3, NIV

Thou shalt bring them in, and plant them in the mountain of thine inheritance, in the place, O Lord, which thou hast made for thee to dwell in, in the Sanctuary, O Lord, which thy hands have established. The Lord shall reign forever and ever.
Exodus 15:17-18, KJV

Chapter 1: Seeing the Mountain

The Idea of the Mountain

One of the most impressive symbols we have is the image of a *mountain*. Its physical immensity and stability can be used to describe the vastness of God's strength[9], the surety of His purposes[10], and the loftiness of His holiness[11]. Imagine standing before any high mountain, and you have a great visual for our Creator's omnipotence, immutability and transcendence.

Beyond this important imagery about mountains in general, God's Word takes matters a big step further: for there will soon come a day when a literal, unique, geological mountain, *His* Mountain, arises on a landscape here on this Earth. If you're around when that happens, you will see this new mountain, along with most people living on the earth then. It will be the most important peak to have ever existed on this planet; and it is this terrain we will be "exploring" in this study.

A good place to begin this expedition is to ground ourselves with the ideas and symbolism that Scripture brings into play here, things that will be clear to all who gaze at this Mountain in days ahead. People such as you or I will easily relate its attributes to Almighty God whose Presence will rest upon it, and the King of Kings who will rule the world from this place.

But before that time, even right now, we can listen to the lessons and let strength be whispered into our souls from He who will reign from this place.

Unmistakable Presence

As we read the Bible, a powerful idea frequently emerges in the background: that a very particular mountain is associated with God. Thanks to this idea, we gain the sense of His overwhelming strength, soundness, authority and holiness. We see it in Sinai, the mountain of God's presence in the Exodus drama. We see it as well in Zion of old, when He made His dwelling place with the first-chosen people, Israel, via the Temple He established there.

---

[9] Seen particularly in Sinai, where God's powerful presence there frightened the Israelites of the Exodus. See also Psalms 65:6, 125:1-2. Further, Psalms 30:7, where David is said to be like a strong mountain.

[10] Seen in the Word of God issuing forth from His mountain, first from Sinai, then Zion of Biblical times, but ultimately from a future Mount Zion: Isaiah 2:3, Micah 4:2.

[11] As seen in many references to Mount Sinai / Horeb as the "Mount of God" from Exodus 3:1 onward. Other references include Psalm 48:1, referring to Zion as the "mountain of his holiness," similarly Psalms 36:6, Jeremiah 31:23, Ezekiel 20:40, Daniel 9:16 & 20, Joel 3:17, and many others.

In both cases, the divine Presence rested upon an actual mountain, and there was no mistaking the connection. In the days of those stories, if someone asked you where God's special Presence resided, you would describe the mountain involved and maybe how to get there.

With Sinai however, one wouldn't carelessly approach the mountain at all. If a human or animal strayed too close, they would suffer death[12]. So powerful was the Lord's manifestation there that the Israelites of the Exodus were absolutely terrified of it[13].

As for Mount Zion, at its apex (contained within Solomon's Temple) was the Holy of Holies. It was no less dangerous, for as with the Tabernacle before it, only the High Priest could enter – and that only once a year[14]. With either Mountain, it is impressed upon us all that to step before God Almighty is no little matter, and generally would mean death for any of us: except for the singular solution, the Son of God, through whom we have access to the Father's throne[15].

Beyond Sinai and historical Zion though, another Mountain of God is destined to be present on this Earth. Like those other mountains, His special Presence *will again reside there*! But also like those other mountains, strict rules are involved, both for the honor of Him and the safety of His people.

Unlike those mountains of the past though, this new one will be central in worship for not only Israel, but all the nations of the world.

Overcoming Power

Here is another "mountain fact" from Scriptures: a mountain also can be symbolic of an *enemy* of the Lord. Some of God's historical nation-adversaries are symbolically linked to their most prominent mountain. For example, Edom had its Mount Seir, which was often seen as physically and arrogantly standing against God's purposes. Because the mountain was symbolic of the people of Edom, Mount Seir had serious prophecies of doom leveled against it[16].

Similar things can be said about "high places" in general, where people (even Israelites) sometimes set up pagan altars, attempting to elevate a false god against the reality of the one true God[17]. These high spots in the landscape received many prophecies against them, because they represented the sinful activities taking place there.

---

[12] Exodus 19:12-13; Hebrews 12:18-20.
[13] Exodus 19:16; Hebrews 12:19,21.
[14] Exodus 30:10; Leviticus 16:34; Hebrews 9:7.
[15] E.g., Ephesians 2:13-18; Hebrews 9-10.
[16] E.g., Ezekiel 35.
[17] E.g., Jeremiah 3:6.

Chapter 1: Seeing the Mountain

So if God is associated with *His* Mountain, and His enemies are associated with their mountain, we can envision a symbolic positioning of one against the other. Before the huge, righteous and immovable peak arises the opponent-mountain, with its spindly loftiness illustrating the towering arrogance of its people. This is what the story of the Tower of Babel[18] is all about: a man-made mountain that sought to rise to Heaven, without the help of God.

This project (and its divine destruction) took place at the very start of our human history, that is, not many generations after Noah and family stepped off the ark. But "Babel" or "Babylon" (the same name) will arise once more. Maybe not with a physical tower; but having a people whose arrogance against God and destructiveness to His creation is foreseen as mountainous and towering as any precedent in history. This political entity will be an ultimate nation-mountain-adversary of the Lord.

> *And I will render unto Babylon and to all the inhabitants of Chaldea all their evil that they have done in Zion in your sight, saith the Lord. 25 Behold,* **I am against thee, O destroying mountain, saith the Lord, which destroyest all the earth**: *and I will stretch out mine hand upon thee, and roll thee down from the rocks, and* **will make thee a burnt mountain**... **53 Though Babylon should mount up to heaven, and though she should fortify the height of her strength, yet from me shall spoilers come unto her, saith the Lord.**
> Jeremiah 51:24-25, 53, KJV

However, in a time yet to come[19], this ultimate "Tower of Babel" and "destroying mountain" will be overthrown by God with a finality never seen in the original drama. In fact, the coming event will be the final chapter in that ancient story of man-made mountains attempting to reach Heaven.

> *And a mighty angel took up* **a stone** *like* **a great millstone**, *and cast it into the sea, saying, Thus* **with violence shall that great city Babylon be thrown down**, *and shall be found no more at all.*
> Revelation 18:18, KJV

With this as a huge example, we see that God will overcome *all* His enemies, and that His "mountain" will prevail against *all* pretenders, a matter spoken of by both Isaiah and Micah.

---

[18] Genesis 11:1-9.
[19] Though ancient Babylon was "punished" for its harm towards Judah, in that its rulers where replaced by those of other nations, the city and region continued to flourish for many centuries. This means that Jeremiah's unfulfilled prophecies remain targeted upon a political entity in the future, one having similar characteristics (attitudes, sins, etc.).

> *And it shall come to pass in the last days, that* **the mountain of the Lord's house shall be established in the top of the mountains, and shall be exalted above the hills**; *and all nations shall flow unto it. 3 And many people shall go and say, Come ye, and let us go up to* **the mountain of the Lord, to the house of the God of Jacob**; *and he will teach us of his ways, and we will walk in his paths:* **for out of Zion shall go forth the law**, *and the word of the Lord from Jerusalem.*
> Isaiah 2:2-3, KJV; see also Micah 4:1-2

This will be the mountain of our expedition: a new sacred peak which has yet to emerge from present-day geography. Among the many visual messages it will declare, the mount will stand as a mighty symbol of God's transcendence over all His enemies. By the time of its arising, the final "Babylon" will have fallen, and the evil alliance of armies gathered at Har- (mountain of) Megiddo, or *Armageddon*, will have been crushed. And arise the new Mountain shall, in a vastness and mightiness surpassing all "mountains" and "towers" that try to stand against it.

Surrounding Protection

We have been working with the idea of the mountain, and how it permeates God's Word in many ways. If we combine the further thoughts of *foundation* and *fortress*, the concept of the ideal and God-made mountain becomes something we can not only go to, but *stand upon* and even *live within*. So if a mountain symbolizes God's omnipresent power, going into a cave or cleft in that same Mountain can be likened to surrounding ourselves with that same power, coming under its protection. No wonder then that we have so many references to our God being our *rock* and *refuge*! Look at these praises from the Psalms.

> **The Lord is my rock**, *and* **my fortress**, *and my deliverer; my God, my strength, in whom I will trust; my buckler, and the horn of my salvation, and my high tower.*
> Psalms 18:2, KJV

> *For* **thou art my rock and my fortress**; *therefore for thy name's sake lead me, and guide me.*
> Psalms 31:3, KJV

> **Be thou my strong habitation**, *whereunto I may continually resort: thou hast given commandment to save me; for* **thou art my rock and my fortress**.
> Psalms 71:3, KJV

Chapter 1: Seeing the Mountain

> *I will say of the Lord,* **He is my refuge and my fortress**: *my God; in him will I trust.*
> Psalms 91:2, KJV

> *My goodness, and* **my fortress; my high tower,** *and my deliverer; my shield, and he in whom I trust; who subdueth my people under me.*
> Psalms 144:2, KJV

David, who knew what it was like to live in caves[20], repeatedly likened his relationship with God to dwelling in a room or cave within His massive rock-like mountain-fortress[21]. This is why our praise songs often contain words such as those cited above, because our Lord's power and love for us is as sure and firm as a mountain, His shelter just as unlimited and immovable as an enormous rocky expanse. In His "fortress" one is not only protected, but made to thrive.

> *You have not come to a mountain that can be touched and that is burning with fire; to darkness, gloom and storm...* **22 But you have come to Mount Zion, to the <u>heavenly Jerusalem</u>, the <u>city</u> of the <u>living God</u>.**
> Hebrews 12:18,22, NIV

As we explore the coming Mountain of God, we should therefore perceive it not like fearsome Sinai, but as a place bursting with life and energy, a City of light and love in fact, reflective of that which flows from Heaven.

The Great Uplifting

Another aspect of any physical mountain, as a section of the earth's surface, is that it has been lifted up by unimaginable forces. Only vast energies of God-created nature can cause any mountain to arise; they are forces far beyond human engineering or perhaps even comprehension. This fact speaks to a broader principle: only God can truly raise that which was low; only He can restore that which was abjectly flattened.

These ideas come together in the coming Mountain which, as we will see, will be physically and dramatically uplifted by God from its surrounding geography, simultaneously symbolizing certain foretold victories that only He could have championed. So in addition to all its other meanings, this new

---

[20] 1 Samuel 22-24.
[21] As did others, e.g., Jeremiah 16:19.

summit will loudly declare that the Lord will have accomplished the impossible: that He will have triumphed over all His enemies, and raised the humbled ones who have made Him their lofty Fortress.

God Will Lift Up His Humbled Servant

Imagine for a moment that you are standing upon a fairly flat plain, looking at a very high and distinct mountain in the distance, a mountain that dominates the horizon now, but wasn't there a few years before. When folks view the new Mountain of the Lord, this will be the sensation. To be sure, it will stand as a massive geological wonder; yet it will also speak to God's healing works, and to those whom His mighty hand will have elevated.

Let's examine this concept at the personal level. We are told many times in the Scriptures that those who humble themselves before the Lord and allow Him to be Master will, in the time of His choosing, be lifted up by Him. Understanding that the word "meek" here refers to a person who has been lowered and humbled[22], consider these verses.

> *When men are cast down, then thou shalt say,* **There is lifting up;** *and* **he shall save the humble person.**
> *Job 22:29, KJV*

> **The meek shall eat and be satisfied:** *they shall praise the Lord that seek him: your heart shall live for ever.*
> *Psalms 22:25, KJV*

> *But* **the meek shall inherit the earth**; *and shall delight themselves in the abundance of peace.*
> *Psalms 37:11, KJV*

> *Thou didst cause judgment to be heard from heaven; the earth feared, and was still, 9 When* **God arose to judgment, to save all the meek of the earth.** *Selah.*
> *Psalms 76:8-9, KJV*

> **The Lord lifteth up the meek:** *he casteth the wicked down to the ground.*
> *Psalms 147:6, KJV*

---

[22] Strong's OT:6035, `anav (aw-nawv').

> *The meek also shall increase their joy in the Lord*, and the poor among men shall rejoice in the Holy One of Israel.
> Isaiah 29:19, KJV

> **Blessed are the meek: for they shall inherit the earth.**
> Matthew 5:5, KJV

> But he that is greatest among you shall be your servant. 12 And whosoever shall exalt himself shall be abased; and **he that shall humble himself shall be exalted.**
> Matthew 23:11-12, KJV (see also Luke 14:11, 18:14b)

> **Humble yourselves in the sight of the Lord, and he shall lift you up.**
> James 4:10, KJV

> **Humble yourselves therefore under the mighty hand of God, that he may exalt you in due time:** 7 Casting all your care upon him; for he careth for you.
> 1 Peter 5:6-7, KJV

Over and over, we are told that our God may permit times of humbling, of crushing even, of our aspirations, resources, even health. At the same time, we are told that if we submit to Him and remain faithful and trusting in Him, He will bring about our "elevation" in His time, and in ways vastly better than what we originally had in mind.

Many of us start out with ideals, objectives and self-opinions that are like a mountain in our own eyes: tall and mighty, like immovable fact. Much of my life has been like that, even as a Christian; and I am sure that I still have such areas. But that's the problem with pride-blindness: you can't see that you have it.

But there is a God, and His ways are far above ours. He, in all His unimaginable holiness and power, is the only true Mountain of strength, life, love and existence itself. And because He truly loves us and wants to engage you and me in a deeply personal relationship, He allows us to discover for ourselves just how lowly our own pile of strength is. He permits circumstances and relationships that reveal how utterly we must depend upon Him. And at the same time, through the Person of His Son, God holds out His hand to lift us up.

Thus the Lord helps us come to an end of our own sufficiency and meaning and timing, and exchange them for His.

In the end, anyone who survives and flourishes into eternity will have come to embrace an abject reliance upon the one and only Creator. They will have seen their own mountain for the lowland it is, and taken shelter in the Mountain that is God.

Those truths will be reflected in a great geological testimony. On the horizon, here on this earth, there will be a physical mountain representing the Lord's uplifting of His humbled servants. In that day, the meek will have inherited the renewed Earth; and they will greatly enjoy this astounding symbol of His faithfulness.

God Will Lift Up His Humbled Nation

This amazing principle doesn't stop at the individual level though. An entire nation can trend toward humbling itself before the Lord, or attempting to raise itself up against Him, or somewhere in between. Similar to the individual, the nation that does honor the Lord as their Master will likewise reap the benefits.

> *... **if then their uncircumcised hearts be humbled**, and they then accept of the punishment of their iniquity: 42 **Then will I remember my covenant** with Jacob, and also my covenant with Isaac, and also my covenant with Abraham will I remember; and **I will remember the land**.*
> Leviticus 26:41b-42, KJV

> ***If my people, which are called by my name, shall humble themselves**, and pray, and seek my face, and turn from their wicked ways; **then will I hear from heaven, and will forgive their sin, and will heal their land**.*
> 2 Chronicles 7:14, KJV

> *For the Lord taketh pleasure in **his people: he will beautify the meek with salvation**.*
> Psalms 149:4, KJV

The entire drama of the First Testament [23] raises Israel as the great example for all nations. In some periods, she obeyed and God's blessings rained down upon her. More often though, bad choices were made, and consequences came. It is the same with any individual or even nation: our loving Creator

---

[23] In this study, the term "First Testament" will generally replace that of "Old Testament." Though the *covenant* inaugurated under Moses is called "old" (e.g., 2 Corinthians 3:14), this is because it gave way to its fulfilling referent in Messiah's sacrifice. The Scriptures involved though are in no way "old" or defunct, for they are every bit "living and active" (Hebrews 4:12, written while the "Old Testament" was still the only recognized Word of God). Indeed, Jesus Himself said that not one least stroke of the pen in those earlier instances of God's messages to us would fail to be fulfilled (Matthew 5:18).

Chapter 1: Seeing the Mountain

expects loving obedience in return for His creating us and taking care of us. But as humans having full freedom of choice and selfish predispositions, our nature is to choose our own ways.

Especially since 70 AD, the nation of Israel has been oppressed. If she were likened to a mountain, she was dramatically de-elevated then. As a matter of fact, Mount Zion of old – which always represented Jerusalem and Israel in general – was very much physically degraded by the Romans. For with the exception of the western wall of the Temple Mount, and certain towers which are now long gone,

> ...*all the rest of the wall, it was so thoroughly laid even with the ground by those that dug it up to the foundation, that there was left nothing to make those that came thither believe it had ever been inhabited. This was the end which Jerusalem came to by the madness of those that were for innovations; a city otherwise of great magnificence, and of mighty fame among all mankind.*[24]

Because of such degradations by the Romans and others subsequently, Mount Zion today, as a geographic feature, is not like the peak it was in Biblical times. It has, in a literal sense, been laid low. Correspondingly, for two thousand years, two "days" in the sight of God, the nation associated with that Mount has been downtrodden as well. But as seen in so many prophecies, that will change.

> *Come, and let us return unto the Lord: for he hath torn, and he will heal us; he hath smitten, and he will bind us up. 2* **After two days will he revive us: in the third day he will raise us up**, *and we shall live in his sight. 3 Then shall we know, if we follow on to know the Lord: his going forth is prepared as the morning; and* **he shall come unto us as the rain, as the latter and former rain unto the earth.**
> Hosea 6:1-3, KJV

God cannot lie[25]; and this "latter rain" must come for Israel. If calculated as we seem to be encouraged to[26], these "two days" are soon to expire. Though some of the prophesied "healing" has already taken place for Israel, any full reviving and raising, in comparison with the prophetic contexts and ideas, remains on the horizon.

This "raising" will transpire *not* by the strength of any man or nation, *not* by the ingenuity of any human army or government or other agency, but by the will of the One True God who calls all nations to Himself. As with an uplifting

---

[24] Josephus, <u>Wars of the Jews</u>, Book VII, Chapter 1, Section 1, as translated by William Whiston, 1737.
[25] E.g., Numbers 23:19.
[26] I.e., one day equating with one millennium: Psalms 90:4; 2 Peter 3:8.

of a real mountain in nature, the forces involved here will be super-human. Yet the uplifting will come; and in each of the following confirmations, it is easy to see Whom will be performing this massive "uplifting."

> *In those days and at that time, when I restore the fortunes of Judah and Jerusalem...*
> Joel 3:1, NIV

> "In that **day I will restore David's fallen tent.** *I will repair its broken places, restore its ruins, and build it as it used to be, 12 so that they may possess the remnant of Edom and all the nations that bear my name," declares the LORD, who will do these things.*
> Amos 9:11-12, NIV

> **"In that day,"** *declares the LORD, "I will gather the lame; I will assemble the exiles and those I have brought to grief. 7 I will make the lame a remnant, those driven away a strong nation.* **The LORD will rule over them in Mount Zion from that day and forever.** *8 As for you, O watchtower of the flock, O stronghold of the Daughter of Zion,* **the former dominion will be restored to you; kingship will come** *to the Daughter of Jerusalem."*
> Micah 4:6-8, NIV

> **The LORD will restore the splendor of Jacob** *like the splendor of Israel, though destroyers have laid them waste and have ruined their vines.*
> Nahum 2:2, NIV

> *The land by the sea, where the Kerethites[27] dwell, will be a place for shepherds and sheep pens. 7 It will belong to the remnant of the house of Judah; there they will find pasture. In the evening they will lie down in the houses of Ashkelon. The* **LORD their God will care for them; he will restore their fortunes.**
> Zephaniah 2:6-7, NIV

> *At that time I will gather you; at that time I will bring you home. I will give you honor and praise among all the peoples of the earth* **when I restore your fortunes** *before your very eyes," says the LORD.*
> Zephaniah 3:20, NIV

> *So when they met together, they asked him [Jesus],* **"Lord, are you at this time going to restore the kingdom to Israel?"** *7 He said to them: "It is not for you to know the times or dates the Father has set by his own authority.*
> Acts 1:6-7, NIV

---

[27] Philistines, with "the land by the sea" referring to the Palestine coast.

Chapter 1: Seeing the Mountain

> *The words of the prophets are in agreement with this, as it is written: 16 "'After this* **I will return and rebuild David's fallen tent. Its ruins I will rebuild, and I will restore it,** *17* **that the remnant of men may seek the Lord**, *and all the Gentiles who bear my name, says the Lord, who does these things 18 that have been known for ages." 19 It is my judgment, therefore, that we should not make it difficult for the Gentiles who are turning to God.*
> *Acts 15:15-19, NIV*

> *And so all Israel will be saved, as it is written:* **"The deliverer will come from Zion**; *he will turn godlessness away from Jacob… as far as election is concerned, they are loved on account of the patriarchs, 29 for* **God's gifts and his call are irrevocable.**
> *Romans 11:26, 28b-29, NIV*

Verses such as these make it clear that the Lord will indeed *fully* restore not only the country of Israel, but also its seat of government: Jerusalem. God the Father will keep His promises to His "firstborn" nation[28], that nation into which all other believing peoples are been grafted by the personal sacrifice of God's Son and Prince[29].

Will this raising up of Israel have a pronounced visible symbol, evident for the entire world to see? Yes it will: the coming Mountain of God, Mount Zion, elevated in the future, and indelibly linked with these sure pronouncements.

Again, what we are now considering is not a symbol of human strength or national power, but a visual monument to *God's* strength, created by that same Power. The coming Mount will declare *God's* faithfulness to His beloved and first-chosen nation, and likewise to all people that come to worship Him there.

God Will Lift Up His Humbled Son

In all these matters, the principle is clear: that to be exalted (raised) by God, one will have been fully humbled (lowered) before Him. It applies to us as individuals, beings created in His image yet born with a will that is at odds with His own. The principle applies to nations as well, peoples created by Him, yet having the same wayward tendencies as a whole. This isn't news. But what is shocking is that God Almighty applied this same principle to *Himself*. For in His plan for redeeming[30] us for eternity, God chose to become one of His human

---

[28] Exodus 4:22.
[29] Romans 11; Ephesians 2:11-20.
[30] "Redeem" refers, in Scriptures, to the act of releasing and regaining someone who has been sold or convicted, by way of paying their debt.

creatures, and ultimately arise as our Savior and ultimate King. Before that though, He was humbled before mankind, and in the most extreme way.

> *He is despised and rejected of men; a man of sorrows, and acquainted with grief: and we hid as it were our faces from him; he was despised, and we esteemed him not. 4 Surely he hath borne our griefs, and carried our sorrows: yet we did esteem him stricken, smitten of God, and afflicted. 5 But* **he was wounded for our transgressions, he was bruised for our iniquities**: *the chastisement of our peace was upon him; and with his stripes we are healed. 6 All we like sheep have gone astray; we have turned every one to his own way; and* **the Lord hath laid on him the iniquity of us all.** *7 He was oppressed, and he was afflicted, yet he opened not his mouth: he is brought as a lamb to the slaughter, and as a sheep before her shearers is dumb, so he openeth not his mouth.*
> Isaiah 53:3-7, KJV

> *Take my yoke upon you, and learn of me;* **for I am meek and lowly in heart**: *and ye shall find rest unto your souls.*
> Matthew 11:29, KJV

> **This Jesus hath God raised up**, *whereof we all are witnesses. 33 Therefore being by the right hand of God exalted, and having received of the Father the promise of the Holy Ghost, he hath shed forth this, which ye now see and hear.*
> Acts 2:32-33, KJV

> **For he hath made him to be sin for us, who knew no sin**; *that we might be made the righteousness of God in him.*
> 2 Corinthians 5:21, KJV

> *But made* **himself of no reputation**, *and took upon him the form of a* **servant**, *and was made in the likeness of men: 8 And being found in fashion as a man,* **he humbled himself**, *and* **became obedient unto death, even the death of the cross.** *9 Wherefore* **God also hath highly exalted him**, *and given* **him a name which is above every name:** *10 That* **at the name of Jesus every knee should bow, of things in heaven, and things in earth, and things under the earth**; *11 And that* **every tongue should confess that Jesus Christ is Lord, to the glory of God the Father.**
> Philippians 2:7-11, KJV

The coming Prince will therefore not be someone who was handed his throne by mere progeniture or inherited fortune, by personal forcefulness, political charm, or any number of human means. Instead, our coming Lord and King will have been humbled beyond imagination; our Savior will have paid the price of our release and redemption, a price none of us could ever pay. Our kinsman-redeemer bought us with His own life; our High Priest offered Himself as the Lamb whose blood would not only cover our sins, but remove them for all eternity.

Thus our Anointed-Christ-Messiah (these terms are equivalent), High Priest of all creation and for all time, will become the King, forever. The meek will inherit the Earth; and the most humbled will be the most exalted. This is the further message of the coming Mountain, declaring that our Lord reigns, and reigns from this very place. Though humbled as no other, no created being or authority in Heaven or Earth will have been able to stand against Him. The mightiest of human and national "mountains," such as Babylon, will have done their best to fight the Humble One. Yet in the coming day, as all will plainly see, His Mountain will arise and prevail; and the Meek One[31] will indeed inherit the Earth, along with all His people.

The Higher Elevations

In addition to the profound symbolism the prophesied Mountain will convey to you or me, it will have the spectacular role of the natural and visible Mountain of God.

Let's pause for a moment though, and ponder this idea of "Mountain of God." As we will see, this next one will be neither the first instance, nor the final. In fact, there is a true progression, an important sequence to these exceptional Mountains. This next one will play an absolutely vital part in that grand story; but to understand its special place, we need to review the drama in an overall sense. The Mountains we need to talk about can be divided into three categories, which I will list in a roughly chronological manner:

- ☐ God's Mountain in Heaven (as it has been, and still is)
- ☐ God's Mountains (plural) on Earth (through human history)
  - o God's (earthly) Mountains in past human history
  - o **God's** (earthly) **Mountain about to come**
- ☐ God's Mountain in Heaven-Earth (in future-eternity)

This entire expedition will be about **God's Mountain about to come**, which is highlighted in the above list. But, we need our frame of reference to understand how it fits into His sequence of the grand story. So we will start with the "bookends," if you will, as an introduction to the Big Picture: the beginning and (un-)ending Mountains of God.

---

[31] Matthew 11:29.

The Mountain of God in Heaven

There is an actual Mountain of God in Heaven, upon which the Heavenly Temple of God stands. Though we are not told much about it, we know that the Mountain exists because of two passages decrying the deeds of Lucifer, while he was free to roam about in Heaven.

> *For thou hast said in thine heart, I will ascend into heaven, I will exalt my throne above the stars of God: I will sit also upon **the mount of the congregation**, in the sides of the north...*
> *Isaiah 14:13, KJV*

> *Thou art the anointed cherub that covereth; and I have set thee so: thou wast upon **the holy mountain of God**; thou hast walked up and down in the midst of the stones of fire... therefore I will cast thee as profane out of **the mountain of God**: and I will destroy thee, O covering cherub, from the midst of the stones of fire.*
> *Ezekiel 28:14,16b, KJV*

Upon this Heavenly Mountain there resides a City, which just happens to have a familiar name.

> *But you have come to **Mount Zion**, to **the heavenly Jerusalem**, the city of the living God. You have come to thousands upon thousands of angels in joyful assembly, 23 to the church of the firstborn, whose names are written in heaven. You have come to God, the judge of all men, to the spirits of righteous men made perfect, 24 to Jesus the mediator of a new covenant...*
> *Hebrews 12:22-24a, NIV*

We see also that the Heavenly Mountain of God and the earthly one of old shared the same name, *Zion*. This name for the one in Heaven is reinforced in the following verse,[32]

> *Then I looked, and there before me was **the Lamb, standing on Mount Zion**...*
> *Revelation 14:1a, NIV*

From the depths of prehistory then, there is this established combination of Divinely-ordained architecture: the Mountain of God (named Zion),

---

[32] In the narrative sequence of this passage, it is clear that the Heavenly Zion is in view. Specifically, since Jesus has yet to come back to Earth at this point (Revelation 19), the activities taking place in Revelation 14, and therefore on the Zion described, are still in Heaven.

supporting the Temple and Throne of God. After His creation of a redeemed race of humans residing in Heaven, there is also a third key element: the City of God, the "higher" Jerusalem.

The Mountain of God through Eternity

On the opposite end of the Big Picture, Lord grants us a small glimpse of the final and eternal Mountain, the culmination of the mountain-drama. We get a hint of this in one of the Psalms which speaks of a Mount Zion that, unlike its Earthly counterparts, will remain high and immovable for eternity.

> *Those who trust in the Lord are like[33]* **Mount Zion**, *which cannot be shaken but* **endures forever.** *2 As the mountains surround Jerusalem, so the Lord surrounds his people both now and* **forevermore.**
> *Psalms 125:1-2, NIV*

Is this the same Mount Zion as is currently in Heaven? No, and we are given specific information on this matter. *After* the second coming of the Lord, *after* His thousand-year reign on this Earth, and *after* the "Great White Throne" judgment at the end of time as we understand it, we are told that the present Earth (and Heaven, with its present Mount Zion there) will pass away and be replaced with something far more glorious.

> *And he carried me away in the spirit to* **a great and high mountain**, *and shewed me that great city, the holy Jerusalem, descending out of heaven from God, 11 Having the glory of God: and her light was like unto a stone most precious, even like a jasper stone, clear as crystal;*
> *Revelation 21:10-11, KJV*

This final Mountain will clearly be the central focus of the new Heaven-Earth creation. Present Earth and present Heaven will have "fled,"[34] their versions of God's Mountain having given way to God's eternal masterpiece. This "great and high mountain" will arise as the finale to all that have come before in Heaven and Earth.

---

[33] Notice the similes: *like* Mount Zion... *as* the mountains... In the Lord's Day, when the Mountain of God is seen and touched and stood upon, Psalms such as this will take on a visceral reality.
[34] Revelation 21:1. See also Jesus' clear prophecy recorded in Matthew 24:35, Mark 13:31 and Luke 21:33.

Note however that the Heavenly City, that in which past believers dwell even now[35], will *not* pass away in that final transition. Instead, this "Jerusalem that is above" awaits that union[36]; and in God's timing, the City will descend to meet the eternal Mountain, and together be the centerpiece of the new and final Creation. In that setting, like its Heavenly version now, the eternal Mount Zion will be the foundation for the City of God, and the Throne of God, forevermore.

The Mountains of God on Earth

We've briefly discussed Mount Zion in Heaven, existing from the deep past, yet present even now. We have also looked to the deep future, when the eternal Mountain of God will be the natural and spiritual highlight of the new Heaven-Earth creation[37]. Chronologically, between these two other-worldly (but nevertheless real) Mountains, there will have stood three representatives of them here on this Earth, and it is to those three mountains we will now turn. They are: Sinai, first Zion, and Zion next to come. The first two, Sinai and (historical) Zion, are in the past, and we will take them on first.

With Sinai came the emphatic symbolism of God's power and holiness. When His presence was upon it, there was thundering, lightning, smoke, and loud trumpet-like sounds[38]. Only Moses could approach the Mountain; and it was terrifying to the Israelites. During that time, Sinai was perhaps similar to the environment of God's throne in Heaven which can likewise have quaking, smoke, thundering and lightning surrounding it[39].

The next earth-based Mountain of God was Zion of Biblical times, and there are a number of connections between it and Sinai. Similar to the Mountain of God in Heaven and its Temple, with Sinai there was the (portable) Tabernacle, and with Zion the (permanent) Temple. Both contained the Most Holy Place, wherein rested the Ark of the Covenant, a terrestrial representation of the actual Throne of God in Heaven. Both Tabernacle and Temple were served by the Priests and Levites, corresponding with the angels ministering before God's Heavenly Throne. With Zion especially, as seen in many Psalms, the Earth was seen as an extension of the Lord's Heavenly dominion, with His rule radiating from the Temple to the benefit of all His people.

From Sinai to Zion, there are huge changes though. Especially from David's Psalms and the narrative surrounding him, Zion was very different from

---

[35] E.g., Hebrews 12:22.
[36] "But the Jerusalem that is above is free, and she is our mother." Galatians 4:26, NIV.
[37] Revelation 20:11, 21:1.
[38] Exodus 19:16-19, 20:18-19; Hebrews 12:18-20.
[39] Isaiah 6:4; Revelation 4:5.

its predecessor. Where Sinai was unapproachable, Zion had dwellings surrounding it. Where Sinai was distant from the camp of Israel, Zion was in the midst of Jerusalem. Where Sinai was associated with fear, Zion was, in its ideal sense, filled with the joy and praise of God's people. Where Sinai's Tabernacle was portable and set apart from God's Mountain, Zion's Temple was permanent and set <u>upon</u> God's Mountain.

With hints such as these, we see portrayed a massive overall progression in God's dealings with His people. God chose Jerusalem for His City and established David, a "man after His own heart," as His favored human king. At the same time, God exchanged Sinai for Zion as His Mountain. In so doing, God demonstrated His great desire: to have a people made in His own image, returning His love; a people with whom He could dwell among and beside.

The Mountain Arising Next

And so we approach the Mountain of God on *our* horizon, the subject of our exploration here. It will not be the final one, for as we have seen, that comes with the new re-creation of Heaven-Earth combined. But it will be the final Mountain of God on this present Earth.

Reflecting the Mount in Heaven, the coming one will be *the* Holy Precinct on Earth as we know it. Like Sinai, it will be a mighty symbol to all mankind of God's Presence and Power. Like Zion of old, it will further emblemize His surrounding protection of and joyous provision for His people. Bearing His Temple at its apex, the Mountain will visually convey that He is the lofty Fortress of His children. Yet being in the midst of their homes, the Mountain will also loudly declare His deep desire to dwell amongst His people.

In the progression of these Earthly Mountains of God, this final one will play a pivotal role, and therefore be unlike historical Zion in several respects. For example, the next Zion will never see unholy practices upon it. Furthermore, though Zion of old (and her people) would experience massive oppressions through history, this coming Mount (and her people) will *never* be downtrodden again. If we need reminders of how first Zion was laid low, we don't have to look hard for Biblical examples.

Even so, there have ever been messages of hope spoken by the Lord who chose this People[40], this City and this Mountain.

> *By the rivers of Babylon, there we sat down, yea, we wept, when we remembered Zion. Psalms 137:1, KJV*

---

[40] Israel, both literally (e.g., Romans 11), and as expanded through the sacrifice of Messiah (e.g., Ephesians 2).

> *To appoint unto them that mourn in Zion, to give unto them beauty for ashes, the oil of joy for mourning, the garment of praise for the spirit of heaviness; that they might be called trees of righteousness, the planting of the Lord, that he might be glorified.*
> *Isaiah 61:3, KJV*

> *But Zion said, "The Lord has forsaken me, And the Lord has forgotten me." 15 "Can a woman forget her nursing child, And have no compassion on the son of her womb? Even these may forget, but I will not forget you.*
> *Isaiah 49:14-15, NASB*

> *Awake, awake, Clothe yourself in your strength, O Zion; Clothe yourself in your beautiful garments, O Jerusalem, the holy city. For the uncircumcised and the unclean Will no more come into you. 2 Shake yourself from the dust, rise up, O captive Jerusalem; Loose yourself from the chains around your neck, O captive daughter of Zion.*
> *Isaiah 52:1-2, NASB*

> *When the Lord turned again the captivity of Zion, we were like them that dream. 2 Then was our mouth filled with laughter, and our tongue with singing: then said they among the heathen, The Lord hath done great things for them. 3 The Lord hath done great things for us; whereof we are glad. 4 Turn again our captivity, O Lord, as the streams in the south. 5 They that sow in tears shall reap in joy. 6 He that goeth forth and weepeth, bearing precious seed, shall doubtless come again with rejoicing, bringing his sheaves with him.*
> *Psalms 126, KJV*

The humbled people and nation *will* be lifted up, with Israel vastly expanded in number. In fact, Israel would eventually encompass all those that have made Messiah their King, whether born of Abraham or not[41]. The humbled Savior will be the victorious King of Kings, with His humbled City, Jerusalem, elevated to be the source of His global rule. In all this, the humbled Mountain of God, Zion, will rise triumphant as well.

> *Thou shalt bring them in, and plant them in* **the mountain of thine inheritance**, *in the place, O Lord, which thou hast made for thee to dwell in, in the Sanctuary, O Lord, which thy hands have established. 18* **The Lord shall reign for ever and ever.**
> *Exodus 15:17-18, KJV*

---

[41] Ephesians 2, especially verses 11-21, show how this expansion of Israel – not replacement! – has taken place through Messiah.

Chapter 1: Seeing the Mountain

> *Thou shalt arise, and have mercy upon Zion: for the time to favour her, yea, the set time, is come.*
> *Psalms 102:13, KJV*

> *"And* **a Redeemer will come to Zion***, And to those who turn from transgression in Jacob," declares the Lord.*
> *Isaiah 59:20, NASB*

> *And it will come about that he who is left in Zion and remains in Jerusalem will be called holy — everyone who is recorded for life in Jerusalem. 4 When the Lord has washed away the filth of the daughters of Zion, and purged the bloodshed of Jerusalem from her midst, by the spirit of judgment and the spirit of burning, 5 then* **the Lord will create over the whole area of Mount Zion and over her assemblies a cloud by day, even smoke, and the brightness of a flaming fire by night; for over all the glory will be a canopy.**
> *Isaiah 4:3-5, NASB*

> *Thus saith the Lord of hosts;* **I was jealous for Zion with great jealousy***, and* **I was jealous for her with great fury***. 3 Thus saith the Lord;* **I am returned unto Zion***, and will dwell in the midst of Jerusalem: and Jerusalem shall be called a city of truth; and* **the mountain of the Lord of hosts the holy mountain.**
> *Zechariah 8:2-3, KJV*

The coming Mount Zion will clearly represent God's victories at many levels. However, it will not only be lifted in concept, but in actual dimensions. We get a hint at this topological exaltation from the prophets.

> *In the last days* **the mountain of the Lord's temple will be established as chief among the mountains; it will be raised above the hills,** *and all nations will stream to it. 3 Many peoples will come and say, "Come, let us go up to the mountain of the Lord, to the house of the God of Jacob. He will teach us his ways, so that we may walk in his paths." The law will go out from Zion, the word of the Lord from Jerusalem.*
> *Isaiah 2:2-3, NIV; also Micah 4:1-2*

> *In the visions of God brought he me into the land of Israel, and set me upon* **a very high mountain***, by which was as the frame of a city on the south.*
> *Ezekiel 40:2, KJV*

We will explore these natural-topographic matters later on. But for the time being, we can appreciate that the mountain that was downcast and downtrodden will become the center of attention for the entire world in the coming "day" of the Lord around the corner.

> *And I will make her that halted a remnant, and her that was cast far off a strong nation: and* **the Lord shall reign over them in mount Zion from henceforth, even for ever.** [42]
> *Micah 4:7, KJV*

> *Great is the Lord, and greatly to be praised in the city of our God, in* **the mountain of his holiness.** *2 Beautiful for situation,* **<u>the joy of the whole earth</u>***, is* **<u>mount Zion</u>, on the sides of the north, the city of the great King.**
> *Psalms 48:1-2, KJV*

> **O Lord***, my strength, and* **my fortress, and my refuge** *in the day of affliction,* **the Gentiles shall come unto thee from the ends of the earth...**
> *Jeremiah 16:19a, KJV*

The next Mountain will stand as a sentinel, declaring all these messages and more, in the sovereign day of our coming Redeemer-kinsman. It will be astounding in its beauty, marvelous in its meaning. It will bear the House of God on Earth, and be center of rule for the Son of God, the coming "King of kings." It will indeed be "the joy of the whole earth," making all other mountains, no matter how big, "envious."

> *Why gaze in envy, O rugged mountains, at the mountain where God chooses to reign, where the Lord himself will dwell forever?*
> *Psalms 68:16, NIV*

So now, let's find out where this next Mountain of God will be.

---

[42] The Mountain coming next to this Earth will give way to its eternal counterpart in the new Heaven-Earth, as discussed in Revelation 21-22. So though the next Mountain only lasts through the Millennial period of 1,000 years, it nevertheless establishes the fact of God's Mountain within creation, in its present and final versions, never again to be downtrodden, and forever to be the seat of His reign.

Chapter 2: Mapping The Sacred

In visions of God he took me to the land of Israel and set me on a very high mountain, on whose south side were some buildings that looked like a city.
Ezekiel 40:2, NIV

...they shall use this speech in the land of Judah and in the cities thereof, when I shall bring again their captivity; The Lord bless thee, O habitation of justice, and mountain of holiness.
Jeremiah 31:22b, KJV

And in this mountain shall the Lord of hosts make unto all people a feast of fat things, a feast of wines on the lees, of fat things full of marrow, of wines on the lees well refined.
Isaiah 25:6, KJV

A Brief Fly-Over

The Gift for the Prince's Use

So let's begin our exploration of the coming Mountain, and start with getting our bearings on approximately where it will reside. In the prior journey[43] in this series we made it as far as the Prince's Province, a special region of future Israel dedicated to our coming Lord. In that study, we saw how Scriptures define the border and internal structure of Messiah's Israel, with the Prince's lands flanked to north and south by provinces allotted to the tribes. And though the north-to-south dimensions of the various tribal provinces are not given to us, those of the Prince's Province are.

> Bordering the territory of Judah from east to west will be the portion you are to present as a **special gift**. It will be 25,000 cubits wide, and its length from east to west will equal one of the tribal portions; the sanctuary will be in the center[44] of it. Ezekiel 48:8, NIV

This north-south width of 25,000[45] "Long" Cubits[46] is about 8.15 miles or 13.1 kilometers, with its western border being the Mediterranean Sea. Though we don't know how far this province will extend to the east, we do know that it will be fully split into western and eastern sections by the Sacred District.[47] In other words, if you were in the eastern part of the Prince's land, you would not be able to travel to the western part without travelling though the Sacred District.

---

[43] The Approaching Country (see bibliography).
[44] Depending on the translation, the word here is variously rendered "center," "middle," "in the midst of," and so forth. The Hebrew term *tavek* (taw'-vek, Strong's OT:8432) is not as exact as our English word "center." So in the sense of east-to-west location, we need not worry that the "sanctuary" must be in the *exact center* of the Prince's Province. Instead, Ezekiel is simply affirming that the Sacred District is in the midst of the Prince's Province, dividing it into east and west sections, just as 45:7 describes.
[45] Affirmed in Ezekiel 45:7 which describes how the Prince's land lies east and west of the Sacred District, with 48:20-21 which describes the latter to be 25,000LC square.
[46] In this study, Ezekiel's cubits are taken to be the "long" (royal) cubit, abbreviated as "LC," with a length equating with:
- 20.64 inches / 524 millimeters
- 1.72 feet / 0.52 meters
- 0.00033 miles / 0.00052 kilometers

[47] Ezekiel 45:7.

Figure 1: The Dedicated Region

Because of its association with Jerusalem, the Prince's Province has a clear north-south anchor point. Unlike the tribal territories, we can know with fair certainty where its northern and southern boundaries will lie. Based on the prior exploration just mentioned, the above map summarizes how this 8.15-mile wide strip might lay across current geography[48]. True, tectonic events will have altered the terrain by that point[49]. But even though the contours will change, the borders of the Prince's land are clearly marked out for us in advance.

Along the way, we have been "windowing in" from a larger area to a smaller one. Beginning with the Middle East region in general, Scriptures allowed us to narrow the view to the borders of future Israel. Within that country is the Prince's Province, and within *that* is the Sacred District. In fact, as the journey progresses, we will be diving ever deeper into this space. Yet in each successive step of magnification, there is – as will become apparent – an increasing amount of prophesied detail. This phenomenon will continue, as we come ever nearer the holier areas. In essence, the closer one gets to the Lord's Temple of the coming age, the more God's Word elaborates on the setting, increasingly emphasizing and detailing the things that will really matter.

Another form of "telescoping" is at work as well: that of *gifting*. At the macro level, it can be said that the Lord gave this creation to mankind to inhabit

---

[48] The background for these topographic figures was obtained from Marine Geoscience Data Systems, and their online GMRT (Global Multi-Resolution Topography) Synthesis software, 6 January 2008, <http://www.marine-geo.org/tools/maps_grids.php>. Ryan, W. B. F., S.M. Carbotte, J. Coplan, S. O'Hara, A. Melkonian, R. Arko, R.A. Weissel, V. Ferrini, A. Goodwillie, F. Nitsche, J. Bonczkowski, and R. Zemsky (2009), Global Multi-Resolution Topography (GMRT) synthesis data set, Geochem. Geophys. Geosyst., 10, Q03014, doi:10.1029/2008GC002332.

[49] E.g., Zechariah 14:4-8; Revelation 11:13, 16:18.

Chapter 2: Mapping the Sacred

and take care of[50]. Within all the land allocations of the nations of the earth, God gave the land of Israel to the people of Israel[51]. Within the ultimate borders of Israel[52], fully obtained only under the coming rule of Yeshua-Jesus, the people are to make a gift of land to their King. We are here referring to that gifted land as the "Prince's Province," *"the portion you are to present as a **special gift**."*[53] Finally, the Prince-King will then make a land-gift from that which was given to Him by the people.

> *The entire portion will be a square, 25,000 cubits on each side.* **As a special gift you will set aside the sacred portion...**
> *Ezekiel 48:20a, NIV*

This "sacred portion," or Sacred District (as we will be referring to it in this study), is the next level of magnification in the prophetic telescope. Though only a portion of the Prince's Province, it receives far more attention in Biblical prophetic emphasis. The Word affords God's astounding insights on this much smaller area, with His message to us becoming increasingly brilliant as we near the epicenter of the story.

The Gift for Sacred Use

This square section in the midst of the Prince's land is said to be the *best* portion of Israel's land[54]. Of all the restored Holy Land to come, that given to God the Son will certainly be among the most wonderful areas; but from within that, this will be the *very* best. This portion will therefore constitute a profoundly great gift from God's people to God, and also from God the Son to God the Father[55].

Though we will discuss details later, we should pause to overview how this most holy of properties is internally organized. With Ezekiel 45:1-7, and amplification in 48:8-22, we are given instruction on how the sacred-plus-city[56] district is to be arranged, with its subdivisions.

---

[50] E.g., Genesis 1:28.
[51] From Genesis 12:7 onward.
[52] Described in detail by Ezekiel, but prophesied by Moses long before him. See *The Approaching Country* for further discussion.
[53] Ezekiel 48:8.
[54] See Ezekiel 48:14.
[55] For God's Temple and City. Ezekiel 48:8, 12, 20.
[56] Strictly speaking, a distinction is made between the northern (20,000 long cubits, north to south) as the sacred portion (48:19), with the southern city section (5,000 long cubits, north to south) being more for "common" use (48:15). However, the entire combined

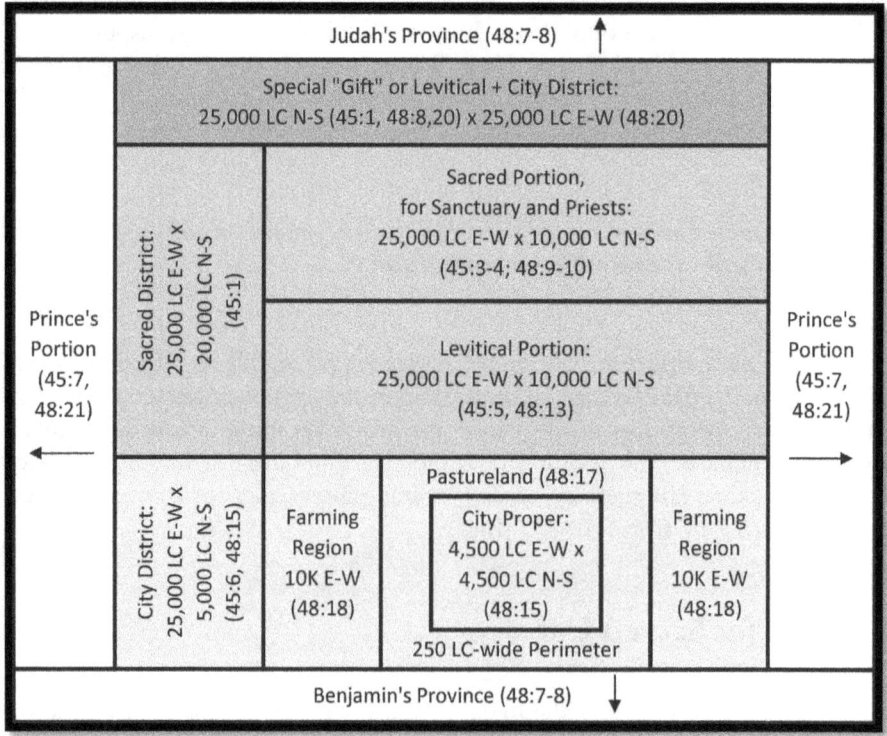

Figure 2: Sacred District Scriptural Diagram

To east and west are the Prince's lands; to north and south lay the tribal provinces, beginning with (respectively) those of Judah and Benjamin. Between all these is the singular square property measuring 8.15 miles (13.12 kilometers) on each side, a most special "gift" of land (48:8). The square is further subdivided, in north-to-south order, into the following:

- ☐ Living area for the priests, with the Sanctuary (Temple) within;
- ☐ Living area for the Levites; and
- ☐ The City (Jerusalem).

Expressed dimensionally, this same data can be presented as follows.

---

square is called the "sacred portion" (48:21) and "special gift" (48:8). Thus for the sake of brevity, "Sacred District," as used in this study, refers to the entire (25,000 cubit) square district that embraces both the sacred portion and City.

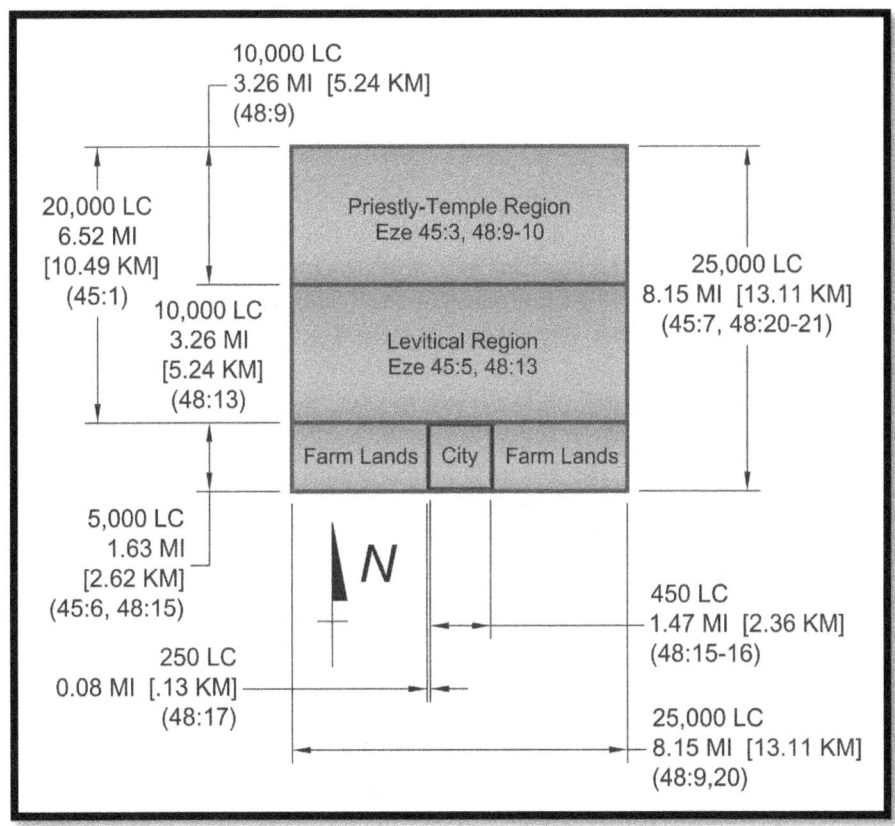

Figure 3: Sacred District Dimensions

Thanks to Ezekiel's careful recordings, we are granted this excellent cartographic view of the coming capitol of the Earth, from which Messiah will reign.

In this map we can almost perceive an enormous version of God's Temple, with its portico (the City), Holy Place (Levitical region), Most Holy Place (Priestly region), and the Ark of the Covenant (the Temple itself) centered in that region. Surely, the similar patterns are no mere coincidence!

And though one would enter the Temple in the order just described, Ezekiel describes this map in a strictly north-to-south sequence of discussion. We will therefore do the same here, beginning with the northernmost section and working our way down.

The Priestly-Temple Region

Holiest of Grounds

Of all the subdivisions, the northern section[57] is clearly the most holy: for within will be the great Temple. Ezekiel's emphasis on the Temple is with good reason: for it will be the dwelling place of the Name of God Almighty[58], the "residence[59]" of the Divine Presence. Once again in history, in a specific and utterly holy geographical area, His profound Presence, as with the Tabernacle and Temple of old, will dwell on Earth. So holy will the coming Temple grounds be that the entire mountaintop will be holy as well:

> *This is the law of the temple:* **All the surrounding area on top of the mountain will be most holy.** *Such is the law of the temple.*
> *Ezekiel 43:12a, NIV*

Of all the characteristics we will discover of the coming Mountain of God, this one is foremost: its unmitigated holiness. We might be reminded of the ground surrounding the burning bush, before which Moses fell prostrate, after being ordered to take off his sandals. We can also recall what the Lord ordained

---

[57] Though Ezekiel was not explicit in saying that the Priestly-Temple region was north of the Levitical region, it is apparent that he was describing it in that fashion, following the same north-to-south pattern of tribal territorial description. However, the phrase "*...and the sanctuary shall be in the midst of it*" (Ezekiel 48:8b) has led some to feel that the Temple (with the Priestly-Temple region surrounding it) should be in the exact center of the 25,000LC square, putting the Levitical region north of the Priestly region. However, as explained in a prior footnote, *tavek* (Strong's OT:8432) does not have to mean "in the exact center of," but can be used to mean from, in, out of, in to, "the midst of" a group, place, or higher conceptual thing. Thus *tavek* is not dimensionally definitive, as in our English language notion of an exact "center." Instead, the word speaks to relative association and proximity. Again, Ezekiel has already been describing land divisions in an obviously north-to-south order (48:1-28). Respecting that order, we will describe the Priestly-Temple region as being northernmost, the Levitical region as just south of that, and the City region as southernmost.

[58] E.g., Deuteronomy 12:5, 11, 21, 14:23, 24, 16:2, 6, 11, 26:2; 1 Kings 5:5, 8:29, 43; 2 Chronicles 6:20, 26; Nehemiah 1:9; Psalms 74:7; Isaiah 18:7; Jeremiah 7:12, 14.

[59] As Solomon made it quite clear: neither Earth nor Heaven can contain the presence of the Lord Almighty, much less an architectural temple (1 Kings 8:27; 2 Chronicles 6:18).

Chapter 2: Mapping the Sacred

for the original Tabernacle built by Moses and the Temple built by Solomon[60], in that those grounds were considered utterly holy as well. All these were places where the special Presence of God resided in this present creation, simultaneously radiating and demanding utter holiness all around. These places are no more, their stories now a matter of history. However, if one seeks the final fulfillment and consummation of the Burning Bush-Tabernacle-Temple-story, and the holy grounds associated with them, one can look ahead to this northernmost section of the Sacred District to come, the Mountain that will form its foundation, and the stories they tell us now.

In fact, we really *should* look forward to the holy Mountain, the holiest area at its summit, and the Temple that area will contain. Without question, there will be big crowds of Jewish folks celebrating then and there, even as they rejoiced when seeing the Second Temple begun[61]. Zerubbabel's Temple, though far less than Solomon's had been, was nevertheless a start of healing for the massive wound left by the First Temple's destruction. Here though, per Ezekiel's descriptions, the final Temple will vastly surpass all its historical forerunners, even Solomon's. We cannot examine that enormous topic in this exploration, but we can, and should, acknowledge that the coming foundation and Mountaintop will be made holy not without cause, but precisely *because* of the Presence of God in the Temple at its apex[62]. Because of His Presence, surrounded by His fully restored creation, *this will be the holiest ground that this world will have ever contained.*

You, I, and all believers of all nationalities can therefore be glad for what the Lord will bring about with the upcoming reconstruction of the Temple[63], and

---

[60] In regards to sacredness, the Second Temple built by Zerubbabel (and later embellished by Herod "the Great") should be included in this list. In regards to God's special Presence with the Tabernacle and original Temple though, we lack evidence that the Ark of the Covenant, and thereby His Presence, returned to the Second Temple.

[61] Ezra 3:10-13, though with weeping as well in that time because Zerubbabel's Temple lacked the glory of Solomon's (Haggai 2:9). However, and in view of Zerubbabel's Temple being a precursor in terms of a 'resurrection' of sorts, this coming and ultimate Temple in Messiah's day will far surpass the glory of even Solomon's (and, as it did not last, Herod's) (Haggai 2:9). There will be no weeping in grief in that day to come, when this Temple in the Prince's day is constructed.

[62] This holiness factor demonstrates that the Temple will not be empty, but fully infused again by God the Father's Presence. The Temple in Messiah's day will therefore be neither a mere monument, nor the place of His (Jesus') residence. The Prince will have His own land; and the Temple will be just that, as Ezekiel is careful to point out. Instead, it will be the renewed seat of the Father's Presence.

[63] As opposed to a short-term one that will be constructed during the "end times." Though yet sacred, and not to be dismissed, the prophets Daniel and John declare that this pending version of the short-lived ("third") Temple will be quickly stained by the actions and effigy of the false-messiah or "anti-christ" in times just prior to Messiah's revealing.

rejoice with all those that have long looked for these culminating events. The coming day of the Prince's reign will be the continuum and fulfillment of God's historical-Biblical promises, the return of the Father's special Presence being the unavoidable exclamation point. God's people will thrive, along with all God's creation[64]. And in all this ongoing rejoicing, the center of attention, *the* focal point of the country of Israel and the entire world, will be this holiest Mountaintop.

Regional Characteristics

The northern and most holy section of the Sacred District provides the real estate for a large population of Temple ministers and their families. This area around the top of the Mountain has specific dimensionality reported to us in the following passage.

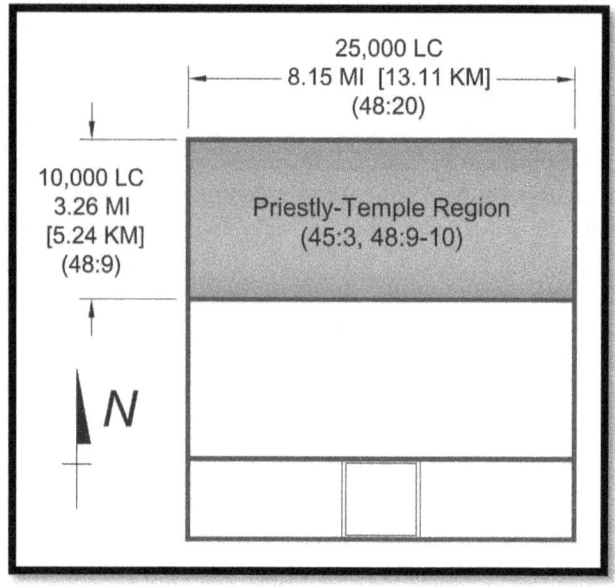

Figure 4: The Priestly-Temple Region

> *The special portion you are to offer to the Lord will be 25,000 cubits long and 10,000 cubits wide. 10 This will be the sacred portion for the priests. It will be 25,000 cubits long on the north side, 10,000 cubits wide on the west side, 10,000 cubits wide on the east side and 25,000 cubits long on the south side.* **In the center of it will be the sanctuary of the Lord.** *11 This will be for the consecrated priests, the Zadokites, who were faithful in serving me and did not go astray as the Levites did when the Israelites went astray. 12 It will be a special gift to them from the sacred portion of the land, a most holy portion, bordering the territory of the Levites.*
> Ezekiel 48:9-12, NIV

---

[64] E.g., Acts 3:21-22; 1 Corinthians 15:23-28.

Chapter 2: Mapping the Sacred

The bulk of this northern subdivision is for dwelling places of the priests that serve Temple functions. For details on what those services will involve (services in which the Prince plays a central role), read Ezekiel 43-46. From that passage – the largest topical section of Ezekiel's Messianic prophecy – there is a huge emphasis on the sacredness of these Temple services *and* the priests that serve them. This is why the facts and requirements of holiness extend, from the Temple in the center[65], throughout the entire northern subdivision.

When we think of who might comprise that priestly population, there are two big changes we should take note of. First, this coming priesthood is primarily defined not by all descendants of Aaron, but only one later descendant of his: Zadok[66]. The other change is that the Lord will make certain exceptions for particular persons who are neither of Zadokite, Aaronic or even Levitical blood:

> *"And they* [people of distant lands] *will bring all your brothers, from all the nations, to my holy mountain in Jerusalem as an offering to the LORD — on horses, in chariots and wagons, and on mules and camels," says the LORD. "They will bring them, as the Israelites bring their grain offerings, to the temple of the LORD in ceremonially clean vessels. 21* **And I will select some of them also to be priests and Levites," says the LORD.**
> Isaiah 66:20-21, NIV

After all these centuries, the Zadokite lineage may well be plentiful – once the Lord sorts out who these people are[67]. But with the special Gentile exceptions known to and chosen by the Lord, this priestly population will be much enlarged. Israel's Aaronic priesthood will have been subjected to God's own filtering, via Zadok. But certain people of other nations will have their roles here, and their residences will be alongside the Zadokite homes in this most holy section of the Sacred District. Whatever the final composition though, it is quite clear that membership in the Temple priesthood in Messiah's time is profoundly selective, and a tremendous honor.

---

[65] Is the Sanctuary (Temple) to be in the exact center of the northern subdivision? Not from the Hebrew word *tavek* used here in 48:10, which (as discussed in earlier footnotes) cannot demand that. However, *tavek* does not preclude the idea either. In fact, other factors give evidence of the Temple being centered within the northern subdivision. We will arrive at that evidence in due course; but for now, centeredness will be assumed, and not because of *tavek*.

[66] As to God's emphasis on this matter, see Ezekiel 40:46, 43:19, 44:15-16. As to why, see, e.g., 2 Samuel 15:24-36; 17:15,17-21.

[67] Such an accurate identification of Zadokites will be no small feat, but its emphasis is nevertheless detectable in Ezra 2:59-62. Presumably the identification will not be without divine enablement, but may well nevertheless involve documentation and scientific means.

Though we don't know how many priests there will be in total (including those from other nations), we are given a number for those coming specifically from the tribes of Israel: 144,000. According to Revelation 7:4-8 and 14:1-4, these priests will be "purchased" from mankind in general (as was Levi was purchased from the tribes of Israel), yet also extracted from *all* twelve natural tribes of Israel – in fulfillment of Exodus 19:6. This number of priests, 144,000, is an exact 500-fold multiplication of the special priest-musicians serving in the time of David (1 Chronicles 25:7).

In addition to their musical service[68], these priests will have a lot of work to do: for this vast Temple, per Ezekiel, will have correspondingly enormous demands for priestly activity, just as in the days of the Tabernacle and Biblical Temples, but multiplied. So it's understandable that there will be plenty of priests to deal with those needs.

The priestly population can be summarized like this: the Zadokite descendants, plus an untold number from all nations of the world, plus the 144,000 from the twelve tribes of Israel. Many priests! And whatever that total number is, it is multiplied when we consider their families, for these men will have wives and children. And in view of the greatly increased longevity in those days[69], these families (as with those of all believers then) may become quite huge.

Will all these families have their homes in this northern subdivision? Not necessarily, for many might come to live and serve in monthly "courses," just as in Biblical days[70], and serve throughout Israel (and other countries) during the major portion of the year. That's for God to say.

The point here is that there will be *no* shortage of priests and their family members inhabiting this northern region and supporting holy Temple services. So it sure won't be difficult to fill this 10.6 square mile (27.5 square kilometer) region with homes!

The Levitical Region

Ministerial Headquarters

Moving southward, the next subdivision we come to is that belonging to the Levites. It is impossible here to do justice to the importance of tribe of Levi, descended from Jacob's third son, but we should refresh ourselves on some of the main points. From all the tribes of Israel, Levi was extracted by the Lord for

---

[68] Revelation 14:2, 15:2.
[69] E.g., Isaiah 65:20.
[70] E.g., 1 Chronicles 28:13; 2 Chronicles 8:14, 31:2.

Chapter 2: Mapping the Sacred

His purposes, to minister before Him. God selected the tribe of Levi way back during the formation of Israel as a fledgling nation, long before Zadok was born.

It's fascinating to realize that Levi was "taken" by God in exchange for the firstborn sons of Egypt slain in the Passover events. The equation is somewhat mysterious, but the gist of it is this: for Egypt's brutal enslavement of Israel, God made them "pay" with their firstborn males, both human and animal. However, Israel would have to "pay" for their own exemption from that punishment, and offer to God all their own firstborn males as well.

> *When Pharaoh stubbornly refused to let us go, the LORD killed every firstborn in Egypt, both man and animal. This is why I sacrifice to the LORD the first male offspring of every womb and* **redeem each of my firstborn sons.'**
> *Exodus 13:15, NIV*

This law applied to Israel for "*both man and animal*"[71]. However, in the wilderness days of Israel's formation, there was a very special path of "redemption" for firstborn sons. The Lord declared that instead of all the tribes offering their firstborn males to Him, He would take *one entire tribe* in payment of that debt.

> **Take the Levites for me *in place* of all the firstborn of the Israelites**, *and the livestock of the Levites in place of all the firstborn of the livestock of the Israelites. I am the LORD...* **Take the Levites in place of all the firstborn of Israel**, *and the livestock of the Levites in place of their livestock.* **The Levites are to be mine.** *I am the Lord.*
> *Numbers 3:41,45 NIV*

> *After you have purified the Levites and presented them as a wave offering, they are to come to do their work at the Tent of Meeting. 16 They are the Israelites who are to be given wholly to me. I have taken them as my own in place of the firstborn, the first male offspring from every Israelite woman. 17* **Every firstborn male in Israel, whether man or animal, is mine.** *When I struck down all the firstborn in Egypt, I set them apart for myself. 18 And* **I have taken the Levites in place of all the firstborn sons in Israel.**
> *Numbers 8:15-18, NIV*

The absolute precision of this exchange[72], firstborn for firstborn, indicates God's exactitude in requiring what was owed to Him in these matters. It also speaks to the pivotal ministerial role the Levites would play in history past, and will do once more in history forward. While Israel remains the Lord's "selected"

---

[71] Exodus 13:2, 12-13, 34:19-20.
[72] Seen in Numbers 3:42-50.

and "first-born" nation amongst all nations[73], the tribe of Levi, quite literally, belongs to God as representative of the entire nation.

From this special tribe would come the priests, whose selection would be further filtered through the bloodlines of first Aaron, and then Phinehas[74], and eventually (as has been mentioned) Zadok. It is only this last sub-sub-sub-division of Levi that will serve as priests in Messiah's coming day, leaving the vast majority of the tribe to find their abodes elsewhere. A portion of Levites, however, will live in this very special and most central section of the Sacred District.

Will these natural-born Levites be augmented in number in some way? Yes indeed! For as quoted above, Isaiah declares quite plainly,

> *And I will select some of them also to be priests and Levites," says the LORD.*
> *Isaiah 66:21, NIV*

As seen in the verses just prior to this, The "them" referred to are "survivors" of "all nations and tongues." Just as the bloodline-selected priests will be enhanced by people from all lands, the Levitical population will be likewise augmented.

What will all these Levites do? With historical precedent for the Tabernacle and Temple in view, they will support the priests in their duties within the Temple[75], performing numerous secondary (though still vital) roles. While the (expanded) Zadokite subset will serve the Lord in His Temple and at the altar there, the broader tribe will enjoy extensive ministry in surrounding and supportive activities.

Regional Characteristics

The Levitical region is, like the Priestly, dimensionally straightforward. Continuing his north-to-south order of description, Ezekiel continues:

> *Alongside the territory of the priests, the Levites will have an allotment 25,000 cubits long and 10,000 cubits wide. Its total length will be 25,000 cubits and its width 10,000 cubits. 14 They must not sell or exchange any of it. This is the best of the land and must not pass into other hands, because it is holy to the Lord.*
> *Ezekiel 48:13-14, NIV*

---

[73] E.g., Exodus 4:22.
[74] Numbers 25:6-13.
[75] E.g., Numbers 3:9, 8:19, 18:6.

Cutting east-to-west, this section splits the Sacred District, having the same north-to-south width as the Priestly-Temple region to the north, and twice that of the City region to the south.

Ezekiel says this section will be "the best of the land," using a word often rendered elsewhere as "firstfruits"[76]. This term indicates this land to be *particularly* good in resources, beauty, or both, even in comparison with other sections of the Sacred District.

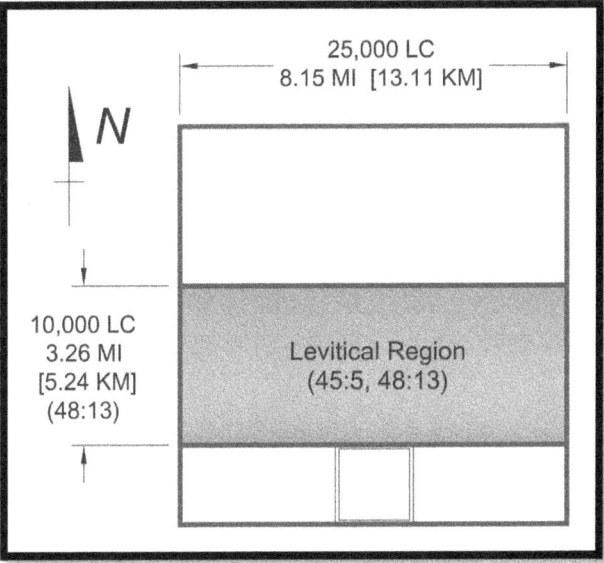

Figure 5: The Levitical Region

We are further informed that this region will likewise be holy[77], along with the Priestly region to the north. This demonstrates that both these regions (and their populations) will act in concert, in service to the Temple. This also shows why both these two larger sections are referred to as a unified whole, "the possession of the Levites," as apart from the city to the south[78]. Like the Priestly region, the central Levitical region proper will be considered "holy to the Lord," which means specially devoted to His purposes.

The holy calling of both the servants and their dwelling areas explains why the Levites must not sell their properties in the Sacred District. For just as in Biblical times, the lands of the Levites must remain theirs in the era to come[79].

One might wonder though, isn't this land area small for a whole tribe? Indeed it is! It will have the same area as the Priestly-Temple region (10.6 square miles /27.5 square kilometers)[80]. Yet in comparison with the average allotment

---

[76] The word for "best" in 48:14 is *re'shiyth* (ray-sheeth'), Strong's OT:7225, the same used to describe "firstfruit" offerings.

[77] *Qodesh* (ko'-desh), Strong's OT:6944.

[78] Ezekiel 48:22.

[79] E.g., Leviticus 25:34.

[80] Minus the comparatively small area devoted to the Temple grounds within the Priestly area.

to the other tribes' provinces, it has merely 1% to 2% of their real estate[81]. Will Levi be that small of a tribe? No. In fact, we can expect that the Levitical population will only be expanded, as we have discussed, via certain Gentile servants of God's choosing[82]. Some of these "foreigners" will most likely also live in this region of the Sacred District, only adding to the "problem." So where will the bulk of the tribe live? This major tribe of Israel, expanded with Gentile members, would easily overflow this holy but small region within the Sacred District, and the necessity of additional property for Levi is plain.

We have a number of clues to the answer, beginning with the fact that, from Ezekiel's territory list, the tribe of Levi has no assigned province in the Prince's day. This might not seem to be a solution at all, but ironically, it is! For historically it was the same situation: that since Levi's inheritance was to minister before the Lord (and *not* to have a tribal territory of their own), they would have no further inheritance of land like other tribes[83]. Since this special service to the Lord will still be present, and since no big province is handed to them, we can anticipate that some different means of property provision will likewise be granted in the Prince's day.

Specifically, with the original tribal distributions under Joshua, additional cities were assigned to Levi[84]. These Levitical towns, with their surrounding areas, were dispersed throughout the other tribal provinces[85]. So we should not be surprised if, under the coming reign of Yeshua-Joshua, the parallel took place, with Levites having dedicated portions *within each of the tribal allocations.*

Furthermore, there is one big additional opportunity for Levites (and priests, for that matter) to have property in the coming time. Keep in mind that many Levites will most likely live in other lands, serving God's purposes in the King's broader worldwide dominion[86]. Though only the Lord knows the details at this point, it will almost certainly be that many foreign-born "Priests and Levites" (as seen in Isaiah 66:21) will serve in their own homeland, in partnership with natural-born Levites co-located there. These servants of the Lord, just like their brethren in Israel, will most likely have their own dedicated lands in every country they minister in.

Since the bulk of the (expanded) tribe of Levi will live in other provinces and perhaps even countries, it may well be that this special location in the Sacred District will be home for those having currently active roles in Temple service –

---

[81] Depending on which tribe, and also land expansions of the provinces to the east, as covered in The Approaching Country.
[82] Isaiah 66:19-21.
[83] Numbers 18:20-24; Deuteronomy 18:1-2.
[84] E.g., Joshua 20, demonstrating the distribution of Levites in their own special cities, throughout the country.
[85] E.g., Numbers 35; Joshua 20.
[86] E.g., assisting in the worship activities that will abound in all lands: Zephaniah 2:11; Zechariah 8:23.

perhaps on a clan-rotation basis, as is reflected in their history[87]. Regardless, those fortunate to live in this portion of the Holy Land to come will clearly see a lot of amazing activity. Without question, it will be a headquarters to which many visitors flock. This central area will truly be a global hub of ministry and praise to God.

The City Region

Home of the Blessed

This southernmost "city" section of the Sacred District is a narrow slice of land that is further split into three segments. The central part is dedicated to the City proper, which is flanked on either side by agricultural lands. "City" here, of course, refers to Jerusalem to come: fully healed, greatly expanded, with foursquare walls and twelve gates just as visited in advance by Ezekiel[88]. Here will be the seat of world government, with the Lord Jesus reigning as King of all kings. The City will be the global focus of praise and celebration to God, with all nations bringing their wealth to it.

The Bible says so much about Jerusalem in these times ahead, that we simply cannot do the topic justice at this point. We will instead defer the City to a further expedition, remaining focused here on the holy Mountain and how the City will be arranged upon it. In the mean time, here are some points to ponder from Isaiah.

> *O afflicted city, lashed by storms and not comforted,* **I will build you with stones of turquoise, your foundations with sapphires. 12 I will make your battlements of rubies, your gates of sparkling jewels, and all your walls of precious stones.**
> Isaiah 54:11-12, NIV

> *Nations will come to your light, and kings to the brightness of your dawn… 5 Then you will look and be radiant, your heart will throb and swell with joy;* **the wealth on the seas will be brought to you, to you the riches of the nations will come… 10 Foreigners will rebuild your walls, and their kings will serve you.** *Though in anger I struck you, in favor I will show you compassion. 11 Your gates will always stand open, they will never be shut, day or night, so that*

---

[87] See 1 Chronicles 24 and 26.
[88] Ezekiel 48:15-20 & 30-35.

men may bring you the wealth of the nations — their kings led in triumphal procession.
Isaiah 60:3,5,10-11, NIV

For Zion's sake I will not keep silent, for Jerusalem's sake I will not remain quiet, till her righteousness shines out like the dawn, her salvation like a blazing torch. 2 **The nations will see your righteousness, and all kings your glory;** *you will be called by a new name that the mouth of the LORD will bestow. 3 You will be a crown of splendor in the LORD's hand, a royal diadem in the hand of your God.*
Isaiah 62:1-3, NIV

"Then they shall bring all your brethren from all the nations as a grain offering to the LORD, on horses, in chariots, in litters, on mules, and on camels, to My holy mountain Jerusalem," says the LORD, "just as the sons of Israel bring their grain offering in a clean vessel to the house of the LORD. 21 "I will also take some of them for priests and for Levites," says the LORD.
Isaiah 66:20-21, NASB

What an astounding city it will be!

Regional Characteristics

In Ezekiel's continuing north-to-south order of description, we find that dimensions are again firmly laid out for this region.

The remaining area, 5,000 cubits wide and 25,000 cubits long, will be for the common use of the city, for houses and for pastureland. The city will be in the center of it 16 and will have these measurements: the north side 4,500 cubits, the south side 4,500 cubits, the east side 4,500 cubits, and the west side 4,500 cubits. 17 The pastureland for the city will be 250 cubits on the north, 250 cubits on the south, 250 cubits on the east, and 250 cubits on the west. 18 What remains of the area, bordering on the sacred portion and running the length of it, will be 10,000 cubits on the east side and 10,000 cubits on the west side. Its produce will supply food for the workers of the city. 19 The workers from the city who farm it will come from all the tribes of Israel.
Ezekiel 48:15-19, NIV

Jerusalem to come, including its surrounding narrow strip of "pastureland [89]," will be 2.65 square miles / 6.87 square km in area. Within that margin, the area of City itself is 2.15 square miles / 5.57 square km. The outer boundary of this margin forms a 5,000 LC square, with a 5,000 LC wide by 10,000 LC long farming area on its east and west sides.

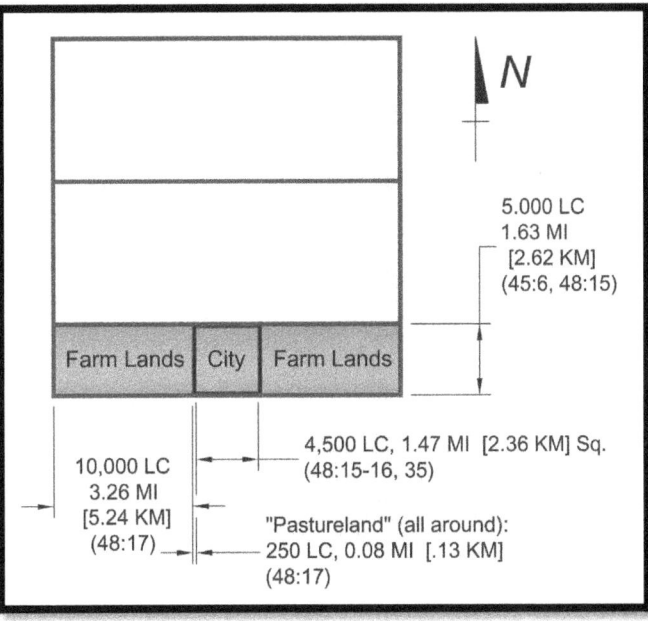

Figure 6: The City Region

Does this arrangement look a little familiar? Yes! It is a miniature of the Prince's Province, which is separated into east and west regions by the Sacred District in the middle. This design connection may well be quite deliberate, with either pattern reminding us of the other.

One might think the City area is quite small, at least by today's standards. For example, see how these modern cities compare[90] with it.

	Sq. Miles	Sq. Km	Mil. Cities
Millennial City	2.15	5.6	-
New York City	303.3	786	141
Los Angeles (city)	469.1	1,215	218

Figure 7: City Area Comparison

---

[89] Though certain translations use "pastureland" here, the term doesn't require animals grazing there. Rather, *migrash* (mig-rawsh', Strong's OT:4054), literally means "cast out," referring to the open areas outside a city's walls where flocks might have been sent for foraging. In the KJV, the word is usually rendered "suburbs" of a city (e.g., Joshua 21; 1 Chronicles 6). In our situation, it only need mean open space outside the walls, perhaps containing farmland, pastureland, parkland, or a mix.
[90] Source: <http://www.city-data.com>, taken on 2/2/2015.

Other major world cities could have been listed here, but you get the point: alongside these two metropolitan giants, Millennial Jerusalem is tiny. You could fit over 200 of them within today's boundaries of LA! So while the coming City won't at all be the largest ever, it will still be the most important and compelling city by far in the coming era.

On the other hand, this is *not* a small area: Millennial Jerusalem will cover 1,376 acres. By the way, it will be 40 times larger in area than the US Pentagon[91], so it will not be an enclosed building, but remain an open-air city. Though not the largest city, it will envelop its ancient counterpart, with an area about six times greater[92].

Millennial Jerusalem will be hugely substantial in many other respects. Surrounded by ministerial regions and provinces, we can foresee the City as the core of civic and governmental activity in tomorrow's Israel, and the apex of concentric levels of praise and worship for all the earth. Jerusalem will be the regal capital of Messiah's worldwide administration, the place of the Creator's rule. Though small by today's standards, this will be a City overflowing with purpose, activity, beauty, and life!

---

[91] The area covered by the Pentagon, including its inner courtyard, is 34 acres. Source: <http://pentagontours.osd.mil/facts-area.jsp>, accessed on 2/2/2015.
[92] The area of the Old City is .35 square miles, equating to 224 acres. Source: <https://en.wikipedia.org/wiki/Old_City_(Jerusalem)>, accessed on 10/24/16.

Chapter 3: Marking the Borders

Beautiful for situation, the joy of the whole earth, is mount Zion, on the sides of the north, the city of the great King.
Psalms 48:2, KJV

So shall my word be that goeth forth out of my mouth: it shall not return unto me void, but it shall accomplish that which I please, and it shall prosper in the thing whereto I sent it.
Isaiah 55:11, KJV

"The days are coming," declares the LORD, "when this city will be rebuilt for me... The city will never again be uprooted or demolished."
Jeremiah 31:38a, 40b, NIV

A Needed Datum

Having worked through the main dimensions of the Sacred District, we end up with a carefully defined geometric grid of sorts. What we don't have though is a firm idea on where it will be positioned on the ground, and how it will be oriented.

The Location Question

Terrain will have undergone serious changes by then, causing some to perhaps ask if placement of the Sacred District over present geography is worth the trouble. But it *is* worth it. Because if we can place this geometry, the borders of the Prince's province would also be known, extending as it will to east and west. Further, we can discover what historical places these borders will embrace, and perhaps gain new insights on Biblical stories about those places, in light of their coming Millennial position.

Furthermore, since God's Word gives us these many careful measurements, it would make a lot of sense if a starting point were likewise granted. In the prior "expedition," we saw that the future borders of Israel were carefully established, using many sites known to this day. We should therefore not be surprised if the Bible also contained critical reference points for the Sacred District's location.

So, what we would like to see is a geographic anchor. If we can discover that, many things follow. But what might it be? How is this grid registered with known geography? Can some key prophesied element be pinpointed to a present-day feature, something knowable and verifiable right now? That is our objective in this next step of the journey: to either acquire such a geometric starting point, or at least perform due diligence in trying to ascertain it.

An Initial Candidate

Actually, we also need a cartographic registration point from *within* the prophesied map-grid, something vital that can be correlated to something on the ground. From what we have seen so far, this anchor position might well be the great Temple seen in Ezekiel's vision. After all, it (along with its surrounding mountaintop) will be the *most holy* of all places on Earth at that time. Without question, the Temple will be the worship focus of the Sacred District, and the entire world for that matter. If we could connect this coming Temple with some known present location, that would be a huge indicator.

Supporting that idea, the prophesied Temple certainly received Ezekiel's rapt attention. The Lord caused him to literally walk its grounds and describe its architecture, recording very precise dimensions and detailed notations. The prophet was actually there on the peak of that holy Mountain, in a "teleportation" of time and distance similar to that recorded in Ezekiel chapters 1-3 and 8-11. In addition to fulfilling his mandate to explain all these matters to us[93], the man's passion was to understand and convey hope about the Temple's *literal* restoration, however distant in the future that might be. More than any other location in his Millennial prophecies, Ezekiel's emphasis is solidly on this holiest of places.

As a location key for the Sacred District's layout, the Temple is – as long as prior calculations here hold true – a reasonable registration point. But can this focus of future worship be independently plotted on a modern map? Can we directly correlate it with a specific known place or locatable feature? One that will remain after the geological turmoil of the "end times" has passed? The answer is, from this author's searches, No. For from the dimensions we've seen, it will be located nowhere near the *historical* Temple site, but about 5.7 miles (9.19 km) to the north of the City's center. We will return to that calculation later, but no matter what, it's a significant distance; and Ezekiel does not tell of some city or other feature north of Jerusalem that the Temple will be related to.

Now if the ancient site of Shiloh were in the vicinity, that finding would be of enormous interest. For we would be reminded of the very, very ancient prophecy of the man Jacob-Israel, speaking to his sons:

> *The sceptre shall not depart from Judah, nor a lawgiver from between his feet, until Shiloh come; and unto him shall the gathering of the people be.*
> Genesis 49:10, KJV

As reflected in the various translations of this verse, some have believed "Shiloh" to be a place name, while others have seen it to be a personal name – specifically, a name for Messiah[94]. Perhaps, in the end, it will be both. For the ancient city of Shiloh (the same word used in Genesis 49:10 just quoted) was home to the Tabernacle in the days of Samuel. And if it were to be co-located with the coming Temple, the symbolic connections would be mighty indeed.

But, Shiloh has been located by scholars much farther to the north, too far it seems for our consideration. Even if an archaeological team were sent to investigate and perhaps improve on traditional understanding, they wouldn't gain access. Tomorrow's Temple, and whatever Biblical sites coincide with it there, are off limits for all practical purposes here.

---

[93] With heavy consequences for him if he did not: see Ezekiel 33.
[94] Shiyloh, (*shee-lo'*), Strong's OT:7886: "tranquil; Shiloh, an epithet of the Messiah."

Therefore the coming Temple does not seem to supply that hard anchor point of mapping, at least at this time, and in this journey. So we need to find something else.

The Other Focus

But is there an alternative? Is there a different dimensional "ground zero" that we have overlooked? Though Ezekiel's prophecies don't directly answer this question, the prophet does begin his vision with a huge clue:

> *In the twenty-fifth year of our exile, at the beginning of the year, on the tenth of the month, in the fourteenth year after the* **fall of the city** *— on that very day the hand of the LORD was upon me and he took me there. 2 In visions of God he took me to the land of Israel and set me on* **a very high mountain**, *on whose* **south** *side were some buildings that* **looked like a city**.
> *Ezekiel 40:1-2, NIV*

These verses form the introduction for Ezekiel's jaw-dropping records of the Messianic dominion to come, with emphasis here in the Sacred District. And, we see an initial clue on how to begin laying out the "grid" of his subsequent measurements for the Sacred District. Though the vision begins with Ezekiel standing upon the Temple Mount to come, his physical gaze is downward and to the south, giving us another focal point: future Jerusalem[95].

Another clue in verse 40:1 is Ezekiel's unmistakable connection with historical Jerusalem, in that this vision of restoration took place on the exact (and to the day) fourteenth anniversary of Jerusalem's fall to the Babylonians. Right from the beginning then, we have these two key points of interest: the Temple *and* the City. And the first thing Ezekiel found himself looking at was the City.

Thus we have not one but *two* key geographic foci to consider. Both are pivotal; and both define, more than any other sacred locale, the nature and purpose of the prophesied Sacred District. If we cannot at this time firmly correlate the Temple with a key place in Biblical history, the City serves as our only alternate geographic anchor point.

---

[95] The fact that this city is Jerusalem is implicit in Ezekiel 48, e.g., in the naming of its gates in verses 30-34. Further, Ezekiel makes it clear that this city is indeed Jerusalem, for its future presence is placed in direct juxtaposition with that ancient city, destroyed just fourteen years prior to this vision (40:1).

Something Has to Move

God declares through Ezekiel that the future Temple and City will be greatly separated – by several *miles!* This is in huge contrast with the Jerusalem we know in history and today, with the position of the historical Temple being *within* the City's borders. A much larger notion of "Zion" is therefore involved here: an enormous Sacred District which now enfolds its cartographically separated centers of attention.

Geographically though, it is clear that one or the other of these two pivotal elements of Zion, Temple or City, will have to *move*. Which of the two is it? Put differently, which of the two will remain *unmoved* through the literally earthshaking events prior to the arrival of Jesus/Yeshua?

Fortunately, we are provided a definitive answer. For in this very context of the Prince's dominion breaking forth, the prophet Zechariah weighs in heavily on this precise matter:

> **On that day** *I will make the leaders of Judah like a firepot in a woodpile, like a flaming torch among sheaves. They will consume right and left all the surrounding peoples,* **but Jerusalem will remain intact in her place.**
> Zechariah 12:6, NIV

And again,

> *The whole land, from Geba to Rimmon, south of Jerusalem, will become like the Arabah.* **But Jerusalem will be raised up and remain in its place,** *from the Benjamin Gate to the site of the First Gate, to the Corner Gate, and from the Tower of Hananel to the royal winepresses. 11 It will be inhabited; never again will it be destroyed.* **Jerusalem will be secure.**
> Zechariah 14:10-11, NIV

In this coming time, and in spite of all the tectonic upheaval, Jerusalem will remain "secure," "intact in her place." We have a confirming witness in Jeremiah, who describes a rebuilding of historical ruins for the coming indestructible City:

> *"The days are coming," declares the LORD, "when* **this city will be rebuilt for me** *from the Tower of Hananel to the Corner Gate. 39 The measuring line will stretch from there straight to the hill of Gareb and then turn to Goah. 40 The whole valley where dead bodies and ashes are thrown, and all the terraces out to the Kidron Valley on the east as far as the corner of the Horse Gate, will be holy to the LORD.* **The city will never again be uprooted or demolished."**
> Jeremiah 31:38-40, NIV

Chapter 3: Marking the Borders

Let's put these facts together. Even after the "apocalyptic" transitional events, in spite of serious geological upheaval therein[96], the Lord makes it quite clear that one will, in days *afterward*, easily detect the sites of certain gates and towers of Jerusalem's ancient architecture, right down to certain gates, wall portions, and the ancient stones that comprise them!

God's emphasis in all this is that Jerusalem, having been ravaged and made desolate in times past, will remain rock solid in its position – not only in the sense of spiritual metaphoric value, but also in terms of literal geography. The fact of a spatial *anchoring* of this city (emphasized in mention of specific gates and other architectural features) is a clear and visible symbol of God's faithfulness in bringing these promises, and so many others, to pass.

Without question then, Jerusalem's physical position remains fixed and inviolable, even after the Trumpets, Bowls and Seals of Revelation. In regards to mapping, this is a vital prophetic fact for us. It requires that the City remains fixed in place throughout any geological upheaval[97].

Such a "movement" of the Temple position does, in fact, have precedent: for the dwelling place of God's name, with the Tabernacle, was *very* mobile, by God's design. The position change further underscores the fact that the Person of the Lord Almighty cannot be contained by *any* structure – not any past Temple, not this coming Temple of the Messianic era, not the Earth itself, not even Heaven[98].

We can know then that the ancient city of Jerusalem will remain the immovable thing "planted"[99] by God and that the position of the Temple representing His Name will geographically move. If we plot Ezekiel's grid based on these facts, and roughly center the Jerusalem "box" over its historic borders, we can more or less understand where the borders of the Sacred District and the Prince's Province will lie.

But we're not done yet.

Ground Zero

---

[96] That is, in spite of the Mount of Olives having been split in half by that time (Zechariah 14:3-5), and global earthquakes having just taken place (e.g., Revelation 16:18).
[97] E.g., Isaiah 29:6; Ezekiel 38:19; Zechariah 14:3-5; Matthew 24:7; Mark 13:8; Revelation 6:12, 11:13, 16:18.
[98] 1 Kings 8:27; 2 Chronicles 2:5-6, 6:18.
[99] E.g., Psalms 80:8,14-15; Isaiah 60:21; Ezekiel 17:1, 19:10.

A Finer Point

We can now, from Zechariah's and Jeremiah's statements just quoted, center Ezekiel's foreseen city *somewhere* over historical Jerusalem. For starters, we could guess at how they correlate by parking Ezekiel's city-square (1.63 miles on each side) over a map of Jerusalem's ancient walls, and call it done. We could calculate the center of ancient city area, place the new City's center over that, and move on. But there's the problem with this sort of approach. At what time in history do you take such a snapshot of Jerusalem's footprint? Which set of walls would you use? King David's, or King Herod's, or something in between? For the City's encircling walls changed dramatically over time; with each stage, the center of area moves, sometimes dramatically. Wall locations are further obscured by subsequent Roman, Crusader and Islamic architecture. Any geographic and definitive "center" of historical Jerusalem, based solely on its borders, would therefore be quite elusive, making this method a quite inaccurate one.

Are we stuck? Hopefully not, because from the city-square, all other major borders of the Sacred District are calculated. With all the prophesied and explicit dimensions, but without a firm starting point, the cartography is blurred. Given the precise nature of Ezekiel's dimensions (conveyed in royal cubits, which are extremely specific), we might expect the Bible to offer a definitive "ground zero" to begin those dimensions from. If we had that, we would be able to more precisely place the 4,500 LC square of the City proper.

Should we bother with understanding these matters? Yes. The Lord gives these dimensions in the form of commands to be acted upon: strict instructions that must be followed by Israelites of that time ahead[100]. Surely *they* will require a cartographic starting point when, say, surveying for the new borders and walls[101]. True, the Lord Himself may well select a certain place and declare, "Begin here with your measurements." But would He do so, in an arbitrary manner? He could; but it would be far easier to anticipate that He confirm and select a place already identified, one already having great meaning in His overall Jerusalem-creation-story.

From that perspective, there is another means of reckoning the center of the City. Let's call this approach the "significant feature method": that there might be some historical spot within Jerusalem that is ultimately defining, regardless of the transitory placement of its walls over time.

---

[100] Especially in Ezekiel 43:11; reflected also in 45:1 & 6, 47:13-14 & 21, 48:9 & 28.
[101] God's people (of all nations) will construct much of this architecture. See Isaiah 60:10-12; 62:6-12.

Feature of Significance

So we want to see if there is a transcendent artifact of historical Jerusalem, important enough to consider it, over time, essential and "central." There are many candidates: within the City are numerous places considered very holy, their aggregate perhaps amounting to more holy-places-per-acre than any other site on earth. But does one momentous spot rise head and shoulders over the rest? Maybe so; but if we are to identify it, we should first consider some criteria.

For the purposes of providing a geographic anchor point to the coming City of Messiah, and thus establishing the cartography of the Sacred District, its three regions, and the Prince's eastern and western lands, such a crucial locale might be characterized as follows:

- ☐ Historical Presence: this position should have been present and identifiable in all the historical stages of the Lord's development of, and interaction with, Jerusalem.

- ☐ Extremely Ancient: this position, per the above, would have been present at least as early as King David's time, since that was when the main Biblical story of Jerusalem as a city came into play.

- ☐ Architecturally Independent: this position would probably be independent of architecture that has come and gone since David's time, such as city walls and other features, and not have been swept away with any of them. It would therefore most likely be natural, not man-made.

- ☐ Covenantal Importance: this position will serve the Lord's purposes in the time of the Prince's reign, being a holy place worthy of being so honored then, reminding all of His covenantal faithfulness toward His people.

- ☐ Identifiable in the Future: this position will have survived great wars through history, and tectonic events of the "end times"; yet it will remain visible as a physical feature from which to measure, in Messiah's Coming Day.

- ☐ Identifiable in the Present: this position, if known in ages past, and also in a day to come, must therefore be identifiable in the present day, and thus locatable on a map we can understand.

From these points, we would like to see a holy place of central, enduring, covenantal significance for Jerusalem, made not by man, but by God. It would be a feature within the Jerusalem *today*, having survived for at least 3,000 years, while stone structures, even massive ones, have not.

A Likely Candidate

There is one holy place that meets all these criteria, and overwhelmingly so. This locale is transcendent of historical walls and borders of habitation, in any historical era. As a matter of fact, it pre-dates David's city, and even the name 'Jerusalem.' That remarkable position is at the apex of God's holy mountain in Biblical times, reckoned so even before Sinai: *Mount Moriah*.

Moriah was the place of Abraham's supreme sacrifice, in obeying the Lord to offer his only son Isaac[102]. Though the Lord stopped Abraham from doing so, that act of faith was part and parcel to God's supreme blessing of him, resulting in the very existence of the nation of Israel[103] and – through his offspring[104], Jesus – the promise that all nations of the Earth would be ultimately blessed[105].

God's redemptive, personal and covenantal interaction, for all mankind, therefore began with Abraham's decision to place *all* his trust in Him. Because of this, Abraham is not only the physical father of his Israelite-Jewish descendants, but also of all those that follow his example in faith, whether Jew or Gentile[106]. Thus people of all nations may join in faith with Abraham's natural and faithful offspring[107], because the Prince, the Son of God, threw open the doors of His covenant to all nations[108]. All Jews and Christians alike therefore find their first roots of faith in this defining act of Abraham, with his near-sacrifice of Isaac his son[109].

---

[102] Genesis 22.
[103] Genesis 22:16-18.
[104] Galatians 3:16.
[105] Genesis 22:18.
[106] Romans 4:11.
[107] Seen throughout the teachings of Moses in the inclusion of the complying non-Israelite into the community, and in the doctrines of Paul (e.g., Romans 4:16ff; Galatians 3:7ff).
[108] The teachings of Paul (e.g., Romans 11, Ephesians 2) make very clear the point that Jesus brings Gentile believers to the Father not in a covenant vacuum, but rather – and explicitly – to a co-membership within an expanded concept if Israel, that is, the entire human population through whom the faith (and therefore fatherhood) of Abraham is the foundation (Romans 4:11-16; Galatians 3:8-9, 14).
[109] The Bible clearly defines God's chosen nation as the descendants of Abraham's barren wife Sarah (Isaac), not the son of his concubine Hagar (Ishmael). At the same time, I will point out two things regarding descendents of Ishmael: that both Jews and

Chapter 3: Marking the Borders

Some time later God tested Abraham. He said to him, "Abraham!" "Here I am," he replied. 2 Then God said, "Take your son, your only son, Isaac, whom you love, and go to the region of **Moriah***. Sacrifice him there as a burnt offering on* **one of the mountains I will tell you about.***"*
Genesis 22:1-2, NIV

That initial and decisive event occurred on a particular mountaintop originally named *Moriah*. It is no wonder then that the Lord directed King David to this *exact spot* for the Temple's design [110], and King Solomon for its construction.

Then Solomon began to build the **temple of the LORD** *in Jerusalem* **on Mount Moriah, where the LORD had appeared to his father David.** *It was on the threshing floor of Araunah the Jebusite, the place provided by David.*
2 Chronicles 3:1, NIV

This hugely special Mount is therefore an immovable anchor point for *all* eras of Jerusalem's definitions, from Abraham, to King David's time, to that of Ezekiel's, to first century times, and to our day; indeed, into Messiah's reign on the horizon. This peak of Mount Moriah was present throughout the Biblical drama of Israel, and provides meaning that surpasses all other geographic and archeological considerations.

Though Calvary is another strong candidate for such a positional marker for the City[111], Moriah can be recommended as the prevalent one. Golgotha was a place outside the city, and not lasting in its geographic understanding. Moriah, within Jerusalem, has enduring centrality through Biblical history.

Going forward, in this expedition at least, Moriah will therefore be considered as the significant anchor point for Jerusalem in history past. It meets the criteria of historical presence, being extremely ancient and architecturally independent, and having tremendous covenantal importance.

Christians can learn respect of law through such historical descendents (Jeremiah 35); and that *all* nations will be represented in the coming kingdom of the Lord Almighty, via Abraham's faithful actions (from Genesis 12:3, 18:18 and 22:18, to Revelation 7:9 and 15:4).

[110] 2 Samuel 24:23-25; 1 Chronicles 21:25.

[111] Without question, some Christians will argue that Calvary is the more defining point. However, we are told that the story of God-breathed faith began with Abraham. As the Prince's City appears as the capstone to that overarching story, Moriah, as the starting place of it, can be argued as the more defining geographic position. Furthermore, the several argued positions for Calvary are conflicting and based primarily on tradition and not on demonstrable fact or Scriptural evidence. It is therefore impossible to pinpoint where Calvary was, there being at least three sites strongly argued for it.

Sharpening the Point

We have a mountain; so where is its peak? In David's later days and Solomon's earlier ones[112], one could readily identify this mountaintop. It was a flat rocky surface recently used as a threshing floor by a Jebusite (non-Israelite) man named Araunah. This was the place[113] that the angel of the Lord was commended to cease his punishing plague upon Israel, a plague brought by David's sin of calling for a census (to build an army, apart from God's strength and blessing). David confessed, and took ownership of his sin; but 70,000 Israelites died in this plague. David actually saw the punishing angel standing at this very spot, on this flat stone mountaintop where Isaac had been promised in sacrifice by Abraham. David purchased this place, built an altar here and made sacrificial offerings. And what had been a mere threshing floor would become the foundation stone for the mighty Temple built by Solomon.

But many things happened thereafter that would obscure this mountaintop from easy view, and alter its appearance as a mountaintop. First there was the excavation and construction involved with Solomon's Temple and its surrounding complex. Then there came the destruction by the Babylonians in 586 B.C. Next there were Zerubbabel's excavations and the construction of the Second Temple, followed by Herod's vast re-architecturing of that Temple and entire site, accompanied by major neighboring Roman constructions during that period (e.g., Fort Antonia). Then, the complete destruction and leveling of the Temple, and Jerusalem in general, by the Romans in 70 A.D. A few centuries later came early Christian architecture. Finally there came the Dome of the Rock mosque, whose construction began in 685 A.D. and stands to this day.[114]

Clearly, the original mountaintop walked by Abraham, upon which Isaac was almost sacrificed, looks quite different now. Its surroundings have been shaped and flattened, its peak covered by varying architecture of several historical ages, the most recent (though still ancient) version of which still stands. Though an impossible proposition today of course, if we had a sort of x-ray that looked past current architecture, the threshing floor of Araunah might be perceived. If that could happen, it would provide a more precise starting point

---

[112] 2 Chronicles 3:1.
[113] See 2 Samuel 24; 1 Chronicles 21 for the amazing story.
[114] Source: Wikipedia article, "Dome of the Rock," <http://en.wikipedia.org/wiki/Dome_of_the_Rock > accessed 26 May 2012.

for mapping purposes. In Messiah's coming day, things will be laid bare, as He sees fit. But for now, we must work with the clues we have.

So, what clues *do* we have? Upon Mount Moriah was a huge, flat stone surface. The Temple of Solomon contained it; and even after the Babylonian devastation, Zerubbabel's Temple (and Herod's) did as well. It is quite possible that this rocky protrusion survived the Roman destruction of 70 A.D. also, and has been preserved within religious architecture ever since. If so, the "threshing floor of Araunah" might well be equated with the "Foundation Stone" beneath the Dome of the Rock mosque even today.

Tradition holds that this was the very rock upon which Abraham almost sacrificed his son. But we have more than tradition to say so: God's Word tells us that Solomon built his Temple on Mount Moriah[115]. Indeed, this stone represents the point toward which many Jews face when praying, for it is still considered the foundation upon which the Holy of Holies was positioned[116].

Moving Forward

For purposes of Messianic era cartography, we now have an arguable and reasonable starting point within Jerusalem: Mount Moriah, overwhelmingly meaningful in God's redemptive Plan, and also a place that is generally locatable in our day. For the purposes of graphic and dimensional layout, a specific point must be picked; and from the evidence uncovered in this expedition, "the Foundation Stone" will be approximated with Moriah's ancient peak. Since the Dome of the Rock is placed directly over that stone, it is that ancient structure – the literal dome, quite visible in satellite photography – that will serve as "ground zero" as this investigation moves forward.

Here's another important mapping question. Will this pivotal marker of *ancient* Jerusalem be necessarily centered within *future* Jerusalem? True, we are not told specifically. However, the prophesied architecture of Jerusalem involves foursquare walls, twelve gates evenly spaced on the four sides, and twelve avenues implicitly running through those gates. All these features produce an unavoidable geometric focus for the City, requiring something to be at its center. A major focal point of history and the beginning of God's redemptive covenant story, Mount Moriah, is argued here to be worthy of such attention, and coincide with the coming geographic and cartographic focal point of the great City to come.

---

[115] 2 Chronicles 3:1.
[116] Wikipedia, "Foundation Stone," as of 26 May 2012, <http://en.wikipedia.org/wiki/Foundation_Stone>.

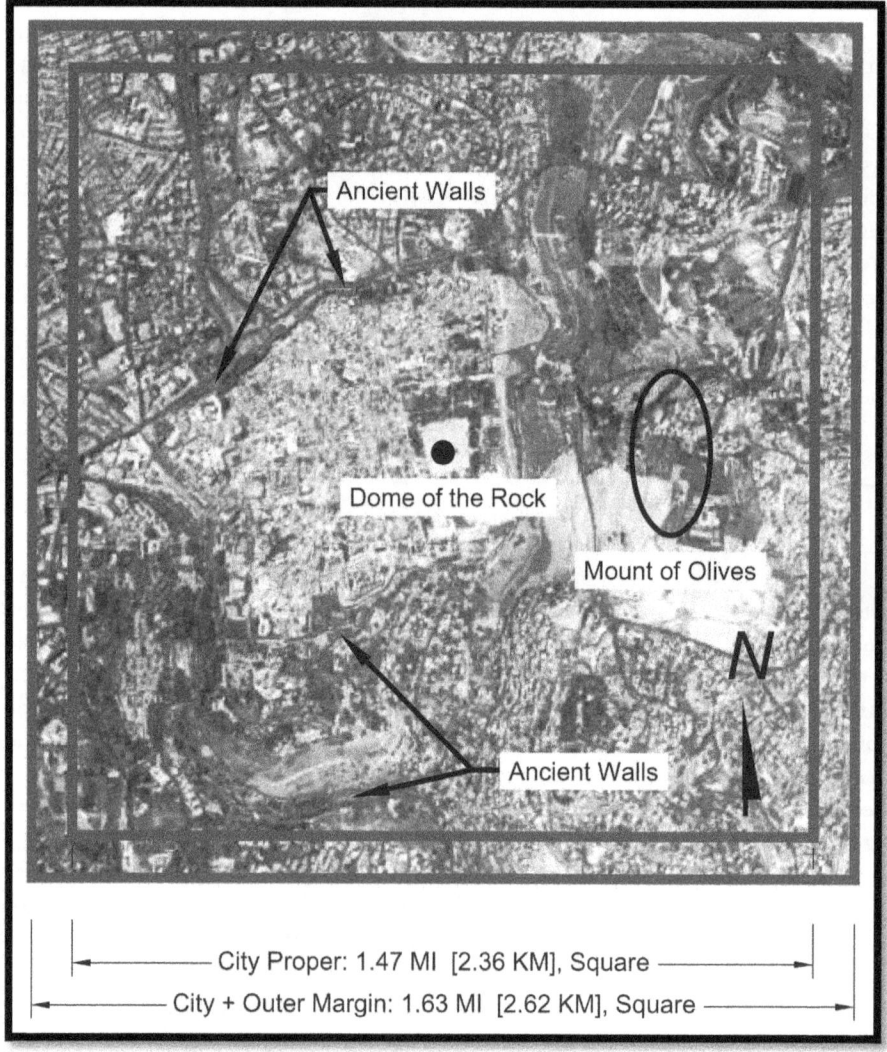

Figure 8: Ezekiel's City Centered on Mount Moriah

In the above figure[117], Ezekiel's 4,500 LC square city border, with its 250 LC outer margin, is overlaid upon a satellite map of Jerusalem. Future surveys will surely improve on these efforts; but for now, centering on Mount Moriah's peak brings a lot of clarity on what will be contained within the walls of coming Jerusalem.

---

[117] Background imagery from DigitalGlobe / GoogleEarth, as of February 2015.

For example, within the coming borders will be the Hinnom Valley (running approximately E-W, near the southern side) and the Kidron Valley (running N-S, east of center). Again, the terrain will be greatly changed by "end times" tectonic events, so these ancient watercourses will give way to new ones (which the prophets also foresaw). We can also see that the coming City walls will envelop those of Jerusalem in all its ancient periods. Furthermore, notice the very important historical site just east of Mount Moriah: the Mount of Olives, key in both David's[118] and Jesus'[119] experiences and actions. No longer outside the city, this key symbolic mountain will also be contained within Jerusalem's boundaries.

Orientation

To complete the plotting of Ezekiel's grid over present-day geography, we need an alignment angle or second reference point to orient things.

The Cardinal Direction

Let's start with angle. The cardinal directions of east, west, north and south are many times emphasized in Scripture, with the eastward orientation being the most significant. This is the general direction of sunrise; and the precision of its directional calculation is witnessed in Egyptian and other ancient architecture. The Hebrew concept of "east" derives from the idea of sunrise[120]. Both Tabernacle and Temple of Biblical days were carefully arranged in an eastwardly-facing fashion, and so will the future Temple have an eastward[121] orientation. It's interesting to understand that "orient" literally means "toward the sunrise." Surely its direction for layout out the Sacred District will be determined with at least as much precision as that employed by, say, the ancient Egyptians[122].

---

[118] 2 Samuel 15:30ff.
[119] As seen throughout the Gospels.
[120] The Hebrew for 'east' is *mizrach* (Strong's OT:4217), referring to the rising of the sun.
[121] E.g., Ezekiel 47:1.
[122] Obviously, the sun was and remains a thing not to be worshipped, as did the ancient Egyptians. However, it remains a God-created marker of time (e.g., Genesis 1:14-16). It is further an important emblem of God's Anointed (Messiah) breaking forth on the earth's activities from that very direction, requiring our vigilance to that event. See Psalm 19:4-6; Isaiah 41:2; Ezekiel 43:2 & 4, 46:1 & 12; Matthew 2:2.

The direction of East is therefore critically important for mapping the Sacred District. Ezekiel clearly describes the coming Temple as facing directly east[123], with many of its related features arranged with that direction as the basis. Moreover, when the prophet referred to certain walls, doors and other items as being be to the south, north or west, all those directions and instructions were based on a proper understanding of *East*, as we will see.

Though the ancients didn't have compasses, they indeed had recognition of precise cartographic and architectural direction. This "compass" of old began with a careful determination of *eastward*, based on the sunrise at a specific point (or two) on the calendar, such as Passover. For example, on Passover of 2015 (April 3), the sunrise was 83° East, while the beginning of the Feast of Tabernacles (September 28) in the same year, it was at 92° East[124]. We do not know what key Millennial date will be used for this calculation of eastward, but it may well be the day that Messiah comes *"as the lightning comes from the east, and flashes even to the west"*[125]. Only the Lord knows.

For the time being though, we can use an average direction of sunrises determined at Jerusalem's equinox dates [126]. For our purposes here, an understanding of East as ninety degrees clockwise from magnetic north is a good enough approximation.

The Right Hand Direction

The Hebrew term for facing towards the 'front' is *qedem*[127], also deriving from the idea of facing the sunrise. While facing east, your outstretched right arm points south. This explains why the Hebrew for "south," *teyman*,[128] derives from the term for *right hand*[129]. *Teyman* is sometimes used in defining certain details of the Tabernacle[130], so it is not surprising that Ezekiel uses it at several points[131] in his Temple descriptions.

Let's take a brief side-path on this "right hand" matter, and the ancient idea that this position is always the place of honor. If you were seated at the right hand of the host of a banquet, this would be the most honored position in relationship to the host. Likewise, to be south (on the right hand) of an

---

[123] E.g., Ezekiel 47:1.
[124] Data acquired from <www.timeanddate.com>, as of 2/18/2015.
[125] Matthew 24:27b, NASB.
[126] From same source and year: March 21, sunrise at 89°E; September 23, sunrise at 88°E.
[127] Strong's OT:6924.
[128] Strong's OT: 8486, *teyman* (tay-mawn'). E.g., Psalms 45:9.
[129] Strong's OT:3225, *yamiyn* (yaw-meen').
[130] Exodus 26:18,35, 27:9, 36:23, 38:9; Numbers 2:10, 3:29, 10:6.
[131] Ezekiel 47:19, 48:28.

Chapter 3: Marking the Borders

important feature in the Sacred District is an honored position relative to that feature. When Ezekiel stood on the future holy Mountain upon which the new Temple will be established, and described the coming city as being "to the south[132]," he described the honored position of the City, relative to the Lord's Presence. There is therefore a strong north-to-south relationship between the coming Temple and City, prophesied by those operating under the direction of King David[133]:

> *Beautiful for situation, the joy of the whole earth, is mount Zion,* **on the sides of the <u>north</u>, the city of the great King.**
> *Psalms 48:2, KJV*

In no other era than the Messianic one can this prophecy have its fullest meaning. First, because Jerusalem has yet to be the joy of the *whole earth*; second, only then will Mount Zion (Jerusalem) be beautifully "situated" on the *southern* slopes of a *higher mountain* to its *north*. This "situation" described by the psalmist is precisely that described by Ezekiel, with the City to the south of God's high and holy mountain[134], and on His "right hand."

Back to *orientation*. In addition to *tayman*, the more common term for 'south' is *negeb*[135], referring to that southern desert region of Israel, and the general direction toward it. *Negeb* is also, however, often used as a strict *cardinal direction*[136], synonymous with *tayman*, and was therefore routinely applied to critical architecture of Tabernacle, Temple and Jerusalem[137].

Between all these words for *east* and *south*, as used by Ezekiel, we can know the following:

- ☐ That the Temple will face strictly east

- ☐ That the Temple and City walls will be carefully positioned toward east, west, north and south in a precise square

- ☐ That the City and Temple have a strict north-south relationship

---

[132] Ezekiel 40:2.
[133] David is considered a prophet (e.g., Acts 2:25), and indeed led the prophecies of all three sub-tribes of Levi in their own prophesying (1 Chronicles 25:1). The Psalm cited here is clearly one where David was either overseeing the prophetic writing, or prophesying directly himself.
[134] Zechariah 8:3b: *the mountain of the Lord Almighty will be called the Holy Mountain."*
[135] Strong's OT:5045.
[136] E.g., Daniel 8:4.
[137] E.g., Exodus 26:18, 27:9, 36:23, 38:9; Numbers 35:5; 1 Chronicles 9:24, 26:15; 2 Chronicles 4:4; Ezekiel 46:9, 47:1, 48:16, 33.

In other words, the arrangement of the Sacred District is indeed very rectilinear and precise, with the City centered east-to-west in its southern section[138] and the Temple being due north of the City (and thus centered east-to-west in the Priestly District).

Ezekiel, having been ordered to carefully convey all this dimensional data to the people, including future surveyors and builders, was certainly concerned with how all this Sacred District geometry would be oriented. Therefore when he declares a compass direction, we can take him at face value, and know that his usage of East, South, North and West are in line with our present understanding.

Centering the Temple

There is another method of alignment though, one even more critical perhaps than using the eastward-sunrise as the basis. We've noticed the strong directional relationship between city and Temple, a north-to-south axis between the two, with the Temple facing due east. If we knew where the Temple will be located within the Priestly region to the north, we would gain an additional clue on how the Sacred District will be aligned.

And so we return to an earlier question: Where is the Temple located within the northern (priestly) section of the Sacred District? We are told, *"and the sanctuary of the LORD shall be in its midst"*[139]. As already pointed out, some Bible translations use the term "center" instead of "midst" here[140]; yet the Hebrew word *tavek*[141] doesn't require that geometric exactness. Though it *can* refer to the very center of something, it more often means "amongst" or "the midst of," in a more general or approximate manner. So while Ezekiel 48:10 might well be one of those cases where *tavek does* convey the more precise idea of literal centrality, we need to look for something more definitive.

Furthermore, in the mighty precedent of the original "camp" of Israel at its beginning, we should look at the arrangement of the tribes surrounding the Tabernacle during the wilderness years. Numbers 2 describes a *strictly square* arrangement of the four sets of three tribal encampments, each effectively forming a "wall" on east, south, west and north surrounding the Tabernacle:

> *The sons of Israel shall camp, each by his own standard, with the banners of their fathers' households; they shall camp around the tent of meeting at a distance. Now those who camp on the east side toward the sunrise shall be…*
> Numbers 2:2-3a, NASB

---

[138] Due to the equal widths of its east and west "pasturelands."
[139] Ezekiel 48:10b, NASB.
[140] Rendered as such in, for example, the NIV and NKJV versions.
[141] Strong's OT:8432.

Chapter 3: Marking the Borders

All four cardinal directions are subsequently addressed, obviously aligned with the firm eastward orientation of the Tabernacle. In the center formed by these "walls" of encampment was a square and sacred region, very analogous to the future arrangement of Temple area foreseen in Ezekiel.

> *But you shall appoint the Levites over the tabernacle of the testimony...* **they shall also camp around the tabernacle.**
> *Numbers 1:50, NASB*

> *The Levites, however, are to set up their tents* **around the tabernacle**...
> *Numbers 1:53a, NIV*

We can learn a number of things from this original wilderness encampment of the Israelites. A deliberate and consistent distance around the Tabernacle was to be kept clear of all dwelling areas, including those of the tribe of Levi. This space radiated all around the Tabernacle, leaving a square clear zone with the holy Tent of Meeting at its center. Around that came the surrounding dwelling areas of the Levites (who included the priests, of course), creating a "priestly perimeter" between the most sacred zone and the "protective wall" formed by the tribal encampments.

This entire arrangement was geometrically centralized on the position of the Tabernacle. The spatial precision symbolized a literal and vital point: that God was central to Israel; and it would only be by His direct leading that Israel would move from one place to another, and find success.

> *Whenever the cloud lifted from above the Tent, the Israelites set out;* **wherever the cloud settled, the Israelites encamped.** *18 At the LORD's command the Israelites set out, and* **at his command they encamped.** *As long as the cloud stayed over the tabernacle, they remained in camp.*
> *Numbers 9:17-18, NIV*

In the surpassingly wonderful manifestation of the "camp of Israel" in the Messianic era, similar symbolic arrangements will also be in play. For example, the Sacred District is set *"in the midst of"* the lands of the Prince, and the Prince's Province *"in the midst of"* those of the tribes, in the general and approximate sense of the word *tavek*.

But then comes the more strictly centered idea. In the holy (and northernmost) section of the Sacred District, we find the dwelling area of the priests surrounding the most sacred area of the Temple. So when we are told that *"the sanctuary of the LORD shall be in the midst thereof"*[142], that is, in the "midst" of the Priestly-Temple northern section, it can be inferred that the principles at

---

[142] Ezekiel 48:10b, KJV.

work in the Tabernacle arrangement are also present in this future one. We again have the central Temple, surrounded by the dwelling areas for the priests, with the idea of literal centrality conveyed from the ancient predecessor of the Tabernacle. Like that earlier arrangement, we may well also have all the twelve tribes "camped" around the Temple grounds, because (as discussed earlier) all twelve tribes will in fact be represented in the priesthood then.

The rectilinear design of the overall Sacred District is very reminiscent of the original camp of the Israelites. It is also the ultimate conclusion to the Exodus drama of God's formation of His people out of any and all forms of wilderness. So it would be reasonable to conclude that the centered, orderly and rectilinear arrangement of the Tabernacle will apply to the Temple to come and the living areas surrounding it.

We can therefore, with good evidence, posit that the Temple will be centered within the Priestly-Temple region to the north of the Sacred District. We have seen that Jerusalem to come will be centered on Mount Moriah, which is in the vicinity of the Dome of the Rock. Between these points, we have confirmation of their explicit north-south relationship, and the orientation of the Sacred District's major features with the four cardinal directions.

Plotting the Grid

Key Parameters

To sum up, the Scriptures appear to reveal certain key points about locating the grid of the Sacred District as foreseen by Ezekiel.

- ☐ Ezekiel's careful dimensions of the Sacred District suggest that a firm starting point and orientation will be available to future surveyors and engineers who will accurately apply the measurements to known geography.

- ☐ Jerusalem will remain unmoved, making it the dimensional starting point for the Sacred District as a whole.

- ☐ Mount Moriah is a prime candidate for Jerusalem's central datum point, having a strong Biblical basis.

- ☐ The Temple's east wall and gate will face due east.

Chapter 3: Marking the Borders

- The Temple will reside at the peak of the coming Mountain, and the City will be due south of that.

- With the Tabernacle (during the Exodus) as a template, the Temple will likely be centered in the northern priestly region of that District, confirming the north-south orientation for the Temple-City axis.

We can summarize and derive the following vital north-to-south distances:

Position or Distance, North to South	Results (North to South)		
	Long Cubits	Miles	Kilometers
Width of the Priestly/Temple Region	10,000	3.26	5.24
Temple Position in the Priestly Region (half the above)	5,000	1.63	2.62
Width of the Levitical Region	10,000	3.26	5.24
Width of the City Region	5,000	1.63	2.62
City Center Position in its Region (half the above)	2,500	0.81	1.31
Distance from Temple to City Center	17,500	5.70	9.18

Figure 9: Key North-to-South Distances

Notice the last 17,500 LC (long cubit) measurement, which is the sum of half the Priestly region's width (5,000), the full width of the Levitical region (10,000), and half the City region's width (2,500).

That summation is fascinating, saying that there are almost *six miles* separating the centers of the City and the Temple! With historic Jerusalem, we are used to a distance much less then that; in fact, we are used to the idea of the Temple being contained *within* the boundaries of the city proper. This, however, will no longer be the case.

Why this large distance? What does the separation between the two indicate? After the Millennial period is concluded, during the eternal time frame, we are told that City and Temple become *one*[143]. The Millennial arrangement may therefore symbolize the fact that things will not yet be complete, because the final "wedding" between City and God[144] will only take place *after* the Millennial period. This distance should therefore not be seen as division for negative reasons, but rather as a reinforcement of the "engagement" between the "Bride" and the "Bridegroom," the Lamb, Messiah, Jesus-Yeshua, in a one-thousand year long "wedding feast"[145].

We can deduce several other things about this distance between Temple and City.

- ☐ The 17,500 LC dimension underscores the huge size of the Mountain of God, with the City being on that mountain's southern slope, yet still contained within the Sacred District's boundary.

- ☐ With the most holy Temple region to the north and with the main residential city region (representative of the entirety of God's people) directly to its south, the "Bride" will be directly on the "right hand" of God, dramatically underscoring her special position of highest honor.

- ☐ The geometry allows for a large priestly population surrounding the Temple and serving its needs, while providing a substantial residential area for the City's population.

- ☐ The north-south dimensions also provide for a generous Levitical living area in between, with that population serving the needs of both the Lord and His people. This region, and that Levitical role, helps keep the two other areas distinct – perhaps as befitting a "bride and bridegroom" arrangement[146].

- ☐ The arrangement of these regions demonstrates a north-to-south progression of holiness and sacredness, inviting people living in or visiting the City of that day to "ascend" both physically and

---

[143] Revelation 21:22, where we see that the City will *be* the Temple.
[144] Revelation 21:2.
[145] Revelation 19:7-9.
[146] Again, the final "wedding" between City (comprising *all* God's people, in Heaven and Earth) and the Lord comes *after* the Millennial period is completed (Revelation 21:2 & 9).

spiritually toward the Lord[147], uphill from the City, through the Levitical area, and finally to Temple.

For reasons such as these, we see that this 5.7 mile / 9.2 kilometer distance between City and Temple will have positive and meaningful purposes in the Day to come.

Refining the Arrangement

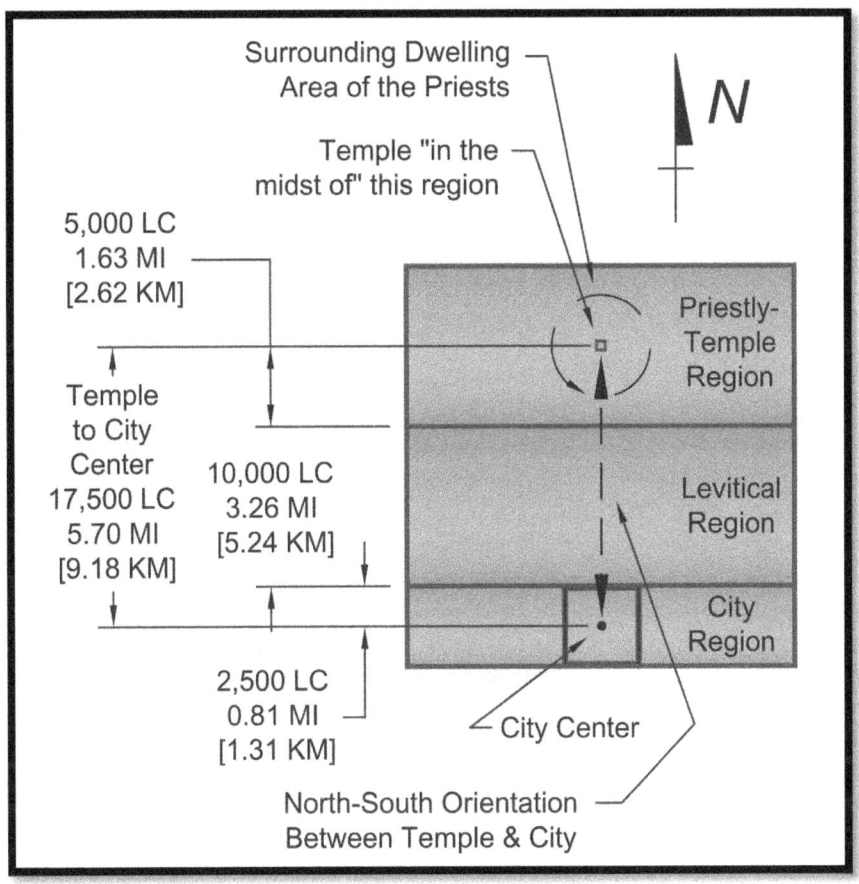

Figure 10: Sacred District Spatial Arrangement

Let's return to actual mapping. The above figure represents the Sacred District as centered upon Mount Moriah, while focusing on the Temple.

---

[147] As is implied in many "ascent" Psalms.

This will be the governmental center of Messiah, the coming capitol of the world from which God's beneficent rule of all creation and mankind will radiate. Like a set of windowpanes hovering over a map we can know now, Ezekiel's grid is a window open between this Earth and Heaven, and between this age and the one around the corner.

This isn't merely ethereal though. Ezekiel's information on the coming Capitol is quite literal, with architecture to be built in this present creation. The placement of the grid is on *this physical earth*, in a time yet to come, and in a continuation of chronology as we understand it. His dimensions describe *real* distances and areas, ones that any crew of civil engineers armed with the proper tools could attempt to lay out, on geography existing in our day. True, the contours of terrain will differ in the Messianic era; but the X-Y positions, east-to-west and north-to-south, apply to both that future map and our present one.

In a sense then, Ezekiel has provided us a sort of treasure map: riches measured not in currency, but in knowledge. And if "X marks the spot" on our treasure map, we actually have two "X's": the City, and the Temple. And, we have good grounds to know where they are. How wonderful it would be to participate with the survey teams plotting out all these actual borders and placing their requisite markers, all under the guidance of the coming Prince!

The Actual Footprint

For now though, we have to be satisfied with being "armchair surveyors," because even if a capable survey team were today assembled and fully financed, it would be an impossible endeavor. The present nation of Israel doesn't have control over most of the territory involved, and tensions in the region are as high as ever. Even so, we can work remotely, in both distance and time, and get a good approximation of how the Sacred District lies upon present-day geography.

The following figure[148] is just such an attempt at staking the borders, with Jerusalem being the heavily populated area in the lower third, and other important sites highlighted with their ancient and modern names. We will explore the implications of these places later. But for now, note where the Temple will be located: almost exactly on the site of ancient Ramah (with modern *Ar-Ram* being slightly offset).

---

[148] The topographic background here is based on maps originally published by the Soviets in 1990, made public by Berkeley University, and downloaded by the author on 11/14/07 from <http://sunsite.berkeley.edu:8085/israel/50k/israel50k.html>. Four source maps, designated as 08-36-011-1, -2, -3, and -4, were cropped, stitched and rotated to true north by the author.

Chapter 3: Marking the Borders 67

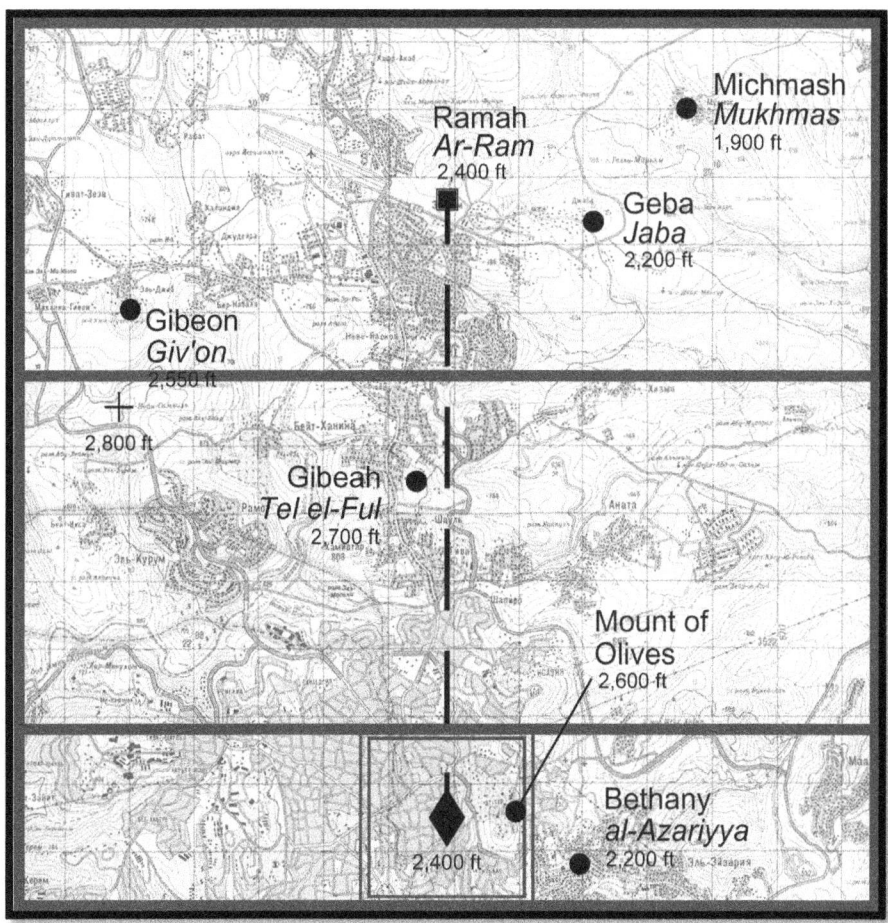

Figure 11: A Topographic Look at the Data

Much of this territory is not part of modern Israel, but contained within the "West Bank." That being the case, some folks might be quite offended by this mapping, others perhaps worried, for this region has long been considered explosively controversial. Isn't it interesting then that such global sensitivity *and* Biblical declaration converge on this very small area of the Earth?

Even so, it must be underscored that the Millennial environment will *never* be realized[149] by human forcefulness, but by <u>divine intervention alone</u>. It is in the Lord's timing, and by His Spirit and power, that these coming borders will be surveyed and marked.

---

[149] Or prevented for that matter, e.g., Isaiah 55:11.

If one doesn't believe in any of this, one should have nothing to worry about. And if one *does* believe, there should likewise be no fear, or any thought of forcing the achievement of these borders. Instead, let us appreciate the dilemma that Zerubbabel faced. While reconstructing the Temple and facing huge opposition, here is what the Lord said to the king through the prophet Zechariah:

> *So he said to me, "This is the word of the LORD to Zerubbabel:* **'Not by might nor by power, but by my Spirit,' says the LORD Almighty.** *7 "What are you, O mighty mountain? Before Zerubbabel you will become level ground. Then he will bring out the capstone to shouts of 'God bless it! God bless it!'"*
> *Zechariah 4:6-7, NIV*

King Zerubbabel, being symbolic of Messiah to come [150], faced a circumstantial "mountain" and a human empire that opposed God's people and His Temple being rebuilt amongst them. Even so, it was only by the interventions of the Lord that success came about. In the same way, the achievement of Ezekiel's borders will not be due to any human effort, no matter how strategized, funded, or politically agreed to in this age. No; the Lord Himself, God the Father through the Yeshua ha Mashiach, Jesus the Christ, will accomplish these things. And only this One God, Father and Son and Holy Spirit, will perform it.

Probing Further

While we lack access for any physical expedition to where God's holy Mountain will be, maybe that's for the best anyway. Yes, it would be thrilling to be part of an archeological investigation, marking out the boundaries and perhaps excavating certain ancient sites it contains. But it would also be easy to get caught up in the intellectual thrill and miss some of what the Lord is still quietly revealing on these matters. In fact, we have much more information from God's Word awaiting us, much more ground to cover than a physical expedition might provide. So if we let the Holy Spirit lead us onward through the Word, we will discover further treasures of knowledge that no actual team in the field could acquire.

Let us therefore probe more deeply into what the Lord has declared, keeping in mind the actual Source of all we are trying to perceive:

---

[150] Zechariah 3:8, with 4:10.

Chapter 3: Marking the Borders

> *...so is my word that goes out from my mouth: It will not return to me empty, but will accomplish what I desire and achieve the purpose for which I sent it.*
> Isaiah 55:11, NIV

Aside from all the amazing things that will be seen in the future, there is this great and central profoundness. It is the Lord's uttering of His Word in times past, releasing an immutable energy that will not be stopped until the One that issued it is satisfied in His purposes – across space and time, no matter how lengthy the process in our eyes.

Even so, our Creator has permitted us innumerable milestones and vast amounts of detail, along the path of His history-plus-prophecy timeline. In doing so, there are many enigmas, many secrets; yet He discloses these things from His Word:

> *The secret things belong to the LORD our God, but the things revealed belong to us and to our children forever, that we may follow all the words of this law.*
> Deuteronomy 29:29, NIV

And that is the point: that we might follow, personally and corporately, individually and as a group, Himself and His intentions for us, *in the here and now*. There are many prophesied facets of Messiah's dominion that may touch our personal interests, be they cartography, engineering, geology, politics, botany, agriculture, meteorology, etc. Since all these prophesied details are *"things revealed"* by God, all of them therefore *"belong to us and our children forever,"* that we might follow our Creator's commands in our present daily life. So let us explore them. For we are *allowed* and *expected* by the Lord to use *our whole intellect* to probe the information He has granted us on the things He has set in motion. Yet let us always honor Him foremost, and give respect to His intentions for us now. For that daily relationship has always been the point, and remains so now and forever.

Like those who gathered around and listened to Ezekiel[151] in the year of about 573 B.C., we too can acquire hope that the Lord's overall Plan *remains absolutely in effect*, and that *His* outcomes will overrule, heal, and make sense of, even the darkest experiences beforehand. And why would we not probe such matters? Why should we not investigate more deeply the secrets of the City to come? The ancient prophets and holy men of the Bible, such as Ezekiel, investigated these matters. They *"searched intently and with the greatest care,"* to know precisely the *"time and circumstances"* of Messiah's coming[152]. Following their footprints, we simply attempt this same form of examination.

---

[151] Ezekiel 40:4, 43:10-11. Though issued in reprimand, God's giving of the plans for the amazing Temple to come are implicitly presented as a tangible source of hope for His people.
[152] 1 Peter 1:10-11.

Even if some of us do not live long enough to see firsthand the coming time of Messianic fulfillment, there is still enormous benefit in this inquiry. It is the same blessing that those prophets of old gained in their study: a confirmation that our Creator's purposes remain *indestructible* and *sovereign*, "*from* everlasting [past] *to* everlasting [future]"; that His ultimate fulfillments will be spectacular and real, at all levels; and that, in the mean time, we are compelled to *"follow all the words of this law."* This law begins with *"Hear, O Israel! The Lord is our God, the Lord is one! 5 And you shall love the Lord your God with all your heart and with all your soul and with all your might*[153]*,"* and also includes the command that *"thou shalt love thy neighbour as thyself*[154]*,"* just as confirmed by Jesus[155].

And isn't that really the ultimate prophetic-eschatological message? No matter how well we think we understand God's workings throughout past and future, His continual purposes for us shine clearly. Even if we could quite clearly detect *everything* about the City in Heaven, its Messianic-era counterpart, and the final-eternal combination of the two, such revelation is only meaningful if we return to our Lord His love toward us, by obedience and love toward others. To paraphrase the Apostle Paul, "If I perceive with the eyes of angels and don't have love, I am just a broken telescope[156]." No matter how excited we get about what God is up to, His Word ever prods us toward these transcendent purposes of His.

Even so, He *allows* us and *invites* us to sink our teeth into these details about future days. Imperfect as this present investigation is, let us therefore embrace the details of what Ezekiel and other prophets described in advance. And while doing so, let it not be merely an intellectual pursuit, but let it also energize our faith, hope and love right now, as we look to and applaud the coming of our King.

> *Therefore you do not lack any spiritual gift as you eagerly wait for our Lord Jesus Christ to be revealed.*
> *1 Corinthians 1:7, NIV*

---

[153] The Great Command (in Hebrew, "*Sh'ma*"): Deuteronomy 6:4-5, NASB..
[154] Leviticus 19:18; Romans 13:9; Galatians 5:14; James 2:8.
[155] Matthew 22:37-39; Mark 12:30-31; Luke 10:27.
[156] Compare 1 Corinthians 13:1.

Chapter 4: Lay of the Land

Many peoples will come and say, "Come, let us go up to the mountain of the LORD, to the house of the God of Jacob. He will teach us his ways, so that we may walk in his paths." The law will go out from Zion, the word of the LORD from Jerusalem.
Isaiah 2:3, NIV

And the glory of the Lord will be revealed, and all mankind together will see it. For the mouth of the Lord has spoken.
Isaiah 40:5, NIV

See, I am doing a new thing! Now it springs up; do you not perceive it? I am making a way in the desert and streams in the wasteland.
Isaiah 43:19, NIV

...the mountain of the LORD Almighty will be called the Holy Mountain."
Zechariah 8:3b, NIV

Chapter 4: Lay of the Land   73

The Current Canvas

So far, we've worked on a two-dimensional map of the Sacred District in the final age of this earth. In the next stretch of the journey, we will examine its elevations and contours.

Present Topology

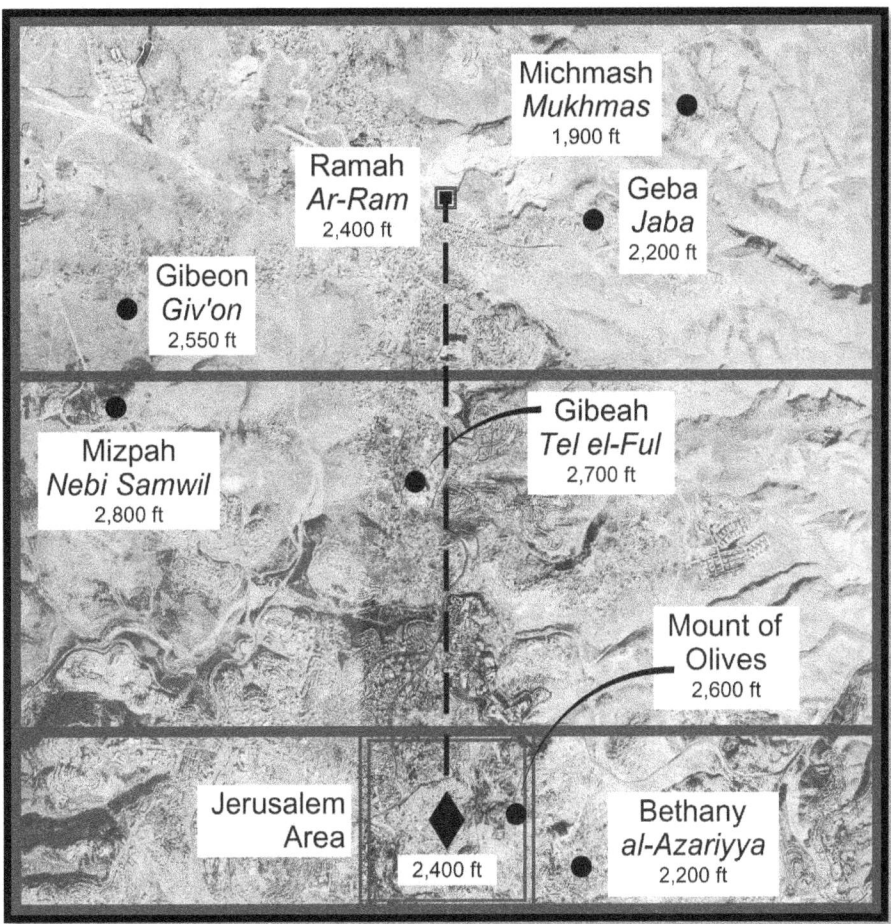

Figure 12: Present-Day Sacred District Topology

The above figure[157] shows Ezekiel's "grid" overlaid on present-day satellite imagery, giving us a hint on just how undulating the area is. In a coming time, many will recall just how arid and wilderness-like the region is at present, just as this image demonstrates. For as we will see, the terrain will be vastly different in the future: relatively smooth, with two distinct peaks arising from these surroundings, and new rivers that have never been seen before.

Terra-Forming To Come

Very big changes are on the way for present-day topography in this area of the Middle East and elsewhere. In the time surrounding Messiah's revealing, the Bible makes it clear that huge and pervasive tectonic events will transpire, with the prophesied "post-apocalyptic"[158] geography reflecting them. This is a large subject in itself, with the Bible speaking of it in many places[159]. For starters, these changes will affect the entire globe:

> ***Every valley shall be raised up, every mountain and hill made low;*** *the rough ground shall become level, the rugged places a plain. 5 And the glory of the Lord will be revealed, and* ***all mankind together will see it.*** *For the mouth of the Lord has spoken.*
> *Isaiah 40:4-5 (also quoted in Luke 3:5-6), NIV*

> *And there were voices, and thunders, and lightnings; and* **there was a great earthquake, such as was not since men were upon the earth***, so mighty an earthquake, and so great. 19 And the great city was divided into three parts, and the cities of the nations fell: and great Babylon came in remembrance before God, to give unto her the cup of the wine of the fierceness of his wrath. 20* **And every island fled away, and the mountains were not found.**
> *Revelation 16:18b-20, KJV*

As described in these last verses, this will be a bigger tectonic event than has ever witnessed by a human being. That's a big earthquake; and its effect on topography will be correspondingly significant, with every island, mountain and hill being affected. Within this same time-frame, other prophets add their voices:

---

[157] Background imagery from DigitalGlobe / GoogleEarth, as of November 2007.
[158] The coming "revelation" (in Greek, *apokalupsis*, or "apocalypse" in English) of Messiah is precisely where the book of Revelation derives its name (Revelation 1:1). Thus the phrases "after Messiah's revealing" and "post-apocalyptic era" are technically synonymous, regardless of how abused and misused the latter term is in our media today.
[159] As but a few examples, preliminary warnings by Jesus in Matthew 24:7 / Mark 13:8 / Luke 21:11, and as directly described in Revelation 6:12, 8:5 & 11:19.

Chapter 4: Lay of the Land

> *But your many enemies will become like fine dust, the ruthless hordes like blown chaff. Suddenly, in an instant, 6 the* **LORD Almighty will come with thunder and earthquake and great noise**, *with windstorm and tempest and flames of a devouring fire.*
> *Isaiah 29:5-6, NIV*

> **The mountains quake at him, and the hills melt, and the earth is burned at his presence,** *yea, the world, and all that dwell therein. 6 Who can stand before his indignation? And who can abide in the fierceness of his anger? His fury is poured out like fire, and the rocks are thrown down by him.*
> *Nahum 1:5-6, KJV*

> *Before him went the pestilence, and burning coals went forth at his feet. 6 He stood, and measured the earth: he beheld, and drove asunder the nations; and* **the everlasting mountains were scattered, the perpetual hills did bow:** *his ways are everlasting.*
> *Habakkuk 3:5-6, KJV*

> *For thus saith the Lord of hosts; Yet once, it is a little while, and* **I will shake the heavens, and the earth, and the sea, and the dry land;** *7 And I* **will shake all nations, and the desire of all nations shall come:** *and I will fill this house with glory, saith the Lord of hosts.*
> *Haggai 2:6-7, KJV*

Using the name "Gog" to summarize the enemies of God's people[160] at the time of Jesus' return, Ezekiel confirms the matter and emphasizes the tectonic activity in the very region of our study.

> *This is what will happen in that day: When Gog attacks the land of Israel, my hot anger will be aroused, declares the Sovereign LORD. 19 In my zeal and fiery wrath I declare that at that time there shall be a* **great earthquake in the land of Israel.** *20 The fish of the sea, the birds of the air, the beasts of the field, every creature that moves along the ground, and* **all the people on the face of the earth will tremble at my presence.** *The mountains will be overturned, the cliffs will crumble and every wall will fall to the ground. 21 I will summon a sword against Gog* **on all my mountains,** *declares the Sovereign LORD. Every man's sword will be against his brother.*
> *Ezekiel 38:18-21, NIV*

---

[160] From internal evidence such as in the burial requirements, "Gog" in Ezekiel 38 differs from the "Gog and Magog" attack of Revelation 20, an event occurring *after* the Millennial period. Ezekiel refers to earthly enemies of the Lord *before* that period.

Furthermore, and specific to Jerusalem in particular, yet another prophet concurs:

> *Then the LORD will go out and fight against those nations, as he fights in the day of battle.... 5 You will flee by my mountain valley, for it will extend to Azel.* **You will flee as you fled from the earthquake** *in the days of Uzziah king of Judah. Then the LORD my God will come, and all the holy ones with him. Zechariah 14:3 & 5, NIV*

We can see in all this that at the time of Messiah's arrival, global tectonic events will have recently transpired, or be underway; and that the land of Israel specifically, and especially the terrain of Jerusalem and its environs, will have been tremendously impacted.

Some of us might actually witness these geographic changes. But all of us, thanks to God's prior descriptions for our benefit, can virtually appreciate them in advance, right now. So it is these transformations we will be investigating next, putting aside for the moment the contours of present-day terrain. Things will be very different after the Lord's return, and the Scriptures have a lot to say about the new look.

Necessary Distinctions

Appreciating the massive earth-moving in days ahead includes understanding the Why of it all. So let's begin with some of the Why's, and examine some key symbolic[161] lessons involved here, in the great arising of the new Mountain of God Almighty.

---

[161] Some might see the predictions of Biblical prophecies as merely a symbolic end in themselves, containing inspirational value that is only figurative or poetic in nature, without any real eventual outworking. Such cannot be the case though: for without the actual fulfillment of the prophecies, the factual truth of the prophecy evaporates, taking with it any symbolic benefit. If one reads a Scriptural passage that declares or implies, "Be glad, for X is on the way," and if 'X' was never intended to come true, then the basis for the gladness is lost. It would constitute false advertising, a lie, which would never be the case with God's words. For as the greatest prophet, Jesus Himself, said: "*Do not think that I have come to abolish the Law or the Prophets; I have not come to abolish them but to fulfill them. 18 I tell you the truth, until heaven and earth disappear, not the smallest letter, not the least stroke of a pen, will by any means disappear from the Law until everything is accomplished.*" (Matthew 5:17-18, NIV).

Lowering of the Lord's Enemies

We come to our first reason why God's Mountain would be specially raised. Many times in the First Testament, idols that led people astray were installed on "high places," literal hilltops on which idolatrous practices were committed. On the other end of the "bad-mountain" spectrum, entire empires that stood against God's program were often likened to mountains[162]. In either case, there is this sense of corporate human arrogance that lifts itself up against the Lord, imagining itself to be more powerful and worthy of honor than He. However,

> ***The Lord Almighty has a day in store for all the proud and lofty, for all that is exalted (and they will be humbled)**, 13 for all the cedars of Lebanon, tall and lofty, and all the oaks of Bashan, 14 for **all the towering mountains and all the high hills**, 15 for **every lofty tower and every fortified wall**, 16 for every trading ship and every stately vessel. 17 **The arrogance of man will be brought low and the pride of men humbled; the Lord alone will be exalted in that day**, 18 and <u>the idols will totally disappear.</u>*
> Isaiah 2:12-18, NIV

In these verses, idolatry, pride and physical loftiness are linked, with the "high place" generally being a natural height combined with something man-made. Near the very beginning of human history and this present age[163] was the mother of all man-made "high places," the Tower of Babel, the builders of which imagined they could build to Heaven. And at the opposite end of this present age[164], another Babylon will arise, committing sins "piled up to heaven[165]," and considering herself utterly independent from God[166]. Whatever this ultimate edifice of arrogance and idolatry will look like, it will be violently thrown down, both figuratively *and* physically:

> *And he cried mightily with a strong voice, saying, Babylon the great is fallen, is fallen...*
> Revelation 18:2a, KJV

---

[162] For example, Isaiah 41:14-15; Jeremiah 51:24-25; Zechariah 4:7.
[163] Genesis 11:1-9.
[164] That is, from Noah to the present time and until Messiah establishes the next one.
[165] Revelation 18:5a.
[166] Revelation 18:7.

> *And a mighty angel took up a stone like a great millstone, and cast it into the sea, saying, Thus with violence shall that great city Babylon be thrown down, and shall be found no more at all.*
> Revelation 18:21, KJV

The demolition of coming Babylon is one of an empire that has stood itself against God Almighty. In that time, the related empire of "the Beast" is likened to a lofty idol-statue[167]; and like Babylon, it too will be destroyed. But look carefully at how the Conqueror is described:

> *Then was the iron, the clay, the brass, the silver, and the gold, broken to pieces together, and became like the chaff of the summer threshing floors; and the wind carried them away, that no place was found for them: and **the stone that smote the image became a great mountain, and filled the whole earth**... 45 Forasmuch as thou sawest that **the stone was cut out of the mountain without hands**, and that it brake in pieces the iron, the brass, the clay, the silver, and the gold; the great God hath made known to the king what shall come to pass hereafter: and the dream is certain, and the interpretation thereof sure.*
> Daniel 2:35 and 45, KJV

The "stumbling stone[168]," Jesus, is indeed our figurative mountain, our rock and fortress, the overcoming King of all kings. He, the "stone the builders rejected," has become the cornerstone of the Father's kingdom[169], and will make this final idol-statue "stumble." Yeshua alone will bring about God's holy mountain that will be exalted over every other man-made high place ever raised against Him. And *this* is why:

> *In the last days the **mountain of the Lord's temple will be established as chief among the mountains**...*
> Isaiah 2:2a, NIV

Though we have only scratched the surface here, it is clear that the Lord will, in the "day" of His reign over this Earth, have completed His victory over all who have stood opposed to Him. Empires of arrogance and idolatry will be crushed; and all the "high places" and "towers" associated with and symbolizing them will be brought down.

Thus it is that the Lord's mountain must, and will be, "exalted" over them all. Whether it will become "chief" in a literal sense of being the highest of all

---

[167] Revelation 13:14ff. Cf Daniel 3:1ff.
[168] Isaiah 8:14; Romans 9:32-33.
[169] E.g., Psalms 118:22; Isaiah 28:16; Ephesians 2:20; 1 Peter 2:6-7.

mountains of the entire earth, we are not told; but it will be "chief among the mountains" in the very real sense of rule, for there will be no other government or religion or power in the world to stand against it. The Mountain of the Lord will arise as the mighty symbol of our Creator's immutable strength, a visible peak reminding all of His surpassing power and faithfulness to His promises.

Healing of the Lord's Land

There is another reason for God's new mountain being raised up, and it has to do with healing of the land. The Lord enlisted Isaiah to proclaim many details of this age's transition to the next, and the prophet dealt with this matter. From a verse recently cited (2:15), we know that in the "apocalyptic" earthquakes, many towers will fall; and from the Revelation record, the multitudinous enemies of the Lord will be slain at the battle of Armageddon. With these points in view, see what Isaiah further has to say:

> ***In the day of great slaughter, when the towers fall, streams of water will flow on every high mountain and every lofty hill.*** *26 The moon will shine like the sun, and the sunlight will be seven times brighter, like the light of seven full days, when the Lord binds up the bruises of his people and heals the wounds he inflicted.*
> Isaiah 30:25-26, NIV

At the very time of Messiah's victory, great shifting of terrain will cause towers to fall, for *"No earthquake like it has ever occurred since man has been on earth, so tremendous was the quake."*[170] Clearly, there is destruction; but it is a destruction of structures that, as with the Tower of Babel, will have been built to defy God[171].

Simultaneously, these same earthquakes bring about healing to the land, in the form of streams of water. As the earth shakes itself free of the evils accumulated upon its surface, *new* sources of fresh water are released from subterranean aquifers, gushing forth not only in valleys, but even from the higher elevations. God reiterates this point again through Isaiah, making it clear that this phenomenon of huge and newly-created springs extends throughout the land of Israel, even the wilderness areas.

> *The poor and needy search for water, but there is none; their tongues are parched with thirst. But I the Lord will answer them; I, the God of Israel, will not forsake them.*

---

[170] Revelation 16:18b, NIV.
[171] This is not to say that all tall buildings are bad (cf Matthew 21:33; Mark 12:1; Luke 14:28). However, at the time of Jesus' arrival, it appears that numerous towering structures will have distinctly "Babel-like" or other God-defying sets of attributes.

> *18 I will make rivers flow on barren heights, and springs within the valleys. I will turn the desert into pools of water, and the parched ground into springs.* 19 I will put in the desert the cedar and the acacia, the myrtle and the olive. I will set pines in the wasteland, the fir and the cypress together, 20 so that people may see and know, may consider and understand, that the hand of the Lord has done this, that the Holy One of Israel has created it.
> Isaiah 41:17-20, NIV

Also,

> I will lead the blind by ways they have not known, along **unfamiliar paths** I will guide them; I will turn the darkness into light before them and **make the rough places smooth**. These are the things I will do; I will not forsake them.
> Isaiah 42:16, NIV

And again,

> Forget the former things; do not dwell on the past. 19 See, I am doing a new thing! **Now it springs up; do you not perceive it? I am making a way in the desert and streams in the wasteland.** 20 The wild animals honor me, the jackals and the owls, because **I provide water in the desert and streams in the wasteland**, to give drink to my people, my chosen, 21 the people I formed for myself that they may proclaim my praise.
> Isaiah 43:18-21, NIV

As we see in these verses, these watercourses will be permanent, allowing new forests of various kinds of trees to be established, and numerous species of wildlife to flourish. But let's be clear: these streams, which will combine into mighty rivers, will have as their source new springs resulting from God's massive alteration of geology, and the subsequent release of subsurface supplies not now understood or accessible.

These healing events will certainly take place in Israel, the focus of Biblical history and prophecy. They will also, in all likelihood, transpire throughout the earth to at least some degree. For as we have seen, the earthquakes and destruction will be world-wide, leaving the entire Earth in need of healing. For indeed, *all* creation has been subjected to the curse, and therefore anticipates its freedom with the "revelation" of "the sons of God,"[172] who will appear with Jesus. This means that all creation will likewise benefit from the "apocalypse" of Yeshua.

---

[172] Romans 8:19-22.

Healing of the Lord's People

Another purpose of God's coming Mountain speaks to the healing of His people. The Holy Land has always been, since Abraham, the "inheritance" of God's people. Parallel with the healing of the Land will be that of the people of Israel, the "inheritance" belonging to God[173]. From the passages from Isaiah just cited, consider these phrases:

> *...when the Lord binds up the bruises of his people and heals the wounds he inflicted.*
> *Isaiah 30:26b, NIV*

> *The poor and needy search for water, but there is none; their tongues are parched with thirst. But I the Lord will answer them; I, the God of Israel, will not forsake them.*
> *Isaiah 41:17, NIV*

> *I will lead the blind by ways they have not known... These are the things I will do; I will not forsake them.*
> *Isaiah 42:16, excerpts, NIV*

> *...because I provide water in the desert and streams in the wasteland, to give drink to my people, my chosen, 21 the people I formed for myself that they may proclaim my praise.*
> *Isaiah 43:20b-21, NIV*

In all these passages, *the healing of the land is inextricably linked with the healing of the Lord's people.* Simultaneous with new water sources pervasively springing forth in even the most barren places will be God's comforting and healing of His children. This connection will be symbolic, in regards to deeper spiritual healing being symbolized by the outward provision. But it will also be practical: the outward provision will come true. The waters will provide drink, enable plants and fish that give nourishment, and allow all to luxuriate in the restored flora and fauna. God's people, and the land He gives them, are therefore connected, their healing intertwined. We are reminded of this promise and prophecy:

> *When I shut up the heavens so that there is no rain, or command locusts to devour the land or send a plague among my people, 14* **if my people, who are called by my name, will humble themselves and pray and seek my face and turn from their wicked ways, then will I hear from heaven and will forgive their sin and will heal their land.**
> *2 Chronicles 7:13-14, NIV*

---

[173] E.g., Deuteronomy 32:9; Isaiah 19:25.

These prophecies will all come true. God's people, wherever and whoever we may be, will someday turn from worldly ways and toward Him and His ways. Healing will then come to their lands; and streams will flow on the mountaintops and in the valleys and even deserts. And marvels of nature will result.

If we wish to see the biggest instance of this, we need look no further than the coming Mountain of God: for from its height, and from beneath the Temple itself, will flow the headwaters of a mighty river, heading eastward[174]. We will explore this river later, and likewise those that will stream from the smaller mount of Jerusalem. For now, in all these matters, it should be understood that *enormous tectonic alterations* will have played a key role in opening these new watercourses; and that with them, healing for both creation and mankind will follow.

Emphasis of the Lord's Government

Another key purpose of the Lord's Mountain is to serve as the visible seat of His earthly rulership. The Word speaks of the place of His reign as being the focal point of Israel, and, since He will be King of all kings[175], the entire world. For example,

> *Thus saith the Lord; I am returned unto Zion, and will dwell in the midst of Jerusalem: and Jerusalem shall be called a city of truth; and* **the mountain of the Lord of hosts the holy mountain.**
> *Zechariah 8:3, KJV*

God's Mountain will thus be "chief" in the sense of governmental dominance over all other literal and symbolic "mountains," as discussed earlier. But, there is more to it than metaphor. Yes, this Mountain will be holy and dominant; but it will also be wondrously impressive in appearance, as befitting its role.

> *They shall not hurt nor destroy in all my holy mountain: for the earth shall be full of the knowledge of the Lord, as the waters cover the sea. 10 In that day the Root of Jesse will stand as a banner for the peoples; the nations will rally to him,* **and his place of rest will be glorious.**
> *Isaiah 11:9-10, NIV*

---

[174] Ezekiel 47:1ff.
[175] 1 Timothy 6:15; Revelation 17:14, 19:16.

Chapter 4: Lay of the Land

Moreover, its glory will involve an arising not only in a figurative sense, but also in altitude.

> *In the last days the mountain of the Lord's temple will be established as* **chief among the mountains; it will be <u>raised</u> above the hills**, *and all nations will stream to it.*
> *Isaiah 2:2 (also Micah 4:1), NIV*

Reminiscent of Sinai and the original Law of Moses, it is from this lofty Mountain that the Lord's reign will extend throughout the earth. But while Sinai forbade anyone to come near, God's coming mountain will beckon all His children, of every nationality.

> *Many peoples will come and say, "Come,* **let us go up to the mountain of the Lord***, to the house of the God of Jacob. He will teach us his ways, so that we may walk in his paths." The law will go out from Zion, the word of the Lord from Jerusalem. 4 He will judge between the nations and will settle disputes for many peoples. They will beat their swords into plowshares and their spears into pruning hooks. Nation will not take up sword against nation, nor will they train for war anymore.*
> *Isaiah 2:3-4 (also Micah 4:2-3), NIV*

Thus it is that the physical elevation of the coming mountain will be figurative of the essential loftiness of the Lord's wisdom and authority as He governs the nations in that day.

Exaltation of the Lord's Majesty

And now, we come to what is perhaps the broadest and deepest "Why" of the future Mountain: a massive and wondrous monument of honor to God Almighty set within, and made from, this creation. When these geological changes occur, it will not be the end of this earth, only the end of the corruption encasing it since the curse commenced in Eden. It will signal the restoration of this planet, wherein its Creator alone will be glorified.

> *Men will flee to caves in the rocks and to holes in the ground from dread of the Lord and* **<u>the splendor of his majesty</u>, when he rises to shake the earth.**
> *Isaiah 2:19, NIV*

In all these aspects we have addressed, and more, it is the Lord God Almighty who is being exalted. And what does that word mean? Here is the definition from the Merriam-Webster dictionary[176]:

1: to **raise** in rank, power, or character
2: to elevate by praise or in estimation: **glorify**
3: *obsolete* : elate
4: to raise high: **elevate**
5: to enhance the activity of: **intensify**

Origin of Exalt: Middle English, from Latin *exaltare*, from *ex-* + *altus* high

Ex-altus, "make high"; raise, glorify, elevate, intensify. The coming Mountain will be the place of God's special Presence, with His Temple at the peak. And with Jerusalem, the Bride-City on its southern slope, the Mountain will also be the place of governance by Messiah, "the Prince," God the Son. This Mount will be glorified, lifted up, "raised above the hills." It will be made "chief among the mountains," literally exalted in a massive manner befitting that highest position.

> *A voice of one calling: "In the desert prepare the way for the Lord;* **make straight in the wilderness a highway for our God. 4 Every valley shall be raised up, every mountain and hill made low; the rough ground shall become level, the rugged places a plain. 5 <u>And the glory of the Lord will be revealed, and all mankind together will see it</u>. For the mouth of the Lord has spoken."**
> *Isaiah 40:3-5, NIV (quoted in Luke 3:5-6)*

Indeed, the glory of God *will* be revealed! His new Mountain, exalted above all others, will magnify His Name before all the nations coming to worship Him.

New Contours

Having looked at the Why's, we will now look at the What's. What will the Lord's Mountain look like? Though we aren't given an explicit picture, the Bible offers a number of fascinating technical points for our consideration.

---

[176] Merriam-webster.com/dictionary, accessed on 4/10/15; emphasis added by author.

Temple Mount Rising

Of all the tectonic events foreseen during this world's transition to the next age, one specific event will cause significant uplifting of our region of investigation. Though quoted before, this key verse bears repeating.

> *In the last days the mountain of the LORD's temple will be established as chief among the mountains; <u>it will be raised</u> above the hills*, and all nations will stream to it.
> Isaiah 2:2, NIV

We have seen numerous symbolic matters involved here; and to bring a truthful foundation to those lessons, the literal must become factual, and the prophecy become realized. The Mountain of the Lord's Temple must be visibly "exalted." The doubled idea of *"chief among of the mountains"* and *"raised above the hills"* is a reinforcement of the point: this is a geological elevation, and not a mere figure of speech. The passage is perfectly transmitted through another prophet, Micah, adding a second witness on the matter [177] and lending even more weightiness to God's message to us here [178].

This geologic phenomenon will take place "in the last days," which we can equate with when the Lord will directly reign over His creation [179]. This new "chief" of all mountains will arise, even as the coming Prince (being the Son of God) will ascend as king over all other monarchs and rulers. It is He, Jesus-Yeshua, who will ultimately submit all earthly authorities and powers to the Father [180]. So when God raises His Mountain at the same time He raised His Son to rule, will the phrase *"chief among the mountains"* involve a literal increase in elevation above at least some other mountains? The simple answer is: absolutely Yes.

If we want to understand how lofty the elevation increase will be though, we aren't explicitly told; but there are a number of points to be pondered.

First, when comparing heights, we should consider the *final* elevation of the other mountains involved. God's Mountain will be raised comparatively higher than many of them, but not necessarily higher than their *current* height. For one extreme example, we cannot simply declare that the Temple site (near Jerusalem's Atarot Airport, which is approximately 2,500 ft/ 760 M in elevation)

---

[177] Deuteronomy 19:15; Matthew 18:16; 2 Corinthians 13:1.
[178] Micah 4:1. Many scholars have argued over which prophet copied the other, in this practically verbatim parallel prophecy of Isaiah and Micah. The often overlooked solution though is that God, choosing to emphasize His statement, spoke the same words through two prophets.
[179] E.g., Revelation 20, which gives a 1,000-year (one millennium) duration to this period.
[180] 1 Corinthians 15:24-26.

will be raised higher than any present-day mountain (the tallest is Mount Everest, at approximately 29,000 ft/ 8,850 M). This would require a more than ten-fold increase in elevation, and the Bible isn't making that demand. In fact, the survival of certain major geographic features, such as the Jordan River and the Mediterranean coast, would be incompatible with such a drastic elevational change; yet they will remain into this final age[181].

Instead, we need to keep in mind that the world's mountains will be generally lowered, and only their subsequent and much decreased elevations are being compared to Lord's Mountain by Isaiah and Micah. As seen earlier, the far-reaching earthquakes beforehand will be larger than any experienced *"since men were upon the earth*[182]*,"* including the cataclysm of Noah's flood; so the coming terra-forming is at least that significant. Since *"all the towering mountains and all the high hills"* are included in this tectonic "humbling[183]" to come, with *"every mountain and hill made low*[184]*,"* all the Earth will clearly be affected, and all mountains and mountain ranges will be lowered to some noticeable degree. How greatly lowered? We are not told, but we can be sure that the result will be significant.

Also, there is the question of geographic scope of the prophecy, regarding what other mountains are being compared to the coming Mount. Is the scope global? Perhaps. However, as with many prophecies (and the bulk of the Biblical narrative), Isaiah's prophecies focus *foremost* upon the Lord's land, the Holy Land. The Mountain of the Lord's Temple will, with fair certainty, become higher than all others in the region, but not *necessarily* higher than all other peaks in the world.

From that perspective, we could anticipate that the coming Mountain will rise higher than others nearby, particularly those of ancient Biblical adversaries such as Edom, Moab and Ammon. We can expect, at a minimum, the mountain range east of the Jordan to subside, and the region of Ramallah and Jerusalem (on the west side of the Jordan) to elevate.

Let's take an example. Many dramatic mountains exist in the greater region of Israel, particularly when its larger ancient borders are considered. Mount Hermon reaches 9,200 feet (2,800 meters)! Though we do not know how much it will be "humbled" (reduced in elevation) in the future, we are told – in a very "messianic" Psalm – that "[mount] *Hermon shall rejoice in thy name.*"[185] So Hermon will still exist and be clearly recognizable, "rejoicing" in the day when "David" is made God's *"firstborn, higher than the kings of the earth*[186]*."* Yet God's Mountain will

---

[181] In The Approaching Country, we saw how these two defining features will be not only visible in the millennial era, but continue to be used as boundary markers.
[182] Revelation 16:18.
[183] Isaiah 2:12-18, especially v14.
[184] Isaiah 40:4.
[185] Psalms 89:12b, KJV.
[186] Psalms 89:27b, KJV. Since Jesus was often called the Son of David, allowing "David" to refer to Jesus in this highly prophetic Psalm.

arise as "chief" over even Mount Hermon[187], over that entire cluster of peaks between the ancient neighboring rivals of Lebanon and Syria. One way or another, Mount Hermon will "bow" to the coming King of Kings and the Mountain He will rule from.

Yes, this might be only a figurative bowing of, say, governmental jurisdiction. But on the other hand, a literal and comparative elevational reversal may be in view. Mount Hermon, like Mount Edom, is a highly symbolic "high place" belonging to an ancient neighbor-competitor of Israel. With regard to the huge geological changes ahead here, Hermon may well be lowered some thousands of feet, with Mount Zion being raised higher than Hermon's "humbled" altitude.

With all this as food for thought, an essential point can be clearly seen. In one way or another, God's Mountain will be "lord" of all mountains of the world. Those we are familiar with will be physically lowered; God's will be very much raised. It will tower over its neighboring mountains and hills, rising as victor, presiding from and over the Land of His great promises. The arising Mountain will, whether figuratively, literally, or both, become chief over every other one on the globe. And **all nations will stream to it.**

The Southern Peak

In his prophecies of the Sacred District, Ezekiel began his observations from near the peak of the coming Mountain, right near the south side of the new Temple. From this great height, Ezekiel saw a city lower down and to the south[188], Jerusalem. Another prophecy echoes this arrangement:

> *Beautiful for situation, the joy of the whole earth, is* **mount Zion, on the sides of the north, the city of the great King.**
> *Psalms 48:2, KJV*

This and other references describe Millennial Jerusalem as being on its own mount which is called "Mount Zion[189]." Is the Mount Zion of the City a completely different mountain than that upon which the Temple will stand? No: the City rests on a smaller peak "on the sides of the north," on the southern slope of the greater Mountain of God[190], while the Temple stands at its highest

---

[187] As a side note, it is interesting that the Arabic name for Mount Hermon is *Jabal Haramun*, meaning Mountain of the Chief." From Wikipedia, "Mount Hermon," accessed 7/15.
[188] Ezekiel 40:2.
[189] Cf 2 Samuel 5:7; 1Kings 8:1; Psalms 2:6, 51:18.
[190] Cf Psalms 20:2, 50:2, 74:2, 99:2, 102:16; Isaiah 8:18, 24:23; Jeremiah 31:6; Joel 3:17.

point. While City[191] and Temple remain distinct elements, their respective peaks can both be called "Zion;" because that is the name of the overall Mountain of God.

So there is this one very large Mountain, with the Temple at its apex, and another lower peak on its southern side. This dual-peak arrangement should be considered a single holy mountain, the entirety of which will be named "Zion":

> *This is what the LORD says: "I will return to Zion and dwell in Jerusalem. Then Jerusalem will be called the City of Truth,* **and the mountain of the LORD Almighty will be called the Holy Mountain."**
> *Zechariah 8:3, NIV*

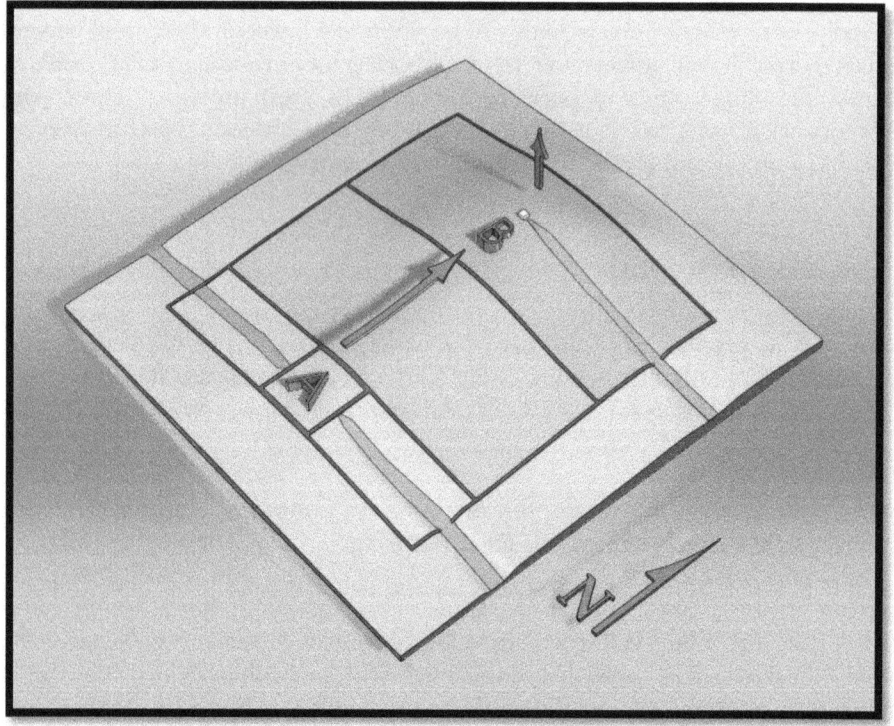

Figure 13: Essential Shape of the Sacred District

---

[191] Jerusalem is sometimes explicitly distinguished from "Zion," e.g., Isaiah 10:12; Ezekiel 40:2; Zechariah 1:14, 8:3.

These then are the first main terrain features of the Sacred District: Jerusalem's mount to the south (labeled 'A' in the above diagram), and the higher Temple peak (labeled 'B') within the priestly region in the north. The relative heights might be moderate and the slopes gentle, as this figure conservatively illustrates. Or, based on a more literal interpretation of matters discussed prior, the elevation changes may be quite a bit more dramatic than was is indicated.

It was theorized earlier that Jerusalem will be centered upon Mount Moriah: the very place where Abraham gave the Lord what he most cared about: his son Isaac[192]. Moriah's peak, the "Foundation Stone," later served as the foundation of the Holy of Holies in Solomon's (and Zerubbabel's) Temple[193]; and, as argued here, it is this that will rest "on the sides of the north" and serve as the City's center. The entirety will be mightily raised – to the point of being considered "chief among the mountains," and "raised above the hills."

> *Many peoples will come and say,* **"Come, let us go up to the mountain of the LORD**, *to the house of the God of Jacob. He will teach us his ways, so that we may walk in his paths." The law will go out from Zion, the word of the LORD from Jerusalem.*
> *Isaiah 2:3, NIV*

Messiah, the King, will reign and rule from the City, drawing people from all the earth to Himself. In such pilgrimages, people will indeed say *"let us go up to the mountain of the LORD…"* and seek the King's wise judgments and advice when in Jerusalem. But they will also wish to go *"to the house of the God of Jacob,"* and make the final uphill stage of the journey to the glorious Temple at the peak of God's Mountain.

A General Smoothing

Here is another key fact for prophesied topography. In stark contrast with the dramatically undulating terrain today (as seen in an earlier satellite image), after all the tectonic upheavals subside, the land of Israel will have been made smooth to a large degree.

> *Speak tenderly to Jerusalem, and proclaim to her that her hard service has been completed, that her sin has been paid for, that she has received from the LORD's hand double for all her sins. 3 A voice of one calling: "In the desert prepare the way*

---

[192] Genesis 22.
[193] Per Hebrew tradition; hence the name, "Foundation Stone."

for the LORD ; make straight in the wilderness a highway for our God. **4 Every valley shall be raised up, every mountain and hill made low; the rough ground shall become level, the rugged places a plain.** *5 And the glory of the LORD will be revealed, and all mankind together will see it. For the mouth of the LORD has spoken."*
Isaiah 40:2-5, NIV

As is written in the book of the words of Isaiah the prophet: "A voice of one calling in the desert, 'Prepare the way for the Lord, make straight paths for him. 5 **Every valley shall be filled in, every mountain and hill made low. The crooked roads shall become straight, the rough ways smooth.** *6 And all mankind will see God's salvation.' "*
Luke 3:4-6, NIV[194]

Over the 2,600 years since Isaiah made this prophecy, many folks have taken his words as spiritually symbolic. As we should! The Lord can and will make our crooked ways straight and smooth, if we but cooperate with His guidance. The Lord will, in the end, bring down that which stands up against Him and bring up those who have humbled themselves before Him. He will make all things plain, removing any "crookedness" or "roughness" in understanding. These examples are perfectly understandable (and vital) symbolic interpretations of what Isaiah said.

On the other hand, for a physical symbol to refer to a higher principle and serve as an adequate metaphor it must at some point exist in some real form, else its symbolic value collapses. This has been mentioned before, but bears reiteration. If a prophecy specifically says that a tangible thing will take place, it must take place; otherwise its figurative benefit disappears. So when Messiah indeed comes to reign over this earth, such prophecies must be visibly fulfilled. God did <u>not</u> say *"every valley* <u>in your mind</u> *shall be filled in,"* or *"every mountain and hill* <u>of your pride</u> *made low."* Those, like many Biblical examples[195], would be explicitly symbolic statements, without any material expectation. But that is not what He said. Spiritual conquering and healing is the more difficult thing; yet to show us His ability and authority to do it, God enacts the tangible counterpart. Just as Jesus reminds us:

---

[194] In a rare instance, all four Gospels reference the same quotation (see also Matthew 3:3, Mark 1:3, John 1:23), underscoring the importance of this "smoothing" of land in relation to Messiah's coming to reign on earth.

[195] Expressly symbolic phrases abound throughout Scriptures. For example, when Jesus said "I am the gate" or I am the vine." Conversely, the Bible contains many statements of God where a primarily physical interpretation is invited, such as those we are studying. To tell the difference, God expects us to use the brains He has given us as fairly as we can.

Chapter 4: Lay of the Land

> *Which is easier: to say to the paralytic, 'Your sins are forgiven,' or to say, 'Get up, take your mat and walk'? 10 But that you may know that the Son of Man has authority on earth to forgive sins . . . ."* He said to the paralytic, 11 "I tell you, get up, take your mat and go home." 12 He got up, took his mat and walked out in full view of them all. This amazed everyone and they praised God, saying, "We have never seen anything like this!"*
> Mark 2:9-12, NIV

It would be easier to say, "God's Mountain will be chief over all others, in only the political sense." It would be easier to declare that "everything will be smoothed out, filled and straightened, but only in a psycho-spiritual sense." It is much more difficult though to visibly demonstrate God's power. On a vastly larger scale than the paralytic man that lay before Jesus two thousand years ago, broad wilderness lands will lay contorted, ravaged and hopeless before Him in the future. In both cases, the easier thing would be to say, "Your sins are forgiven." "Peace be with you." But the hard thing, the thing that God alone is really good at, would be to remedy the matter at all levels. So Jesus issues the command: "Get up! Be healed!" In both cases, as with countless others, God visibly demonstrates His power to perform not only the physical solution, but the far more difficult spiritual solution[196].

In a time to come, people will be just as amazed as in the time and story of the paralyzed man, though on a scale far more vast. *"We have never seen anything like this!"*

Now back to the tangible aspects of topography. Real valleys will indeed be lifted up, real high points pushed down, real crooked paths made straight. The result will be a general smoothing in the land of Israel, at least (and especially) near the "epicenter" of the Lord's geographical focus, His coming Mountain. As a matter of fact, we are told explicitly that this will be the case.

> *The whole land, from Geba to Rimmon, south of Jerusalem, will* **become like the Arabah...**
> *Zechariah 14:10a, NIV*

The ancient city of Geba is located about five and a half miles to the north of Jerusalem, right near the future Temple. There is scholarly dispute over where Rimmon was, but "south of Jerusalem" is pretty clear. So the scope of this prophetic necessity applies at least to the region near or around the Temple, and

---

[196] The irony in the story of Jesus and the paralyzed man is that forgiving sins is a far more difficult or weighty matter than physical healing, yet easier to talk about. Jesus made this clear, in that his performing the physical healing demonstrated his authority and ability to perform the spiritual healing.

all the way down to the City and somewhat beyond. We already know that this same area will involve an uphill slope from Jerusalem to the Mountain's peak. So, now we know that it will *"become like the Arabah."*

The "Arabah" is the flat plain of the Jordan Rift Valley, south of the Dead Sea, a comparatively level expanse. So, very unlike the rifts and undulations we see in the terrain today, this still very much sloped region between City and Temple will also be very much smoothed out.

From what we have heard from Isaiah, this phenomenon of gentle terrain will not be limited to the Sacred District, but be pervasive throughout Israel. From Zechariah though, we see that the smoothing will be particularly present in the Sacred District, between these two peaks of the Mountain. And how fitting! For pilgrims of all nations will make this City-to-Temple procession, and witness the marvels of God's reshaping of His Land. To underscore what Isaiah foretold,

> *And the glory of the LORD will be revealed, and all mankind together will see it. For the mouth of the LORD has spoken.*
> Isaiah 40:5, NIV

Capital Landscaping

Further Features

The Bible isn't at all silent about additional topographic elements that will shape the future Holy Land. Some of these elements are simply ones that are here in the present day, and preserved into the future age. Take Ezekiel's boundary-mapping journey of Millennial Israel, for instance. As we walked those borders with the prophet[197], we observed such things as:

- ☐ The Mediterranean coast
- ☐ Ancient Zedad / modern Sadad
- ☐ Ancient / modern Damascus
- ☐ The Jordan River
- ☐ The "eastern" (currently Dead) Sea
- ☐ Ancient Kadesh
- ☐ Ancient Wadi of Egypt / modern Wadi el-Arish

---

[197] Discussed in The Approaching Country, Chapter 2, "Border Reconnaissance," examining Ezekiel 47:15-27.

Chapter 4: Lay of the Land 93

Since Ezekiel saw these things from the perspective of that future place and time, all these *presently existing* features will also be *present in the day of Jesus' reign*. That tells us that the landscapes here will not be simply obliterated. Even though elevation changes and re-contouring will be involved, they will still remain as visible witnesses of Biblical geography, and God's faithfulness that continues through the next age.

In addition to things preserved, many geographically high places may be lowered and re-shaped – as already discussed. But there will also be numerous new features of geography, not only in Israel, but also in neighboring countries[198]. We will continue our focus on the coming Sacred District though, where we are told of striking new things on the landscape.

City Terrain

The following figure illustrates the area of future Jerusalem described by Ezekiel, as being a square with each side measuring 5,000 Long Cubits (1.47 mi / 2.36 km).

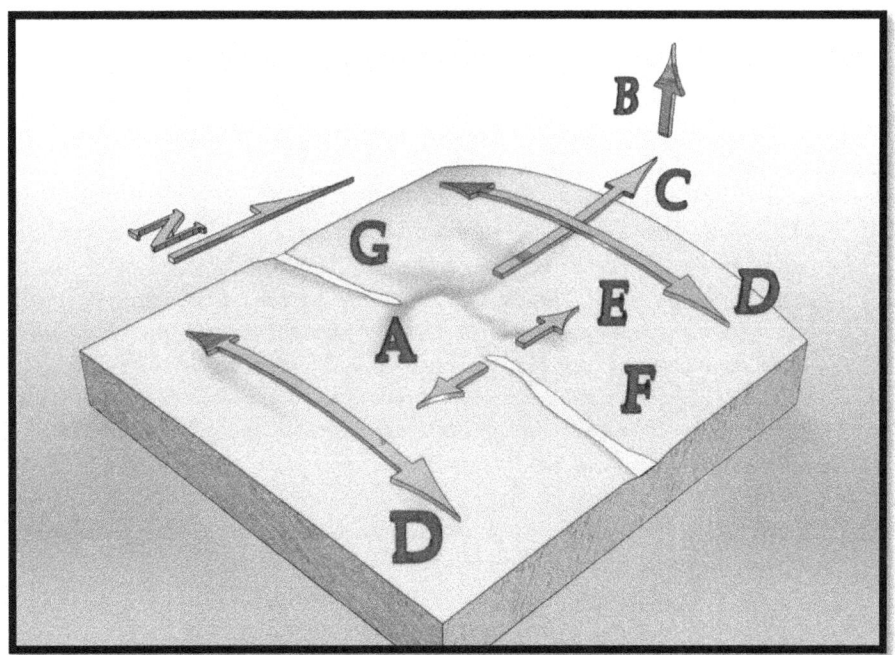

Figure 14: Terrain Features of Future Jerusalem

---

[198] E.g., Isaiah 19 describes a number of changes pertaining to the lands of Egypt and Assyria.

At the center is Mount Moriah: the place of Abraham's demonstration of ultimate faith in the Lord, the place around which stood the Holy of Holies of Solomon's Temple, and upon which rested the Ark of the Covenant[199].

The central peak of the City is labeled 'A', while the Temple peak, far to the north (and not shown in this diagram), is indicated as 'B'. We have talked about the upward slope from A to B, here labeled as 'C'. We don't know how small or great that angle will be, but we do know that the 'A' of the City will rise on the south side of that slope, and in a noticeable fashion.

The general smoothing of the entire area is twice marked as 'D', and this will be a prevalent phenomenon throughout. North-to-south, there is the general upward slope overall, perhaps as gentle as shown, but perhaps much more extreme in the outworking.

The Split Mount

There remain additional elements to think about, and for those we turn to the prophet Zechariah. Referring still to the above diagram, just east of Jerusalem's peak ('A') is a lesser peak, the Mount of Olives ('E'). But notice that this smaller mount is divided in two, with a valley cutting through it. Zechariah describes this in the same passage where he foretells the general smoothing of terrain at this time. From these verses we know that the Mount of Olives will remain on the scene, but now in two parts.

> *Then the Lord will go out and fight against those nations, as he fights in the day of battle. 4 On that day his feet will stand on the Mount of Olives, east of Jerusalem, and* **the Mount of Olives will be split in two from east to west, forming a great valley, with half of the mountain moving north and half moving south.** *5 You will flee by my* **mountain valley**, *for it will extend to Azel. You will flee as you fled from the earthquake in the days of Uzziah king of Judah. Then the Lord my God will come, and all the holy ones with him. Zechariah 14:3-5, NIV*

Uzziah has come and gone, but these events have not in any sense taken place yet. But they will indeed come to pass. There will be a new and "great" valley running from Jerusalem's center eastward, cleaving the Mount of Olives in two, with its new halves literally moving toward north and south.

This is a poignant example of how the Lord will perform His terrain alterations: by way of natural fissures and tectonic motion, as He sees fit, and

---

[199] If you haven't done so already, please read 2 Chronicles 3:1ff for correlation between the Temple Mount and the Mount Moriah of Abraham's story.

under His control. The resultant valley will be broad enough for multitudes to escape through just before King Yeshua's coming. Subsequently, a "highway" will most likely be built through this new valley to serve the eastern gate of future Jerusalem[200] and travelers coming from that direction.

This rift through the Mount of Olives will be no minor thing. As Zechariah says, a significant earthquake will result in this new valley which the Lord himself will call "my valley." It will be created by His explicit intervention, a true gorge dividing two mountaintops where there once was only one.

There is, however, another purpose for this valley.

Twin Rivers

Continuing with Zechariah's vision, we learn of one of the most fascinating features of the coming Mountain's topography: a pair of new rivers, flowing from Jerusalem in opposite directions. These are entirely different from the ancient Kidron brook we might be familiar with, which lies just east of Jerusalem, flowing north to south. Instead, these new streams will spring up "on that day" when Messiah comes to defeat His enemies, save His people, and establish His earthly reign. Here is how Zechariah describes them.

> **On that day living water will flow out from Jerusalem, half to the eastern sea and half to the western sea, in summer and in winter.** *9 The Lord will be king over the whole earth. On that day there will be one Lord, and his name the only name.*
> *Zechariah 14:8-9, NIV*

These two new rivers will emerge from Jerusalem's peak, or at least from somewhere near and almost as lofty. We can see in them striking examples of Isaiah 30:25 ("*...upon every high mountain, and upon every high hill, rivers and streams of waters...*") and 41:18 ("*I will open rivers in high places...*"). As opposed to seasonal rivers, these will flow continually, all year long. Their water will never be motionless or stagnant, but "living," that is, *flowing*, from one or more springs.

As a side point, these watercourses confirm that the City will indeed be centered on a significant peak of its own. One of its rivers will flow to the Mediterranean, the other to the "eastern sea," that is, the Dead Sea (though it will no longer be "dead" then), via the Jordan Valley. The City and Mountain of God will therefore be situated on a geological ridge, a dividing watershed, even as Jerusalem is situated now. These peaks will be the highest points in the

---

[200] Apparently the Benjamin Gate: Ezekiel 48:32.

heightened ridge that even today separates eastward-flowing from westward-flowing watercourses in the region.

For both rivers, there will be new valleys cutting eastward and westward from Jerusalem's peak, providing interesting contours in the newly smoothed landscape. Because of this, the river valleys may well be gentle in slope, and not too deep in comparison with surrounding terrain. It is hard to say. However, when the eastward river passes through the split Mount of Olives, the gorge will have to be quite deep, for the river to continue flowing eastward. The chasm there will be dramatic!

The new valley will permit the new watercourse for the river flowing toward the Jordan Valley. And here's a fascinating point about that. Near Jerusalem's east side, the eastward river will span what is now the Kidron valley; and in doing so, we have a prime example of valleys that will be "raised up"[201]. For the east-flowing river will not be diverted by that deep and ancient north-south rift, but instead find a freshly-formed course towards the sunrise.

With these twin rivers streaming from Jerusalem, we can be reminded of Eden and the headwaters of the four major rivers arising from that original garden[202]. And with that, we begin to see a theme that will be often repeated in our journey here: that Jerusalem to come will not only be central in our Lord's dominion, but also be the epicenter of His re-created Garden on this Earth.

---

[201] Isaiah 40:4.
[202] Genesis 2:10-14.

Chapter 5: River and Tree

And he will be like a tree firmly planted by streams of water, which yields its fruit in its season, and its leaf does not wither; and in whatever he does, he prospers.
Psalms 1:1-3, NASB

For as the earth bringeth forth her bud, and as the garden causeth the things that are sown in it to spring forth; so the Lord God will cause righteousness and praise to spring forth before all the nations.
Isaiah 61:11, KJV

"...whoever drinks the water I give him will never thirst. Indeed, the water I give him will become in him a spring of water welling up to eternal life." "Whoever believes in me, as the Scripture has said, streams of living water will flow from within him."
John 4:14b and 7:38, NIV

Streams for Bookends

At both the very beginning and very end of the Biblical record, there is a fascinating pair of natural (yet *super*-natural) features: a life-giving river, and a life-giving tree. Chronologically situated between these garden-like settings will be another "Eden," with a river flowing from the peak of the Lord's Mountain, and very special trees growing beside it. This approaching watercourse will be the next thing we explore in the Sacred District. As a bit of preparation, we will first view its relatives flowing in the deep past and further future.

Fluid Foreshadows

Eden, the original garden of God, was the gem of all creation before it was subjected to the curse[203]. This wonderful place wasn't watered by rain, but by a mist that regularly came out of the ground[204]. So we can imagine a lush region of boisterous vegetation, unencumbered by "thorns and thistles" and exuberant with greenery, flowers, fruits and vegetables. In our mind's eye, we can picture the other feature that watered Eden: its river, springing forth from within.

> *And the Lord God planted a garden eastward in Eden; and there he put the man whom he had formed. 9 And out of the ground made the Lord God to grow every tree that is pleasant to the sight, and good for food; the* **tree of life** *also in the midst of the garden, and the* **tree of knowledge of good and evil. 10 And a river went out of Eden to water the garden...**
> Genesis 2:8-10b, KJV

Eden's unnamed river is strongly related to two very extraordinary trees: the Tree of Life, and the Tree of the Knowledge of Good and Evil. Eating the fruit of the latter forbidden tree was the start of all the problems on Earth. But after that catastrophe, eating of the Tree of Life wasn't allowed either: for the resultant eternal life would be corrupted by the new-found capacity for evil[205]. These two trees have therefore characterized mankind's need ever since: remedying the eating of the tree of knowledge of good and evil, and seeking the fruit of the Tree of Life.

---

[203] Genesis 3:17-18, where because of sin, the ground would thereafter produce thorns and thistles, and be otherwise difficult to farm.
[204] Genesis 2:5-6.
[205] Genesis 3:22-24.

Because of the life-giving tree, the river of Eden can be also thought of as a special life-giving watercourse, a "river of life" sharing miraculous properties with the Tree it nourished. Together, this Tree and this River form a consistent pair of Biblical metaphors for eternal life that comes from God alone.

Eternal Fountainhead

But these are no mere metaphors. After the future Millennial era, in eternity forward, another quite real River will flow from God's garden and His City-Temple, and nourish equally special Trees.

> *Then the angel showed me* ***the river of the water of life, as clear as crystal, flowing from the throne of God and of the Lamb*** *2 down the middle of the great street of the city.* ***On each side of the river stood the tree of life,*** *bearing twelve crops of fruit, yielding its fruit every month. And the leaves of the tree are for the healing of the nations. 3 No longer will there be any curse.*
> Revelation 22:1-3b, NIV

As in Eden, this everlasting setting will be free of the curse, free of any evil degrading its marvels. As in Eden, alongside God's River will flourish once more the Tree of Life. No mere icons, these trees will bring eternal-life-nourishment and healing in an ongoing manner to people from every nation, to all who have sought their vitality in their Creator.

> *He that hath an ear, let him hear what the Spirit saith unto the churches; To him that overcometh will I give to* ***eat of the tree of life, which is in the midst of the paradise of God.***
> Revelation 2:7, KJV

> *Blessed are they that do his commandments, that they may have right to* ***the tree of life,*** *and may enter in through the gates into the city.*
> Revelation 22:14, KJV

In that eternal Day, this Tree[206] of Life will stand along the mighty River of Life flowing from the Throne of God. Forever there will be this strong river-symbol of His life being the wellspring of our own, just as even now He alone is our source. For as Jesus said,

---

[206] Per Revelation 22:2 just quoted, it may be that there will be multiple Trees of Life, growing on both sides of the River of Life. Or, it may be that there will be a single vast Tree, spanning the River. Either way, it will be fascinating!

> ...*but whoever drinks the water I give him will never thirst.* **Indeed, the water I give him will become in him a spring of water welling up to eternal life.**
> John 4:14, NIV

> *If anyone is thirsty, let him come to me and drink. 38* **Whoever believes in me, as the Scripture has said, streams of living water will flow from within him.**
> John 7:37b-38, NIV

Here we see a powerful image of "livingness," a mighty and living "river" that God the Father would have flow in and through us, via His Son and His Spirit. This is a clear spiritual truth. However, the symbol used here points to the real thing: for the "river of life" *did* exist in Eden; and it *will* overwhelmingly exist in the eternal City, plainly evident for all to see and partake of.

Two Life-Symbols

Both Eden past and Eden eternal share these two life-giving wonders: the Tree and the River. Both of these physical features are also iconic symbols permeating Scripture, encouraging us all to find our life in the Lord and His ways. For example,

> *Blessed is the man that walketh not in the counsel of the ungodly, nor standeth in the way of sinners, nor sitteth in the seat of the scornful. 2 But his delight is in the law of the Lord; and in his law doth he meditate day and night. 3 And* **he shall be like a tree planted by the rivers of water, that bringeth forth his fruit in his season; his leaf also shall not wither; and whatsoever he doeth shall prosper.**
> Psalms 1:1-3, KJV

Thus the symbol, lesson, and physical referent will be forever intertwined. In eternity forward, God's children will always sense the flow of His life within, being "planted" and "rooted" in Him forever. At the same time, we will see and enjoy these physical features, the River and the Trees[207], as living symbols of that life and love.

Notice, however, that before the eternal setting there comes the victorious reign of Messiah. And in that era, we are informed of very real reminders of the

---

[207] The "Trees" are being capitalized here, not to say that they will be actual instances of the Tree of Life, but to draw attention to their special supernatural properties as heralds of that eternal Tree.

final Eden of eternity: for in the Mountain of God, there will also be a life-giving River, with its life-giving Trees growing beside it.

Returning Garden

Healing Trees

The first thing we notice about the river flowing from the coming Temple is its fascinating live-giving nature. Wherever it flows, good things happen – beginning with a beyond-natural vibrancy in botanic life.

> *Now when I had returned, behold, on the bank of the river there were very many trees on the one side and on the other…* 12 ***And by the river on its bank, on one side and on the other, will grow all kinds of trees for food. Their leaves will not wither, and their fruit will not fail. They will bear every month because their water flows from the sanctuary, and their fruit will be for food and their leaves for healing.***
> *Ezekiel 47:7&12, NASB*

In confirmation, we have this from the prophet Joel:

> *In that day the mountains will drip new wine, and the hills will flow with milk; all the ravines of Judah will run with water.* ***A fountain will flow out of the Lord's house and will water the valley of acacias***[208].
> *Joel 3:18, NIV*

These are very special trees! They are like deciduous trees, in that they bear leaves and fruit. But since their leaf and fruit production continues year-round, they are almost like evergreens – except that they have leaves, not needles as a conifer would. So right from the start, we know that the trees growing along the Temple River will have super-natural properties: when creation is restored, these trees will have new characteristics beyond what we see in our environments.

---

[208] Strong's OT:7851, *shittiym*, acacia trees. Though not a known place name, the desert acacia wood was used to construct the Ark of the Covenant and other Tabernacle elements (Exodus 25-27). The environment of this ancient, thorny, arid-climate tree will be touched by God's new River, with the new and accessible "trees of life" arising in dramatic contrast to the thorny desert acacia.

Chapter 5: River and Tree

It also seems that there will be "all kinds" of trees, not just one kind. Perhaps these will be species familiar to us, though simply made to continuously flourish because of the presence of God's life-giving river. We should also remember that, in the "edenic" conditions of Messiah's reign, the curse upon creation will have been substantially lifted[209]. Present-day species, relieved of repercussions of "the fall," and especially when planted beside this River, will likely explode into the botanic vitality witnessed by Ezekiel. This will be a big example of how and why present-day creation is said to "groan" under current conditions, looking forward to the coming day of rejuvenation under Jesus, and "the glorious freedom of the children of God"[210]. As Joel prophesied, the thorny and arid-climate acacias will be watered by this new River flowing from the Temple of God, and give way to wondrous trees that bear fruit all year long.

Where Eden had only a single Tree of Life, Ezekiel observed that many of these vigorous trees will be present on both sides of the Temple River. He further mentions that their purpose is to bear fruit for food, fruit of all kinds and at all times – just as in the original Garden of Eden[211] and the eternal one[212]. The other main purpose is in their non-withering leaves, which are specifically useful for healing. Again, we are reminded of the original Tree of Life, which would have permitted eternal bodily health[213]. But in the coming Day of the King, all those who partake of the leaves of these trees can find healing for various maladies. This is all a foreshadowing of the eternal version of these Trees and their leaves:

> *In the midst of the street of it* [the city of New Jerusalem], *and on either side of the river, was there* **the tree of life**, *which bare twelve manner of fruits, and yielded her fruit every month: and* **the leaves of the tree were for the healing of the nations.**
> Revelation 22:2, KJV

We see that eternal tree strongly reflected in its Millennial cousin in many major features: growing on both sides of God's River, bearing fruit for food in

---

[209] See 1 John 3:8 and 1 Corinthians 15:24-25. The Devil's works must be overturned by Jesus, including elements of the curse caused by the Enemy and affecting creation (see Romans 8:20-22). This reversal is exemplified in passages demonstrating at least pre-Noahic conditions for the messianic reign: for example, peaceful and herbivorous behavior of present-day carnivores (Isaiah 11:6-8, 65:25), and human lifespans of up to 1,000 years (Isaiah 65:20). There is the distinct possibility though that the original curse will not be completely overturned until the New Heaven-Earth is realized after the Millennial period (see Revelation 22:3).
[210] Romans 8:20-22.
[211] Genesis 2:9.
[212] Revelation 22:2.
[213] Genesis 3:22.

all twelve months of the year, and having leaves especially designed by God to heal His people of any ailment or injury. The connections are therefore unmistakable: that the coming trees foreseen by Ezekiel will be hugely foretelling of their eternal counterparts. With every partaking of their fruit or use of their leaves, people will be reminded of the final and everlasting Kingdom to come.

There are differences though, between the coming forerunner and the final Tree of Life. While the Millennial trees grant bodily healing, those subsequent and eternal trees are, emphatically, *Trees of Life*. As in the original Garden of Eden, eating the fruit of those trees brings not just healing, but immortality[214]. Even so, the special trees growing beside God's coming Temple River will be more than adequate symbols of what is to come. Though the ultimate Trees of Life will grow in a wonderful creation that does not yet exist, their foreshadowing versions will flourish in our present earth, and on our continuing timeline.

In the mean time, we can appreciate a final truth toward which all these trees, even those we are familiar with in our present day, point.

> *How blessed is the man who does not walk in the counsel of the wicked, Nor stand in the path of sinners, Nor sit in the seat of scoffers! 2 But his delight is in the law of the LORD, And in His law he meditates day and night. 3* **And he will be like a tree firmly planted by streams of water, Which yields its fruit in its season, And its leaf does not wither; And in whatever he does, he prospers.**
> *Psalms 1:1-3, NASB*

In "planting" ourselves in the Lord, we are completely analogous with these very trees of the Millennium, and eternity: residing beside the river of God's own life, we bear "fruit" in the proper season, "watered" by Him so that our "leaves" of faith and works do not wither. Only when rooted in the Lord and sustained by Him will we, like a strong tree, prosper. This will be true after Jesus comes to reign; yet it is just as true right now.

River Overview

Many Bible verses teach that the coming Sacred District will be spectacularly garden-like. For example,

---

[214] Genesis 3:22; Revelation 22:14.

Chapter 5: River and Tree

> *The Lord will surely comfort Zion and will look with compassion on all her ruins;* <u>*he will make her deserts like Eden, her wastelands like the garden of the Lord.*</u>
> Isaiah 51:3a, NIV

> *They will say, "This land that was laid waste* <u>*has become like the garden of Eden...*</u>*"*
> Ezekiel 36:35a, NIV

Though this massive garden will be geographically dominated by the Mountain of the Lord, its terrain will still be greatly influenced by three new and significant rivers prophesied to flow from within the region. Like its forebear in the Genesis story, the coming garden of God will have rivers beginning from within, proceeding outward to surrounding regions. The following figure summarizes these watercourses.

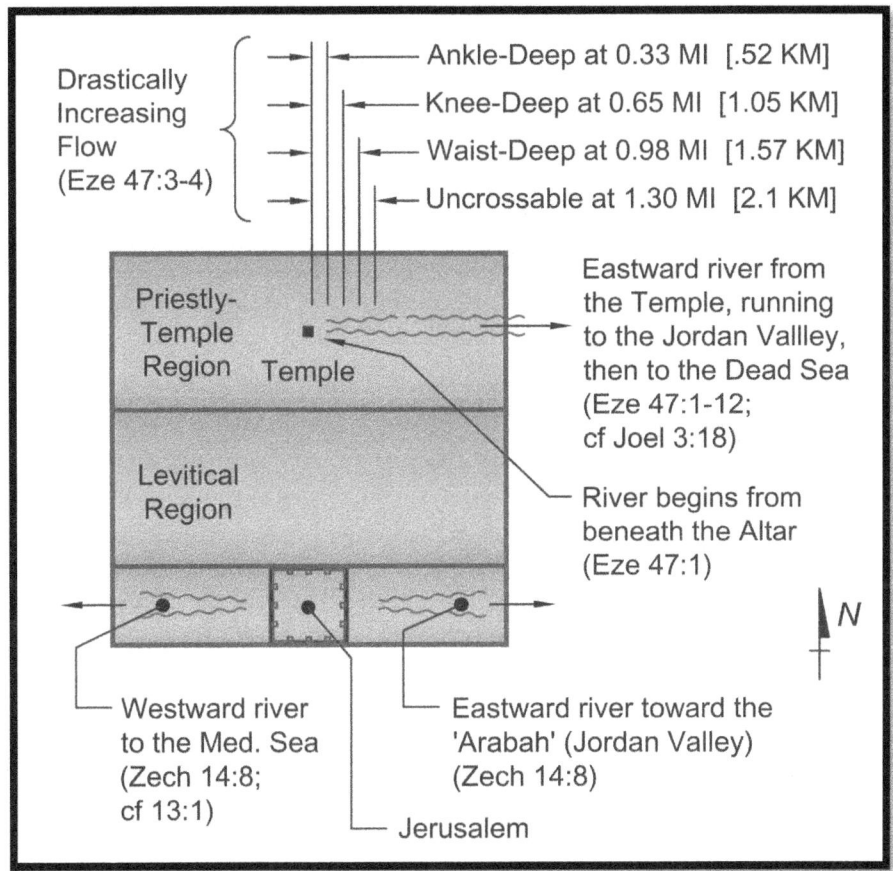

Figure 15: Primary Sacred District Rivers

Twin Streams

In the last chapter we discussed an amazing example of how streams will emerge "from every high hill [215]": the twin rivers from Jerusalem, running eastward and westward from the City's mount. With these new watercourses, this Eden-like place of the Lord's coming reign will indeed be glorious [216].

One name is common to both the Genesis account and Jerusalem's geography: the *Gihon*. This spring arises from within the City of David on the southwest side, and has been the major water supply for historical Jerusalem. The river's name was also given to one of the four that Eden's river divided into [217].

We've seen that the Mount of Olives will be split by a new eastward valley, and that a new river will flow through it from Jerusalem. Will this eastward river be named after the ancient spring nearby, and also the river originating from Eden of old? If so, one wouldn't be surprised: "Gihon" seems to be a clear candidate. Whatever its name though, this new river will not run southward (as does the present Gihon), nor have its watercourse located in distant regions (as with Eden's Gihon). Instead, it will continue east and down to the Jordan Valley and soon join with the Jordan River, where it will turn south toward what will become known as the "Eastern Sea [218]."

We are told less of its westward-flowing sister river, though we can safely say that there will be a watercourse and valley, containing and forming its banks as it travels all the way to the Mediterranean Sea. One wonders what its entry to that Sea will look like, for example, how the new landscape and coastline will appear, and whether there will be an important port there. Without question, many discoveries await Jerusalem's and Israel's future inhabitants, and many great stories will told by them about these two rivers from the City.

We can, however, know a lot more about one other river flowing from the coming "Eden," the third one described by the prophets that will flow in the Sacred District.

Living River

It isn't every day that a major new river bursts onto the scene, but that is exactly what will happen on a future day that will also be remarkable for severe

---

[215] Isaiah 30:25.
[216] E.g., Isaiah 11:10, 60:13.
[217] Genesis 2:13.
[218] Zechariah 14:8.

Chapter 5: River and Tree

earthquakes [219]. On that very day, new streams will open from Israel's mountaintops, with the twin rivers of Jerusalem being key instances. But one river will be, by far, the most important: the Temple River.

Though a name for the river is not declared in the Word, we will refer to it here as the "Temple River" because that is where it will originate: from the south side of the altar, within the coming Temple of God.

Like Eden's river in the deep past, and the eternal river to come, the Temple River will not merely convey water. For as we will see, this mysterious stream will convey life-giving attributes as well.

Supernatural Spring

Within all Ezekiel's observations for coming terrain in the area, this watercourse figures highly. Flowing from the Temple at the Mountain's peak, it cuts across the northeast quadrant of the Sacred District, flowing in the cardinal direction of *East*.

> *Afterward he* [the angel-guide] *brought me again unto the door of the house; and, behold,* **waters issued out from under the threshold of the house** [the Temple] **eastward**: *for the forefront of the house stood toward the east,* **and the waters came down from under from the right side of the house, at the south side of the altar.** *2 Then brought he me out of the way of the gate northward, and led me about the way without unto the utter gate by the way that looketh eastward; and, behold, there ran out waters on the right side.*
> *Ezekiel 47:1-2, KJV*

Right from its source we see something mysterious about this river, in its very headwaters. Instead of emerging from some random crack in the landscape, Ezekiel says that the stream will emerge from the southern side of the Temple's altar. This is a very precise location, with the altar being centered within the Temple grounds[220], at (or near) the apex of the future Mountain of God, the most "exalted" point upon the most "exalted" mountain. Nothing random about that location! No one will doubt that this geographical feature will have been designed and arranged by God Himself.

But this begs the question: how could any major river spring up from the *top* of a mountain? Generally, a spring results from surface water seeping down into an underground aquifer that, eventually, discharges its overflow at a lower

---

[219] A day when towers fall: Isaiah 30:25.
[220] Working through the dimensions of Ezekiel 40-42, we see that the three gate pairs (inner and outer instances of north, east and south) and the portico of the Temple proper (to the west, but facing east) all face the altar, making it central in the Temple area.

elevation. Here though, a large spring emerges at the top of a mountain that happens to be the "chief" of mountains, presumably having no higher rival nearby. Clearly, something special must be going on here.

What could be that energy source, one so great that it lifts a significant and sustained underground flow to the elevation described by the prophets [221]? Perhaps there is some ancient, deep, enormous, but presently trapped aquifer that is pressurized by the geology above it. In that scenario, gravity would be the potential energy source. Could something like that body of water be released with a major earthquake occurring at the Lord's return, forcing the prophesied fountains up through newly-opened fissures? We are not told exactly. Nor do we know all about the subterranean structures and aquifers of Israel now, let alone their rearrangement during cataclysmic events occurring with Messiah's arrival. But we can expect that natural forces will remain very much at work in this creation, and that the outcomes will be understandable to geologists or other scientists that investigate further in that time.

The design of the Temple River is deliberate, just like that of the eternal River of Life. To begin with, the concept of flowing water is a huge symbol for us: for water is what we are primarily composed of, and often symbolizes life itself. Its flowing nature speaks to a dynamic relationship between us and our God; and an abundance of flowing water is a river. So when a river flows from the Lord's Temple, springing up fresh and pure, the messages are fairly obvious! For example: our life comes from our Creator; He wishes us to immerse ourselves in Him; He desires to flow to and through us. Like its counterparts in the deep past and eternal future, the coming River will shout out that *all* life stems from *Him*, in symbolic and visual-natural clarity.

This stream will therefore be carefully determined by God to emerge where He says, flow in the direction He declares, and have the flow characteristics He describes. The Temple River is thus an intentional precursor, in this *present* Earth and creation, to the eternal river:

> ... *the river of the water of life, as clear as crystal,* **flowing from the throne of God and of the Lamb.**
> *Revelation 22:1b NIV*

We know though that the Temple River will not be the only symbol of life streaming and flourishing because of God. Already we have seen the twin rivers emerging further down to the south, from Jerusalem's lower mount. But it doesn't stop there, because this phenomenon and message will pervade the country:

---

[221] E.g., Ezekiel 40:2, "on a very high mountain."

> ... *streams of water will flow on every high mountain and every lofty hill.*
> Isaiah 30:25b, NIV

> *I will make rivers flow on barren heights, and springs within the valleys. I will turn the desert into pools of water, and the parched ground into springs.*
> Isaiah 41:18, NIV

> *So shall ye know that I am the Lord your God dwelling in Zion, my holy mountain: then shall Jerusalem be holy, and there shall no strangers pass through her any more. 18 And it shall come to pass in that day, that the mountains shall drop down new wine, and the hills shall flow with milk,* **and all the rivers of Judah shall flow with waters...**
> Joel 3:17-18a, KJV

Throughout Israel healing waters will flow, turning the barren and stricken areas into gloriously foliated lands. With remarkable frequency the new water sources will be from hilltops, as opposed to valleys or hillsides. Yet in all the wonders of this restoration and re-creation, one watercourse will remain by far the most astounding: the one associated with God Himself, the mighty River flowing from His Temple and from the peak of His Mountain.

Astonishing Flows

The next mystery of the River lies in its "behavior" as it flows outward and eastward from the Temple. Ezekiel observes that as soon as it proceeds from the Temple area, it quickly and dramatically increases in breadth and depth, soon getting to a point where it becomes impossible to wade across.

> *And when the man that had the line in his hand went forth eastward, he measured a thousand cubits, and he brought me through the waters; the waters were to the ankles. 4 Again he measured a thousand, and brought me through the waters; the waters were to the knees. Again he measured a thousand, and brought me through; the waters were to the loins. 5 Afterward he measured a thousand; and* **it was a river that I could not pass over** *for the waters were risen, waters to swim in,* **a river that could not be passed over.**
> Ezekiel 47:3-5, KJV

Let's walk this location with the prophet. Heading from the eastern wall of the Temple, Ezekiel is led eastward for a distance of 1,000 long cubits, about 1/3 mile or 1/2 kilometer. The river here is but a shallow stream – shallow enough to only get one's feet wet, say, two to six inches. With another 1,000 LC walk, the water is to the knees, say, 18 inches at least. Another 1,000 LC, it is up to the waist, call it three feet. Then another 1,000 LC, and now the river is deep enough to swim in; say, four and a half feet at least. These numbers can be tabulated, as in the next figure.

Distance from the Temple			Depth Estimate	
Long Cubits	Miles	Kilometers	Inches	CM
1000	0.33	0.52	3	7.6
2000	0.65	1.05	18	45.7
3000	0.98	1.57	36	91.4
4000	1.30	2.10	54	137.2

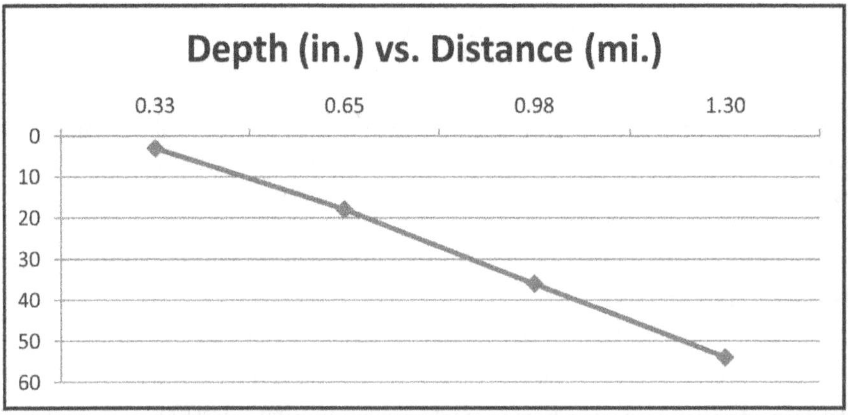

Figure 16: Temple River Depth vs. Distance

In a distance of only one and one-third miles (2.1 km), this very shallow stream has grown into a serious flow. Here is how the NIV version translates the result (for verse 5b): *"now it was a river that I could not cross, because the water had risen and was deep enough to swim in — a river that no one could cross."* The river is plenty deep now, and the prophet didn't attempt any more depth measurements.

At this point it was also observed to be *"a river that no one could cross."* Why would that be? Why impassable? Since no obstacles are mentioned, velocity would be the logical swim-stopper. After all, there is a drastic elevational change from Jerusalem to the Jordan Valley, even today: about 3,800 feet (1,158 meters) in 20 miles (32 km)[222].

---

[222] Starting from Jerusalem, about 2,400 feet (732m) elevation, going eastward to the Jordan brings one near the Dead Sea's mouth, about 1,400 feet (427m) *below* sea level.

Chapter 5: River and Tree

When God's Mount is raised far higher than Jerusalem today, the vertical difference will be increased even more, producing an average flow velocity that is quite extreme.

This would easily explain why Ezekiel said that, one and a third miles out from the Temple's eastern wall, the Temple River will be not only too deep to wade across, but impossible to swim across. On its downhill run towards the Jordan and Dead Sea valley, the Temple River may often be a roaring flow that cannot be crossed by swimming[223].

Referring back to Ezekiel's data expressed in the previous figure, how might this steady increase in water volume take place? The answer cannot be that it begins shallow and broad, and just gets deeper and narrower (with the same volume of water involved), because that would require too broad a starting stream[224]. What makes more sense is that as the River proceeds eastward, it gains additional volume from other sources on the eastern side of God's Mountain. Though starting as a shallow stream, it is joined by other flows along its course, with the growing confluence being a major river that is significant in depth, breadth, and speed.

But where will that additional water come from? We've seen the answer already: for God *"will make rivers flow on barren heights, and springs within the valleys"*[225], such that *"streams of water will flow on every high mountain and every lofty hill"*[226]. Though applying to all Israel and perhaps beyond, the phenomenon especially applies for the Temple River and the area around it. So we should expect a lot of springs bursting forth from hilltops and hillsides and valleys in the vicinity, all over God's Mountain.

There are two great nearby candidates for "barren heights" to have water flowing from them: Geba and Michmash. These two ancient "high places" lie on either side of where the coming watercourse appears to run, a short distance due east of the Temple area. These two mountain "pillars," remarkable in their elevation and standing to the left and right of the Temple River, would surely qualify as "barren heights." If the Lord chooses to leave these intact as historical landmarks, streams will apparently flow from them as well as other peaks.

---

[223] Though we are not told, there may well be pools and lakes along the Temple River's course. But the main point of Ezekiel 43:5b is that at a particular distance from the Temple the river was not crossable by swimmers, and implicitly remained so from that point onward.

[224] If a 3" deep channel becomes impassable at 54" deep, with the same flowing volume involved, the starting stream would be 18 times as wide as the deeper section. For example, if the impassable river of 43:5b is a mere 50 feet across, the "stream" at the start would have to be 900 feet wide. That's wider than any of the Temple walls (500 LC or 860 ft: Ezekiel 42:16-20), so that wouldn't work.

[225] Isaiah 41:18a, NIV.

[226] Isaiah 30:25b, NIV.

What a wonderful sight it will be, with waterfalls adding their flows to the glorious River from the Temple. Combining into a mighty, boisterous and roaring flow, the River will cascade down the eastern slope of God's Mountain, toward the sunrise.

Breathtaking Scenery

Though Ezekiel's commentary may seem peaceful and tame, we shouldn't kid ourselves: the Temple River will be a roaring whitewater in at least some stretches, and probably a vast waterfall in others, for in a very short distance it must undergo simply magnificent changes in elevation. So let's read between the lines a little, and appreciate this natural wonder to come.

As mentioned earlier, a hypothetical present-day river flowing from Jerusalem to the Dead Sea would drop nearly 3,800 feet in 20 miles. But when the new headwaters emerge from near the peak of the "chief of the mountains," the height difference may well be *thousands* of feet greater. True, the Dead Sea will be raised in level[227]; but the change in elevation for the River will still be astounding. Anticipate then that this River from the Temple of God may well have some of the most spectacular waterfalls mankind will ever have witnessed.

Because of the prophesied trees growing on both sides, and the fact that people will need to regularly and safely access them to pick leaves and fruit, we can also expect there to be broad places that the River traverses more gently. Being reminiscent of the Garden of Eden, and prescient of the eternal Garden to come, these riverside opportunities may well be glorious park-like spaces, designed by "One greater than Solomon[228]," knowing that the first Solomon having designed some fairly amazing gardens himself[229].

However, the more frequent the calm stretches in the River, the more dramatic the waterfalls between them will be. For example, if the River drops 5,000 feet in twenty miles, and much of that distance is devoted to accessible trees and garden spaces and so forth, one or more *very* spectacular waterfalls would be involved. Our present-day record holder is Angel Falls in Venezuela, at 2,648 ft (807 m) in a single drop[230]. But the Temple River may have at least one waterfall surpassing even that magnificent feature of present-day creation.

---

[227] The water level of the Dead Sea will be heightened, because the constant and significant flow of the Temple River (in addition to the Jordan) will enter it. A result will be that the Jordan River becomes broad and navigable by larger vessels (Isaiah 33:21), requiring the Dead Sea (with which that river communicates) to rise as well.
[228] Matthew 12:42; Luke 11:31.
[229] Read Ecclesiastes 2:4-6, in view of the many astounding building projects that Solomon conducted (e.g., the Temple, palaces, palace gardens, etc.).
[230] Per <www.guinnessworldrecords.com>, accessed 6/9/2015.

Chapter 5: River and Tree

Adding to the scene will be streams from adjacent hills, as we observed earlier. Surrounding all will also be many kinds of trees, flowers and other botanic life in abundance. Not to mention playful and tame animals of *all* sorts that will be particularly present here on the Mountain of God.

> *The **wolf** will live with the **lamb**, the **leopard** will lie down with the **goat**, the **calf** and the **lion** and the **yearling** together; and **a little child will lead them**. 7 The **cow** will feed with the **bear**, their young will lie down together, and the **lion** will eat straw like the **ox**. 8 The **infant will play** near the hole of the **cobra**, and the **young child** put his hand into the **viper**'s nest. 9 They will neither harm nor destroy on **all my holy mountain**, for the earth will be full of the knowledge of the Lord as the waters cover the sea.*
> Isaiah 11:6-9, NIV

> *The **wolf** and the **lamb** shall feed together, and the **lion** shall eat straw like the **bullock**: and dust shall be the **serpent**'s meat. They shall not hurt nor destroy in **all my holy mountain**, saith the Lord.*
> Isaiah 65:25, KJV

When we think of this awesome stream to come, we shouldn't at all limit our mind's eye to the diagrams and figures presented in this study. The watercourse flowing from the Lord's Mount will be filled with exciting scenes and beautiful vistas, with high waterfalls, lush foliage, and amazing wildlife. For all the pilgrims that visit, it will also have peaceful places where one can pick and partake of wonderful fruit and healing leaves, and also just enjoy the scene, immersing oneself into this all-embracing symbol of God's eternal love, sustenance and life itself.

Reviving Waters

Maybe the most striking thing we read about the coming Temple River is the life-giving nature of its waters. We have seen how it gives boisterous life to the trees near it, enabling them to produce leaves that heal, and bear nourishing fruit in all seasons of the year. This livingness will benefit not only human beings, but flow also into the animal realm.

> *Then he said to me, "These waters go out toward the eastern region and go down into the Arabah; then they go toward the sea, being made to flow into the sea, and **the waters of the sea become fresh**. 9 And it will come about that **every living creature which swarms in every place where the river goes, will live**. And there will be very many fish, for these waters go there, and the others*

become fresh; so everything will live where the river goes. 10 "And it will come about that fishermen will stand beside it; from Engedi to Eneglaim there will be a place for the spreading of nets. ***Their fish will be according to their kinds, like the fish of the Great Sea, very many.*** *11 But its swamps and marshes will not become fresh; they will be left for salt."*
Ezekiel 47:8-11, NASB

What an amazing (and very specific) prophecy! The Dead Sea will be "resurrected," finding itself absolutely teaming with animal life, both saltwater and freshwater species. How spectacular will that be, here in the lowest and naturally "most dead" sea in the world!

We can picture why this would happen. A large freshwater river will empty into a major landlocked body of salty water. That river will, for some appreciable distance, produce a fresh water section in that saltwater body, presumably with some brackish area in between. That is what we have here. The influx of freshwater, for a lengthy expanse, precludes and dilutes the otherwise deadly saltiness, creating waters amenable to freshwater species. So we see prophesied here a far greater phenomenon than a mere Jordan-like flow would produce: only the huge volumes resulting from the prophesied Temple River could do this. It will bring fresh water not only to the northern portion of the Dead Sea, but all along its western side all the way down to at least its midpoint[231].

Why does the entire Dead Sea not become fresh water with all this influx? By way of topography, and per God's intention, certain eastern portions will specifically remain as salty. This is for the production of salt, an ancient industry present in the area even to our present day. So even the Lord's limitation of these fresh waters in the Dead Sea, and their prophesied affect therein, has great purpose.

The result for this deadest of seas will not only be many species of fish, but fish in such great numbers that a significant and ongoing fishing industry will be present. But ponder this fact: not only will there be fish species known to inland bodies of fresh water, but also species like those in the "Great Sea." That is, like aquatic life in the Mediterranean Sea (in ancient times). That will keep fishermen busy. But here is another point we must deduce: that there will be a transitional zone in these waters of the Dead Sea, between fresh and deadly-salty, where the salinity will be analogous to regular seawater.

The three zones of the renewed waters of the "Eastern Sea" will therefore be freshwater, seawater, and very salty – the latter being such as it is now, in the areas retained for salt production at least. But the first two will be created by the Temple River, permitting both freshwater and saltwater species. The Eastern Sea will support perhaps the most varied congregation of aquatic life ever known.

---

[231] At En Gedi. The position of En Eglaim, though in dispute, is apparently further south of that known point.

Chapter 5: River and Tree

How could a single river flowing from the Temple to the Jordan, and only about 20 miles (32 km) long, turn the deadest of seas into perhaps the liveliest body of water that creation has ever known? The answer clearly relates to the source of the water involved: the Temple of God Almighty, soon to reside on His arising Mountain. This natural phenomenon will be a visible, tangible and immersive symbol of our Creator who is the source of all life. In this we are, and will be, reminded of Jesus' words:

> *"If you knew the gift of God and who it is that asks you for a drink, you would have asked him and he would have given you living water." 14 "…whoever drinks the water I give him will never thirst. Indeed,* **the water I give him will become in him a spring of water welling up to eternal life."**
> *John 4:10b & 14b, NIV*

> *"If anyone is thirsty, let him come to me and drink. 38 Whoever believes in me, as the Scripture has said,* **streams of living water will flow from within him.***"*
> *John 7:37b-38, NIV*

Amen. With each of the mysterious qualities of the Temple River, we see emphatic illustrations of the Lord's life-giving nature. As to *how* this great spring will emerge from the high peak of God's Mountain, one could debate factors of surface topology, subterranean aquifers, differential water pressures, climate and rainfall, relative elevations, and so forth. But beyond such technicalities, the more important things are clear. A factual "River of Life" will indeed spring from the Temple of God, *here on this present earth*. In that day on the horizon, the River's divine attributes will be clear to all who gaze upon it and partake of what it brings forth. All will understand what this River from the Temple, like Eden's River of the deep past and the eternal River of Life, flows with the life of God Almighty.

The New Sea

We will end this chapter by continuing what will arguably be one of the most manifest resurrection stories in nature to come. As you know, the Dead Sea is the lowest point on the Earth's surface. In future days, as now, it will continue to accept the flow of the Jordan River[232]. But in addition, it will receive a comparably enormous perpetual flow from the Temple River. This entirely

---

[232] The Jordan River will not be obliterated by the new Eastern Sea, for it will continue to be a significant boundary-marker in the Millennial period: Ezekiel 47:18.

new freshwater system, fed from the coming Mountain of God and supplemented by significant streams along its eastward path, will change everything for the lowest and deadest water expanse on the planet. We have talked about the new life that will emerge here, and we can assume that the botanic exuberance experienced throughout Israel will be present as well. Those are two forms of "resurrection" coming to the Dead Sea.

But there is a more literal kind, that is, a factual arising. With all this new inflow, this lowest coastline will rise quite a bit, and expand outwardly as a result. How much will it rise? How large will it become?

As a matter of fact, we are granted a few good clues on the matter. We have just seen that the water level will stabilize, and thereafter permit an ongoing fishing industry on the western shore. So the Eastern Sea will still be bounded by a shoreline that is at least reminiscent of how the Dead Sea has been historically defined. But we are given more clues.

> *But there the glorious Lord will be unto us* **a place of broad rivers and streams**; *wherein shall go no galley with oars, neither shall gallant ship pass thereby. Isaiah 33:21, KJV*

With the term "broad rivers," how broad is broad? Broad, like the Jordan is now? Or in a completely different category, unlike anything people were familiar with in Isaiah's day, such as the Mississippi or Amazon? Clearly, Isaiah was seeing rivers that were much wider than the Jordan, and is inviting us to imagine a much broader watercourse. No, we don't know just how wide. But, we can understand that the Jordan River – the clear front-runner for exemplary fulfillment here[233] – will be much wider than it is now.

Another implication from the above verse is that large ocean-going ships of Isaiah's day – huge oared vessels such as those used by the Phoenicians – would be technically able to ply the Jordan's waters in the future. Though such means of transport will be specifically disallowed, these kinds of big ships *could* apparently sail on the future Jordan River *if* permitted to do so. And that would require an enormous deepening and broadening of the Jordan's waters. Keep in mind that as the Eastern Sea deepens and widens, so does the Jordan as it enters in the north end.

The technical possibility of large ocean-going ships sailing on the Jordan may well indicate that the Eastern Sea will communicate with the larger oceans. But, we have already seen the much stronger argument to this same point: that

---

[233] Additional broad rivers may well develop in the plains, with the westward river from Jerusalem being a prime candidate. But given that the Jordan River will remain as such, that the ridge dominated by God's Mountain will arise even more than at present, and that the Jordan Rift Valley (parallel to, and just east of that ridge) is enormous, broad and deep, the river therein provides a clear opportunity for the enlargements Isaiah describes.

marine life *"like the fish of the Great* [Mediterranean] *Sea"* will abound here, in what is now the Dead Sea. How can fish of the deep oceans get into the Dead Sea? By providing a way for them to swim in.

From all these clues, it appears that the Dead Sea (and the Jordan River upstream of it) will fill up with in-flow of the Temple River, perhaps stabilizing at sea level. This would help the new "Eastern Sea" to communicate with the ocean to the south, via the eastern fork of the Red Sea (the Gulf of Aqaba)[234].

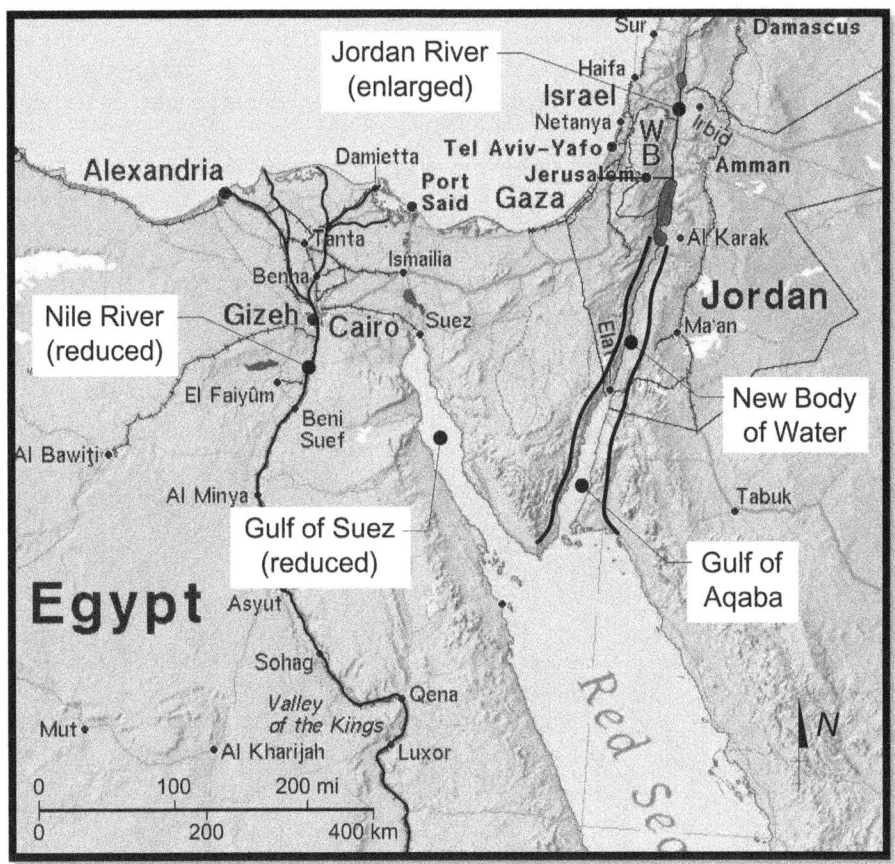

Figure 17: Changes in the North Red Sea Area

Still, the intervening rise in the valley, north of that Gulf, would be in the way, and massive geological barriers would have to be removed for any full communication with the Red Sea and oceans beyond. For that, the "New Body of Water" indicated in the above figure would need to be created. And actually,

---

[234] Background of the following figure is a public domain map, accessed 02-09-16, from: <http://ian.macky.net/pat/map/mide/mide.html>.

that might occur quite "easily," if the Jordan Rift Valley, south of the Dead Sea, were slightly widened.

What might trigger such a widening? A likely cause is the largest earthquake to ever happen since before even Adam walked the earth[235]. The Jordan Rift Valley is an enormous fault line and depression that forms the Sea of Galilee in the north, the entire Jordan River, the Dead Sea, and the Gulf of Aqaba, even before it comes to the Red Sea and continues toward Africa. It is one of the world's greatest fault lines, and therefore very prone to activity and alteration with the foretold tectonic events.

We are told elsewhere that major earthquakes will dramatically affect terrain and water flow in this very region, and in this very time frame:

> ***And the Lord shall utterly destroy the tongue of the Egyptian*** [Red] ***sea;*** *and with his mighty wind shall he shake his hand over the river, and shall smite it in the seven streams, and make men go over dryshod.*
> *Isaiah 11:15, KJV*

The "tongue" of the Red Sea[236] will be greatly altered, while the Nile will be split and made shallow. These two bodies of water, clearly symbolic of Israel's original oppressors, will be greatly diminished. At the very same time, the Jordan will be made deep, broad and navigable. Will the "humbling" of the Nile and Red Sea, and the "exaltation" of the Jordan, be mere coincidence in the time of Israel's final healing? No: at long last, these things will all be part of the final chapter of Israel's Exodus story.

Again, huge earthquakes will reorganize the geography here. And a comparatively slight parting of the Jordan Rift Valley, at the northern tip of the Gulf of Aqaba and northward to the Dead Sea, would open up that entire section of the Rift to the waters of the Red Sea. This would bring seawater in from the south, allowing marine life to enter the Eastern Sea from the oceans. At the same time, the Temple River from the north will bring in freshwater, all along the western side to about its middle. Thus would the prophesied variety of saltwater and freshwater species be provided for, with the eastern side of the much-enlarged Eastern Sea still being maintained for production of salt.

With this new Eastern Sea being no longer at -1,401' (-427 m) below sea level, but instead *at sea level*, its coastline will be quite different than today's. In fact, this new water incursion – though still called the Jordan River – might well proceed all the way up to the Sea of Galilee. Even that lake's surface is presently

---

[235] Revelation 16:18.
[236] There are two "tongues" forking north of the Red Sea, to either side of the Sinai Peninsula. On the east is the Gulf of Aqaba; on the west, the Gulf of Suez. The Gulf of Suez, being much larger, and also the scene of the parting of the Red Sea in the Exodus story, is most likely the "tongue" referred to in this verse.

Chapter 5: River and Tree

far below sea level, for it is the earth's lowest freshwater lake. Will the Temple River "exalt" the Sea of Galilee, raising its level with "living" fresh water? Only God knows for now.

When the Dead Sea becomes significantly larger, that will explain why it will be renamed the "Eastern Sea." With the Jordan on the east, it will be the counterpart to the "Western Sea"[237] opposite. The two bodies of water will cradle the country of Israel for much of its north-south length.

Only the Lord sees how the terrain details will be formed; sees how high the waters will rise in the day of His coming reign; sees the size and shape of the Eastern Sea and Jordan then. We can know though that His River will flow through those bodies, and greatly transform them. The great stream flowing from the Temple, as evidenced in the great trees growing along its banks, will bring life and healing to all it touches.

Whether firsthand or from afar, everyone that experiences God's River will come away nourished, encouraged, healed and inspired by it, and the amazing Trees growing alongside. All will be taking in the very life of God, in a way never experienced on this earth since Eden.

---

[237] The Mediterranean Sea: Deuteronomy 11:24, 34:2; Joel 2:20; Zechariah 14:8.

Chapter 6: Neighbors and Borders

'...you [Israel] will be for me a kingdom of priests and a holy nation.' These are the words you are to speak to the Israelites.
Exodus 19:6, NIV

But you are a chosen people, a royal priesthood, a holy nation, a people belonging to God, that you may declare the praises of him who called you out of darkness into his wonderful light.
1 Peter 2:9, NIV

And foreigners who bind themselves to the LORD to serve him... these I will bring to my holy mountain and give them joy in my house of prayer. Their burnt offerings and sacrifices will be accepted on my altar; for my house will be called a house of prayer for all nations.
Isaiah 56:6a & 7, NIV

District Review

As we have noticed along the way, there will be big differences between the main subdivisions of the Sacred District, such as who will live in them, and what roles those people will have. Between these three regions, City, Levitical and Priestly-Temple, Ezekiel would only have described their clear demarcation unless God Almighty had commanded him, and with good reason. And in so doing, our Father-God invites our honest questions: Why these divisions of areas and residents, and what will be the physical indication of their borders?

Many layers are at work here. So instead of attempting a single pass at explaining the differences and borders between the regions, we will take three distinct excursions through the Sacred District, each of them starting at the coming City and walking toward the coming Temple.

These three uphill treks will deal with who the people are, what roles they will play, and what borders will exist between their regions.

But first, two reminders are in order.

Reminder of the Layout

The following figure and its key information is shown once again for your reference while navigating what we're about to go through. In this 3D diagram, the Sacred District is the larger square (shown with a broad margin of surrounding territory), being 8.15 miles (13.1 km) on each side. The highlighted features are:

A. **The City**, Millennial Jerusalem
B. **The Temple Area**, centered within the northern Priestly region)
C. **The Priestly Region**, inhabited by those that perform the main services of the Temple
D. **The Levitical Region**, inhabited by Levites who support all Temple activities
E. **Farmland**, to either side of the City, with Jerusalem's twin rivers flowing through them
F. **The Temple River**, extending from the Temple to the Jordan Valley and Dead Sea

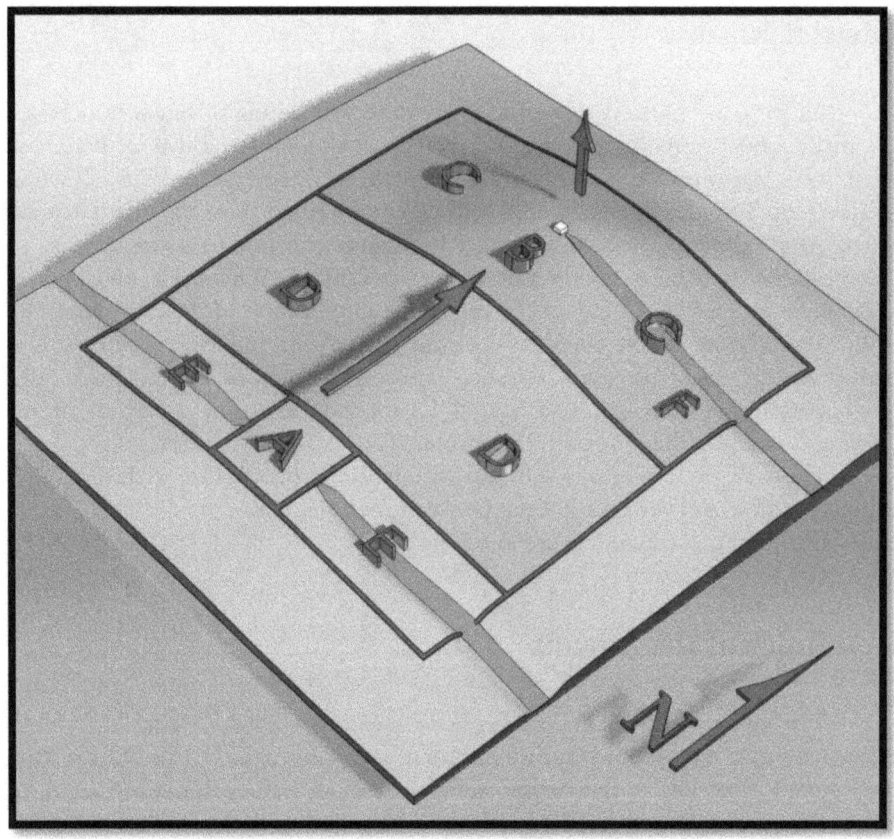

Figure 18: Schematic Model of Millennial Zion

On the downhill side, we have looked briefly at the City and farmlands. We have also discussed the fascinating twin rivers flowing from Jerusalem (**A**), and can see that their watercourses (**E**) will flow directly through the farmland areas to either side. Without a doubt, these areas east and west of the City, whether used as farmland or parkland, will be very well watered and lushly vegetated!

Much more can be said of the City. In fact, The Bible contains a treasure chest of information about it, far too much to take on in our present expedition. The same can be said about the millennial Temple. So though we will still repeatedly touch upon these foremost features of God's Mountain, we must retain an emphasis on the Sacred District as whole. That is, we will continue a focus on the land we would be hiking through, from point **A** (City) to point **B** (Temple).

In this chapter's uphill treks, we will journey from the City's northern gates to the Temple's southern gate, essentially following the sloped center arrow in the above diagram. The bulk of this hike will be through **D** and **C**, the Levitical and Priestly regions, so it is those that will be particularly in view.

Reminder of the Slope

As discussed in Chapter 4, and indicated with the up-sloping and vertical arrows in the last figure, these will truly be uphill hikes – if we were one the scene, in the time to come. So as we discuss particulars of the Sacred District's regions, let's keep in mind that there is a significant slope to the terrain, in almost any direction we look. For the vertical nature of these walks will be dramatic, because the Mountain of God is to be geologically uplifted in a severe manner:

> *In the last days* **the mountain of the LORD's temple will be established as chief among the mountains;** *it will be raised above the hills, and all nations will stream to it.*
> *Isaiah 2:2, NIV*

This "mountain of the Lord's Temple" equates to Zion[238] in general, embracing not only the Temple but also Jerusalem on its southern slope. But there is a great vertical difference between the two key elements of Zion to come, between Temple and City. This is implicit in what Ezekiel described:

> *In the visions of God He brought me into the land of Israel, and set me on* **a very high** *mountain; and* **on it to the south there was a structure like a city.**
> *Ezekiel 40:2, NASB*

This is why the Psalmist can prophetically describe the city of Zion as *"the joy of the whole earth,"* and as being *"on the sides of the north*[239]*."* As we have discussed, the entire Sacred District, the bulk of the Mountain's surface, will therefore be greatly pushed upward, with the Temple's pinnacle rising high. That peak will be at a greater altitude than the City on its southern slope, which will itself surround its own high point of Mount Moriah.

---

[238] Zion encompasses Jerusalem (e.g., 2 Samuel 5:7; 1 Kings 8:1; Psalms 2:6, 51:18). Zion also encompasses the Temple Mount (e.g., Psalms 20:2, 50:2, 74:2, 99:2, 102:16; Isaiah 8:18, 24:23; Jeremiah 31:6; Joel 3:17). City and Temple remain two distinct components (e.g., Isaiah 8:18, 10:12; Ezekiel 40:2; Zechariah 1:14, 8:3) of this overarching concept of Zion; yet the name surrounds both.
[239] Psalms 48:2.

Only the Lord sees how high either of those peaks will be and their difference in final elevation. This is why the above figure should be taken only as a schematic indicator: for the actual slope between City and Temple may well be <u>drastically</u> greater than what is indicated in the diagram.

This, then, is the second reminder: that when all is said and done, Zion will be no mere foothill. The arising Mountain will be chief of all mountains, in a literal sense that has yet to be fully appreciated. Jerusalem will be on its southern slope, but the Temple, and apex of God's Mountain, will rise high above.

What we are about to do is take three consecutive hikes up this Mountain, starting at the City, and climbing to the Temple.

Yes, they will be in a virtual sense, because that's the best we can do at this point. But rest assured: God's Word is fact. In a day soon to come, people will make this uphill climb, and do so by the means of physical legs. They will appreciate the Scriptural nuances we are about to probe. But in the mean time, in advance, we can attempt some glimpses.

Copious Communities

In our first excursion from God's coming City to the top of God's coming Mountain, we will focus on one big aspect: who will be living here? As we move from one section of the Sacred District to the next higher one, what kinds of people will make up the population?

A Full City

We begin at future Jerusalem, somewhere near its center. How crowded will the City be? And will everyone there be Semitic in racial background, or will there be other genetic heritages involved? The Bible isn't explicit on the first question. But in attempting to answer it, we will find the answer to the second one.

Firstly, it is clear that the area will be *heavily* populated. After all, it will be the renewed Jerusalem from which the great King, Yeshua-Jesus, will literally rule this world. As the nerve center of global government, it will involve a great number of officials from every nation that need accommodation in, or at least near, this greatest city. Many other people will need to live here because of their occupations, or simply want to do so out of devotion or other personal reasons. For many reasons then, a huge population will find the City, and nearby areas of opportunity, to be attractive places in which to make their home. In raw terms, the "market" for this real estate will be immeasurably high.

Chapter 6: Inhabitants and Borders

But let's talk about the size of the City. In fact, the coming version will have much less area than what is calculated for present-day Jerusalem, and will be *greatly* less in area than what we consider large cities today. Ezekiel informs us that Millennial Jerusalem will be 450 long cubits square, which works out to be 2.15 square miles (5.57 square kilometers) in area. Contrast that with present-day Jerusalem, whose area is 48.3 square miles[240] (125.1 square kilometers), which is 22.5 times larger! So while the four-square Millennial Jerusalem will be more distinctly defined than today's, it will also be far more compressed.

Though we cannot know how many people will be housed within these tight boundaries, we can consider the kinds of populations that will live here. In so doing we can confirm the sense of density, and also begin to answer the "who" element of the composite population.

Population Type 1: Native born. Due to Jerusalem's twelve gates being named after the twelve tribes[241], we can infer that each of those tribes will be represented in the permanent population of Jerusalem. These will include many Jews, that is, "natural" Israelites by bloodline, wanting to live there, or needing to because of their role in the King's administration.

Population Type 2: Foreign Born. Almost as long as there have been Israelites born of the patriarch Israel (Jacob), there have been Israelites considered to be so by conversion-integration[242]. Especially because of Messiah's work as our High Priest[243], people of all nations have been "grafted"[244] into the nation of Israel, and many of these will live in Messiah's day to come. Keep in mind that many such "foreigners" will be explicitly chosen by God for duty within the coming administration, sometimes being called for the even higher Temple duties[245]. Like their natural-born Israelite brothers and sisters, they may either need, or want, to live in Jerusalem.

Population Type 3: Service-Cyclical. We have seen already the interesting number of those chosen for special service in Revelation 7 and 14: the 144,000. Per 1 Chronicles 23-27, the various service courses established by David involve the multipliers of twelve tribes or twelve months or both. In the 144,000 number, we are told of the twelve tribes, and can easily infer the same multiplying intent of monthly courses of service. Though only God knows what their assignments will be, the "rhythm" of Davidic math seems clearly maintained. And though these 144,000 are declared as native-born from one

---

[240] Per Google data, accessed 7/2/2015.
[241] Ezekiel 48:31-34.
[242] Foreigner conversion and inclusion in Israel begins as early as the original exodus from Egypt, e.g., Exodus 12:48-49 and the many subsequent laws applicable to Israel and "the foreigner that lives among you."
[243] Hebrews 8-10.
[244] Romans 11:17-24; Ephesians 2:12-13.
[245] Isaiah 56:4-8, 66:19-21.

tribe or another, we know that foreigners will sometimes settle within their provinces [246] and also be called to service with them [247]. When these tribal representatives, however comprised, are called upon for service in their appointed month, they will need establishments for eating and places to stay.

Population Type 4: Pilgrimage-Cyclical. Many people will come here from all over the world, especially on the main Feast days. We can expect there to be facilities present for these folks as well.

From all the above, it should be clear that many people will want, or need, to live here in this 2.15 square mile plot of land. And, it should be equally clear that the population will represent all of Messiah's people, that is, a portion of each of the nations of the earth:

> *"You are worthy to take the scroll and to open its seals, because you were slain, and* **with your blood you purchased men for God from every tribe and language and people and nation. 10 You have made them to be a kingdom and priests to serve our God, and they will reign on the earth."**
> *Revelation 5:9b-10, NIV*

So, there will be a lot of people here.

And to close the subject, we will ask one more question. How crowded will the coming Capital City be? Will it have a greater population density than the most heavily populated cities on earth now? Most likely not: for the next Jerusalem will be pleasant for its inhabitants, not unpleasantly overcrowded. But for the sake of discussion, here are some city densities to consider[248].

---

[246] Ezekiel 47:23. Since foreigners will settle within Israel's various tribal provinces, we can expect a corresponding portion of them to be included when their adoptive tribe has special duties towards the City's or Temple's purposes.

[247] E.g., Isaiah 66:21.

[248] From <https://en.wikipedia.org/wiki/List_of_cities_by_population_density>, accessed 7/2015, with Density columns being added by me (as a division of Population by Area). See also <http://www.demographia.com/db-worldua.pdf>.

Chapter 6: Inhabitants and Borders

City	Country	Population	Area		Density	
			mi^2	km^2	People /mi^2	People /km^2
Manila	Philipp.	1,652,171	14.88	38.54	111,033	42,872
Titagarh	India	124,213	1.25	3.24	99,370	38,368
Baranagar	India	248,466	2.75	7.12	90,351	34,886
Serampore	India	197,857	2.27	5.88	87,162	33,654
Pateros	Philipp.	64,147	0.81	2.10	79,194	30,578
Mandaluyong	Philipp.	328,699	4.35	11.27	75,563	29,176
South Dumdum	India	392,444	5.23	13.55	75,037	28,973
Kamarhati	India	314,507	4.23	10.96	74,352	28,708
Caloocan	Philipp.	1,489,040	20.6	53.35	72,283	27,910
Levallois-Perret	France	63,436	0.93	2.41	68,211	26,337
Jerusalem (present-day)	Israel	809,112	48.3	125.1	16,752	6,468
Millennial Jerusalem Population What-	Israel	144,000	2.15	5.6	66,977	25,861
		100,000	2.15	5.6	46,512	17,959
		35,000	2.15	5.6	16,279	6,286

Figure 19: Comparing Major City Populations

The world's most densely populated cities, where a lot of overcrowding-related hardship exists, exceed 50,000 people per square mile. So perhaps we should expect a far lesser density for the coming Capitol. In other words, if God's coming City is to be pleasant to live in, it probably won't have capacity issues like the direst situations today. The Lord will have better and much more workable plans.

Here's an example on the high side. If all the 144,000 "sealed servants" from each tribe[249] were packed into a 2.15 square mile area, that would result in a density of 67,000 men per square mile, and not even including their wives and children! If each man had a wife and two kids, that would result in a density of 268,000 per square mile, which is clearly a not reasonable scenario. Thus we can expect that not all the 144,000 (with their families) will have homes within Millennial Jerusalem, and nor does the Bible say they will.

Here is another hypothetical, on the lower end. If the density of modern-day Jerusalem strikes one as being a reasonable comparator, the population of

---

[249] Revelation 7:3-8, 14:1-5.

Millennial Jerusalem, by an extrapolation of area, would be around 35,000. In comparison with any city today, this is quite a small number of total inhabitants. So perhaps we wouldn't be surprised if tomorrow's density is greater than today's.

I have cited these numbers only as food for thought. Clearly, only our Lord knows how many residents will live within the great City, and who they will be. However numerous though, they will be Jew and Gentile, with various roles in the King's service, rejoicing together in this amazing City on the horizon. The remainder of the Lord's children on Earth will have their homes elsewhere in His restored creation, and happily make pilgrimage to this place and rejoice before the Lord[250]. Between the permanent and visiting populations, we can rest assured that this 2.15 square mile / 5.6 square kilometer area of land will be quite packed with exuberant culture and meaningful activity.

As wonderful and colorful as this City's life will be, we must extricate ourselves and start walking uphill.

Borders of Bloodline

Looking uphill from the City area, we gaze upon the main block of the Sacred District, approximately 53 square miles (138 square kilometers) [251] surrounding the high peak of God's Mountain above us. There is not much doubt about who the main inhabitants are: families belonging to the tribe of Levi (in the central "Levitical" region)[252], and families descended from special priest-clans of that same tribe (in the northern "priestly" region)[253]. Unlike the City, where people of all Israel's tribes (including "adopted" Gentiles within each) will live, this much larger area is for priests and Levites, that is, people dedicated to and commissioned for the service of God Almighty.

Perhaps some today can trace their lineage back to Zadok; and certainly *many* can trace back to Levi. Even so, residence here will be of the Lord's calling. In this central place on Earth to come, what matters will not be human preference, but what God wants and says. He will choose who serves at His Temple[254], and these, with their families, are those destined to live in these regions. Since their activities will surround the Temple, close proximity is vital.

Just north of the City then, we will see the homes of Levite clans and families who will play supporting roles for Temple purposes, and perhaps

---

[250] E.g., Isaiah 56:6-7; Zechariah 8:23.
[251] 25,000 LC wide x (10,000+10,000) LC north to south.
[252] Ezekiel 45:5, 48:13.
[253] Ezekiel 45:3-4, 48:9-10.
[254] Isaiah 56:4-8, 66:19-21.

administrative and other special roles in the City. Around the mountaintop and Temple area, we can expect to see dwellings of the Priests and their families.

There is therefore a dramatic visible difference in the populations, as we walk northward from the City into the Levitical region: in ethnicity and culture. Where Jerusalem will involve a boisterous multi-cultural aspect, this region just uphill from it will be primarily indwelt by families descended from the Hebrew tribe of Levi. When moving from Levitical to Priestly regions, the difference may be all the more evident, given the much narrower bloodline of Zadokite descendents.

Some of us might not be used to seeing an ethnic group being singled out for honor, especially in view of today's political correctness. If so, let's take the opportunity to better grasp the Lord's greater story here. All humanity will witness God's faithfulness to His first-chosen nation, as He fulfills His many promises to them made thousands of years ago. As the Apostle Paul said regarding Israel, "God's gifts and his call are irrevocable."[255] Therefore we see Israel's elevated position throughout this journey; and along the way, we see heightened roles for certain descendents of Israel-Jacob, when they are granted special roles. In these border distinctions then, actual bloodlines therefore indeed come into play.

When these distinctions emerge, God's people from other nations won't waste time complaining, but instead celebrate the massive and tangible instances of God's faithfulness they are witnessing. For if He is faithful to His Word and to His people in such minute detail and over such a long period of time, one can see that there are no barriers to His faithful love toward all His children. In His remembering the promises He made thousands of years ago to Israel, it becomes clear that His promises are sure *for all eternity* and *for all His children*.

Levitical Expansions

Though the genetic filters declared through Ezekiel are absolutely true, God has elsewhere pointed out that the populace will be expanded in several senses, increasing the candidates for residents of the Levite and Priest regions. We can start with the fact that, preceding the prophecies of Ezekiel, there is this overarching declaration spoken through Moses:

> *...you [Israel] will be for me* **a kingdom of priests and a holy nation.**' *These are the words you are to speak to the Israelites.*
> Exodus 19:6, NIV

---

[255] Romans 11:29, NIV. See 16-29 for Paul's further explanation.

This clear promise of the Lord is likewise immutable[256] and unbreakable[257]; and it has not yet seen fulfillment in any full or practical sense[258]. So the indication is that at some point in time ahead, *all* tribes of Israel will be somehow represented in a global ministry of "priesthood." From that perspective, an otherwise puzzling text in the New Testament may have great bearing on this very matter.

> *"Do not harm the land or the sea or the trees until we put a seal on the foreheads of the servants of our God." (4) Then I heard the number of those who were sealed: 144,000 from all the tribes of Israel.*
> - *(5) From the tribe of Judah 12,000 were sealed,*
> - *from the tribe of Reuben 12,000,*
> - *from the tribe of Gad 12,000,*
> - *(6) from the tribe of Asher 12,000,*
> - *from the tribe of Naphtali 12,000,*
> - *from the tribe of Manasseh 12,000,*
> - *(7) from the tribe of Simeon 12,000,*
> - *from the tribe of Levi 12,000,*
> - *from the tribe of Issachar 12,000,*
> - *(8) from the tribe of Zebulun 12,000,*
> - *from the tribe of Joseph 12,000,*
> - *from the tribe of Benjamin 12,000.*
>
> Revelation 7:3-8, NIV

This fascinating passage describes a ministerial population comprised of *all twelve tribes*. This prophesied quantity of 144,000 is not delivered as a metaphor or symbol, but as a specifically computed population of men from distinct tribes of Israel that will be "sealed" for special service[259] to God when Messiah comes to reign. We have noticed the special math in the 144,000, and that service to God is implicit in the number. But there is another and perhaps more compelling reason why we might consider the 144,000 as being in a Levitical role. The clue is contained in this key verse describing those special servants.

> *Then I looked, and there before me was the Lamb, standing on Mount Zion, and with him 144,000 who had his name and his Father's name written on their*

---

[256] E.g., Psalms 145:13, Isaiah 55:11.
[257] E.g., Romans 11:29.
[258] Though the expansion of covenant (and this promise) through Jesus' blood embraces all peoples, the plain reading of Exodus 19:6 applies explicitly for Israel.
[259] See Revelation 14:1-5. These are described in highest terms, as special servants of the Lamb.

Chapter 6: Inhabitants and Borders

> *foreheads… They follow the Lamb wherever he goes. They were purchased from among men and offered as **firstfruits** to God and the Lamb.*
> Revelation 14:1, 4b, NIV

The *firstfruits* term is telling, for its Biblical use consistently refers to an offering of initial strength and blessing, with a firstfruits offering simultaneously representing the larger harvest or group. The "firstfruits" concept is related to that of firstborn[260], in that both belong to God[261]. So note this. The entire tribe of Levi was extracted for the Lord's purposes *as representative of all Israel's firstborn sons*[262].

> *Take the Levites instead of all the firstborn among the children of Israel, and the cattle of the Levites instead of their cattle; and the Levites shall be mine: I am the Lord.*
> *Numbers 3:45, KJV*

The tribe of Levi was extracted from Israel and represented all the other tribes, specifically their firstborn[263]. Along this same pattern, but on a much bigger scale, Israel is seen as God's "firstborn son" and nation[264], and as such it represents all other nations[265]. Jeremiah confirms that Israel is chosen by and for God as a firstfruits offering, representing all the peoples of the world[266].

So here we see a clear fulfillment: the future "offering" of the 144,000, purchased not from among Israel, but "purchased from among men." They are called a firstfruits offering, just like the Levites originally were. But since they will be representative of all peoples, these ministers will be taken from Israel in general, that is, from each of the tribes.

These events will have an impact on the residency of at least the Levitical region of the Sacred District. We have a representative "firstfruits" portion of Israel, called in the same manner as the tribe of Levi, fulfilling a ministerial role in that time. The population will therefore be augmented by these special servants, even though extracted from all the tribes.

Will all 144,000 live there? Due to the overcrowding that would result, as discussed prior, most likely not. Moreover, remembering the monthly nature of the courses established by David, we might expect to see one tribal course of

---

[260] The firstborn is the sign of the father's strength: Genesis 49:3, Deuteronomy 21:17.
[261] E.g., Deuteronomy 18:4 (firstfruits) and Exodus 13:2 (firstborn).
[262] Numbers 3:39-51.
[263] Numbers 3 describes the exact means of purchasing of the Levites, down to the exact shekel.
[264] Exodus 4:22.
[265] Deuteronomy 32:8-9.
[266] Jeremiah 2:3.

12,000 men (and their families) here at any given time, but rotating to the next tribe each month. These would be in addition to the land-owning Levites who serve and dwell here permanently[267].

In our uphill walk through the Levitical region, we see plenty of residences. Most inhabitants will be just as Ezekiel describes: descended from Levi, and having properties that permanently remain in each family's possession. We would also see their diverse activities in support of Temple events, furnishings, equipment and supplies. But a large number of "Levites" from the other tribes will increase the numbers here, and they will also have homes – though probably shared with others. Perhaps serving on a monthly rotation, and on a temporary residence basis, their presences will be easily noticed. And, maybe we would notice evidence of their special roles, in particular service to the King: *"They follow the Lamb wherever he goes"* (Rev 14:4b, NIV).

Priestly Expansions

For the northernmost Sacred District sector, Ezekiel is very explicit as to who will reside there and serve God in His coming Temple.

> *It shall be for the **priests that are sanctified of the sons of Zadok**; which have kept my charge, which went not astray when the children of Israel went astray, as the Levites went astray.*
> *Ezekiel 48:11, KJV*

This is a quite specific limitation, which we should honor with an equally strict interpretation: that in a coming time, God will identify certain descendents of Zadok (who are Levites having that particular lineage), choosing them to fulfill the highest callings of Temple ministry.

However, there may again be some redefinition in that day. Though the core priestly population will consist of Zadok's physical descendants, a big a caveat must be pointed out. We return to a verse recently cited, and add its New Testament application.

> *And **ye shall be unto me a kingdom of priests, and an holy nation.** These are the words which thou shalt speak unto the children of Israel.*
> *Exodus 19:6, KJV*

---

[267] Ezekiel 48:14. Note the connection between Levites and the "firstfruits of the land" in this verse.

Chapter 6: Inhabitants and Borders

> *But* **you are a chosen people, a royal priesthood, a holy nation**, *a people belonging to God, that you may declare the praises of him who called you out of darkness into his wonderful light.*
> 1 Peter 2:9, NIV

God declared this first through Moses to the Israelites (of mixed tribes), and then through Peter to Christians (of mixed nationalities). And though these statements are often applied in the spiritual-symbolic sense, there is good reason for us to appreciate their face-value interpretation. For just as we have seen that all tribes of Israel may well be involved with the ministerial population (via the 144,000), we can likewise see expansions, through Messiah, to all nationalities – as witnessed in the above two verses. God declared this expansion of priesthood around two and a half centuries ago:

> **And foreigners who bind themselves to the LORD to serve him**, *to love the name of the LORD, and to worship him, all who keep the Sabbath without desecrating it and who hold fast to my covenant — 7* **these I will bring to my holy mountain and give them joy in my house of prayer.** *Their burnt offerings and sacrifices will be accepted on my altar; for my house will be called a house of prayer for all nations."*
> Isaiah 56:6-7, NIV

> *"And they [Gentile peoples] will bring all your brothers, from all the nations, to my holy mountain in Jerusalem as an offering to the LORD — on horses, in chariots and wagons, and on mules and camels," says the LORD. "They will bring them, as the Israelites bring their grain offerings, to the temple of the LORD in ceremonially clean vessels. 21* **And I will select some of them also to be priests and Levites," says the LORD.**
> Isaiah 66:20-21, NIV

Here then are two prophecies that distinctly describe Gentiles being selected by God and brought by Him to the Sacred District to serve Him – and in the latter verse, in fact *become* Levites and even priests! These statements by the Lord are just as truthful as all His Word, so we can take them to be factual and worthy of shaping our expectations.

As we walk through the southern half of the priestly region, towards the Temple, we would witness the residences and communities of the native-born Zadokite priests. We would notice also their difference in activities, for their services differ from those of the Levites.

When either population is enlarged by foreigners selected by God, will there be any big visual difference? In skin color and other physical features, of course, yes. But will cultural expressions differ from the "native" population, such as with costume? Probably not: for when these non-Jews are selected, they will become "priests" and Levites," very likely adopting the dress and culture of their adoptive clan.

A Population Summary

God described through Ezekiel the residents in these main sections of the Sacred District, and we cannot discount the weightiness of these explicit declarations. However, we must also respect other Scriptures showing that these Levitical and priestly populations will be expanded, through Messiah-Christ, and at the Father's choosing.

Putting these elements together, we can reasonably expect that Ezekiel's prophecies describe the norm for inhabitants of the main regions of the Sacred District. But we can also expect additions, which to at least some degree result in a mix of tribes and even ethnicities. Based on what we have seen, this mix can be summarized as follows. Note that most of these elements should be understood as including their families.

1. City Region:
    a. Core population: representatives of the twelve tribes of Israel
    b. Additional core population: people of all nations who wish to be adopted into one of the tribes, and also to live here
    c. Visiting population #1: Officials from all over the world, and their retinues, seeking audience with the King of Kings
    d. Visiting population #2: Pilgrims from all nations, especially during the main feast times (particularly Tabernacles: Zechariah 14:16-19)

2. Levitical Region:
    a. Core population: A small portion of all Levi's descendents, having permanent properties here (with the bulk of these descendents living in towns dispersed throughout Israel)
    b. Additional core population: non-native Levite adoptees, selected by God on a case basis
    c. Additional population: a portion of the 144,000 special servants of the King, extracted from all 12 tribes, perhaps rotated on a monthly basis and therefore having shared residences

3. Priestly Region:
    a. Core population: Descendents of Zadok (subset of Levites) called as priests

b. Additional core population: non-native priests selected by God on a case basis, perhaps adopted into the clan of Zadok

Standing near the Temple and looking back downhill, we would see all these populations, and how they will glorify God in joyful harmony. And we will surely know that only the Lord Almighty could have brought these wonders to pass.

Purposeful Partitions

This will be our second hike from City to Temple, where we will look at reasons behind the separation into these regions in the first place. After all, historical Jerusalem, with the Temple area directly adjacent to it, was home to priests, Levites, and general citizenry alike. So why would there now be these dwelling areas distinctions in the coming Mountain of God?

City Regional Purposes

To appreciate Jerusalem's unique purposes in the Millennial era, we need to first step back and distinguish between the City's differing "versions" across time (historical and prophesied).

From the very start there has been a divine emphasis on a physical "City of God" where His Name and special Presence dwells with, and amongst, His people[268]. We see hints of the idea in Eden, where God walked with Adam and Eve in that garden[269]; and we see it taking structure and arrangement in the wilderness encampment of Israel[270]. Since before King David's time, God's City on Earth took on a permanent place and name: *Jerusalem*. On the opposite end of the Biblical time-spectrum this name will remain for the ultimate Heavenly-eternal City, toward which all earthly versions point: the "New" and eternal Jerusalem[271].

Between these extremes, we can perceive a progression of "God's City" from earthy to Heavenly, from imperfect to complete, from mortal to immortal. This progression of God's City on earth is still ongoing; its story is still in the unveiling, for there are two more versions to come.

---

[268] E.g., Deuteronomy 12:21, 16:11; 1 Kings 8:44, 11:36; 2 Kings 21:7
[269] As evidenced in Genesis 3:8.
[270] E.g., Numbers 2-3.
[271] Revelation 21-22.

So before examining the upcoming version here on this Earth, let's talk a little about the final one. Heavenly-eternal Jerusalem is already designed, built and populated, needing only God's timing for it to merge with a brand new Earth. This concluding City in Heaven will therefore endure forever, and is mentioned many times in the Bible.

> *I am going there to prepare **a place for you.** 3 And if I go and prepare a place for you, I will come back and take you to be with me that you also may be where I am.*
> *John 14:2b-3, NIV*

> *But the **Jerusalem that is above** is free, and she is our mother.*
> *Galatians 4:26, NIV*

> *For he [Abraham] was looking forward to the **city with foundations, whose architect and builder is God.***
> *Hebrews 11:10, NIV*

> *Instead, they were longing for **a better country — a heavenly one.** Therefore God is not ashamed to be called their God, for he has prepared **a city** for them.*
> *Hebrews 11:16, NIV*

> *But you have come to **Mount Zion, to the heavenly Jerusalem**, the **city of the living God**. You have come to thousands upon thousands of angels in joyful assembly,*
> *Hebrews 12:22, NIV*

> *For here we do not have an enduring city, but **we are looking for the city that is to come.***
> *Hebrews 13:14, NIV*

This final version of Jerusalem exists right now, in Heaven; it is where all those in the Lord go to dwell now, just as they always have done[272].

Though this place resides in Heaven's space and form, it is not at all diminished in its reality and tangibility for those experiencing it. For example, it has literal foundations (seen above in Hebrews 11:10). They are very real, in

---

[272] Before the sacrifice of God's Lamb, First Testament saints went to an afterlife-place we see mentioned in Luke 16:19-25. After that sacrifice, the Lamb, our coming King, freed those spirits from captivity (Ephesians 4:7-10), taking them to this City in Heaven. Subsequently, when any believer dies, they go to this same Heavenly abode. So when Jesus said "I go to prepare a place for you" (John 14:2-3), the "you" He referred to includes *all* believers: First Testament, New Testament, all since then, and all to come in days ahead (including those born in the Millennial era).

Chapter 6: Inhabitants and Borders

every way; and we even see them described by the prophet John[273]. Their big difference with foundations we can see and touch now is that the ones in Heaven were designed and built by God Himself.

How will Heavenly Jerusalem merge with God's "earthy" creation? We aren't given details, but we are shown an overview. Eventually, the *present* Heaven and *present* Earth will pass away, an event hinted at several times in Scripture[274]. Both will give way to an entirely *new* creation, a permanent and eternal one[275]. During the transition to that state, the Jerusalem that is now in Heaven will perfectly survive, becoming the centerpiece of God's eternal Heaven-Earth creation.

> *Him who overcomes... I will write on him the name of my God and the name of the city of my God, the* **new Jerusalem, which is coming down out of heaven from my God***...*
> *Revelation 3:12, portions, NIV*

> *I saw the Holy City, the new* **Jerusalem, coming down out of heaven from God***, prepared as a bride beautifully dressed for her husband.*
> *Revelation 21:2, NIV*

> *And he carried me away in the Spirit to a mountain great and high, and showed me* **the Holy City, Jerusalem, coming down out of heaven from God. It shone with the glory of God***,*
> *Revelation 21:10-11a, NIV*

This *eternal* Jerusalem will surely be *the* most amazing and glorious place of *all* time! However, a lot of very important things need to happen before that ultimate confluence, which is approximately 1,000 years in the future[276]. Way before that, in a time very soon to come, the Lord will reign victoriously over all the Earth; and His enemy, Satan, will have been fully vanquished and banished[277]. The nation first chosen by God will become "the head and not the tail"[278]; and Jerusalem, as the place of Messiah's reign, will arise as the beloved focus of all peoples and nations. This is the gist of so many prophecies.

So let us be clear about which expression of Jerusalem is which. Between the Jerusalem of history and Jerusalem of eternity, there will emerge a link

---

[273] Revelation 21:19-20.
[274] See Psalm 102:26; Matthew 24:35; Hebrews 1:11-12; 2 Peter 3:10.
[275] 2 Peter 3:10-12; Revelation 21:1.
[276] The cited passages regarding eternal Jerusalem are fulfilled only after the Millennial reign of Messiah, the duration of which, per Revelation 20:2:6, is 1,000 years.
[277] E.g., Genesis 3:15; Isaiah 45:23; Corinthians 15:25.
[278] Deuteronomy 28:13.

between them: the Jerusalem of the coming Millennial period. The Word is not at all silent about this City soon to come to our present creation, with the following verse as but one example that could be cited:

> *Beautiful for situation, the joy of the whole earth, is mount Zion, on the sides of the north,* **the city of the great King.**
> Psalms 48:2, KJV

This is the City of our expedition, the place of our focus here. Standing between the historical acts of God and the eternal acts of God, Jerusalem of Messiah's Day will answer all prophecies and conclude the earthly story of God's redemption of Israel and all mankind. As the continuum of historical-earthly Jerusalem, it will be the victorious centerpiece of the renewed Earth, the epicenter of the King's wise and perfect dominion, and the jewel of God's seventh-Sabbath "day" of creating an eternal people for Himself.

This next version of Jerusalem, the final one on *this* Earth, will therefore abound with continual celebration of what the Lord has accomplished through history past, and will accomplish – with His City-Bride – through eternity forward. Between its permanent residents, regular servants and perpetual pilgrims, Jerusalem will be multi-tribal, multi-national, and multi-cultural. The "joy of the whole earth" will emulate the eternal praise heard within its Heavenly counterpart, boisterously proclaiming *in this creation* the salvation of our loving God and Creator from "every nation, tribe, language and people"[279].

God appreciates, even "inhabits," the praise of His people [280]. When praises to Him emerge from all the nations He created, from all their languages and voices, the adoration will unite with His Presence and be wonderful indeed. All this will arise from God's City, from all Israel's tribes and all the world's pilgrims; the worship will be breathtaking in its variegated and passionate expression. Though similar adulation is taking place in Heavenly Jerusalem even now[281], this communal praise we are discussing will stem from *this* Earth and *this* creation. It will loudly announce our Lord's mighty victory over all His enemies and proclaim the many facets of His love and faithfulness across all history of this planet.

Of all Jerusalem's versions on *this* earth then, the next one (before the eternal) will signify God's triumphant and immutable plan for His City-Bride. Composed of all nations, it will reside in this creation; and it will indeed be a place of jubilation for all God's people here!

But now, we return to our uphill hike. With all these findings we can understand why Jerusalem of tomorrow should be separated from its ministerial

---

[279] Revelation 5:9, 7:9, 14:6.
[280] Psalm 22:3.
[281] Exemplified in Revelation 5:9-10.

neighbors to the north. The Levites and priests up there will be devoted to the Temple's activities and service to God's Presence there. In contrast, as we have seen, people of all Israel's tribes will be in the City. Jerusalem will furthermore be the pilgrimage objective of all peoples[282] and a place devoted to ongoing feasts and celebrations – especially during the Feast of Tabernacles[283]. To preserve all this diversity and activity, there needs to be a quite firm boundary between the City and the Levitical region just to the north.

As we travel from the City upward to the Levitical-Priestly regions, we can sense a number of differences. Celebration gives way to dedicated service; transient pilgrim gives way to resident servant; multilingual gives way to a single language; variegation gives way to ordained pattern. In these and many other aspects, we would see differences in art, language, dress. For as we journey nearer God's holy Temple, the purposes and activities of participants become correspondingly selective.

Levitical Regional Purposes

Walking uphill, we'll start at the center gate of the three arranged along Jerusalem's northern side. Emerging from that gate, we first cross the City's 250-LC-wide perimeter. This isn't a huge distance to cross, only 143 yards or 131 meters. But it is still an adequate expanse for, say, really nice parklands. However this stretch of garden will appear and be utilized, we soon reach its northern edge and the border of the region belonging to the Levites. Thus we exit what will be perhaps the most energetic enclave of the Sacred District, and move into more "ministerial" sections.

Levi was the tribe that was extracted from all the others, and replaced by God with one of Joseph's sons[284]. From earlier observations we know this to be a comparatively huge area. The City has only 5,000 x 5,000 long cubits for its dimensions[285]. But, with dimensions of 25,000 x 10,000 long cubits, the Levitical region has exactly *ten times* the area of the City.

Why so much space for the Levites? True, we have seen that plenty of them will live here. However, there will also be many people living in, and especially visiting, the City. So, what is so important that ten times the land of

---

[282] E.g., Zechariah 8:22-23.
[283] Zechariah 14:16-19.
[284] To replace Levi, Joseph became two tribes: Manasseh and Ephraim. Generally speaking (and there are exceptions), when Levi is mentioned in a list of the twelve tribes, it is a list of the original twelve brothers, where Levi and Joseph replace Manasseh and Ephraim. But in a list of tribal land allocations (for example), Joseph and Levi are replaced with Manasseh and Ephraim.
[285] Equating to 25,000,000 sq LC / 2.65 square miles / 6.87 square km.

the City is dedicated to Levitical families and their purposes? Why such a massive difference in real estate, especially since the tribe of Levi will already be represented within the City[286]?

The reason is that the purposes for the Levitical ("pertaining to Levi") area are very different than those for the City, with said purposes requiring much more land. Our understanding here will, once again, be improved if we look back at the Scriptural drama. For starters, consider the original tribal land divisions, where the tribe of Levi was *not* to be granted a regular tribal portion of land:

> *It is the Levites who are to do the work at the Tent of Meeting and bear the responsibility for offenses against it. This is a lasting ordinance for the generations to come.* **They will receive no inheritance among the Israelites. 24 Instead, I give to the Levites as their inheritance the tithes that the Israelites present as an offering to the LORD.** *That is why I said concerning them:* **'They will have no inheritance among the Israelites.'** *Numbers 18:23-24, NIV*

> *At that time the LORD set apart the tribe of Levi to carry the ark of the covenant of the LORD, to stand before the LORD to minister and to pronounce blessings in his name, as they still do today. 9* **That is why the Levites have no share or inheritance among their brothers; the LORD is their inheritance***, as the LORD your God told them.*
> *Deuteronomy 10:8-9, NIV*

> **The Levites, however, do not get a portion among you, because the priestly service of the LORD is their inheritance.**
> *Joshua 18:7a, NIV*

In the Millennial period as well, we see no allocation for Levi amongst the provinces of the other tribes. Let me repeat that. In the detailed list of Israel's future provinces given by Ezekiel[287], each being carefully assigned to a particular tribe, none are assigned the tribe of Levi. This blatant omission is a simultaneous declaration that similar land apportioning principles will be at work in the coming era. So, just as shown in the verses cited above, we can expect Levi's land provisions to be according to the original pattern: that certain towns *within each tribal area* will be given to the tribe of Levi.

Thus this chosen tribe was, and will be, "sprinkled" throughout the nation of Israel, living in dedicated city areas within each other tribal portion.

---

[286] As seen in Levi's gate being one of the twelve listed (Ezekiel 48:31-34). Note that this list of gates represents the original sons of Jacob, in that Levi is present, and Ephraim/Manasseh are "compressed" into their father Joseph.
[287] Ezekiel 48.

Chapter 6: Inhabitants and Borders

Still, there remains a need for a central gathering place for Levi's descendents, at a minimum for internal tribal administrative purposes. Where might this larger place be? Right here, in the heart of the Sacred District. This Levitical region, near the God Who chose them, readily fulfills that function. Here is how Ezekiel describes the property:

> *Alongside the territory of the priests, the* **Levites** *will have an allotment 25,000 cubits long and 10,000 cubits wide. Its total length will be 25,000 cubits and its width 10,000 cubits. 14 They must not sell or exchange any of it.* **This is the best of the land and must not pass into other hands, because it is holy to the LORD.**
> *Ezekiel 48:13-14, NIV*

The area described is 3.26 x 8.15 miles, or about 26.6 square miles (69 square km, 17,000 acres). Though big in comparison with the City, it is quite small when compared to the other tribal provinces. Now, if the tribe of Levi is average in population in comparison with the other tribes, how could they all fit in that small area? Of course, they won't be required to. As just mentioned, the Biblical pattern of city-gifting for Levi will apply in Messiah's day, as it did in Moses' day:

> **Command the Israelites to give the Levites towns to live in from the inheritance the Israelites will possess.** *And give them pasturelands around the towns...* **8 The towns you give the Levites from the land the Israelites possess are to be given in proportion to the inheritance of each tribe**: *Take many towns from a tribe that has many, but few from one that has few.*
> *Numbers 35:2, 8 NIV*

Though we are not told what other particular cities the Levites will receive in the future, we do know of this central region of the Sacred District; and we can be sure that it will be the nerve center for that exceptional ministerial tribe of Israel.

As for what special services these specially-chosen Levites will offer to God in this time to come, we can review what they constituted in Biblical times, and extrapolate them toward the duties required for the glorious Temple to come. A big example is that the Levites had full responsibility for the Tabernacle, its furnishings and its implements[288]. With those patterns in mind, and as we read and infer from Ezekiel[289], their tasks will evidently revolve around a massive and holy facility to care for, enormous numbers and kinds of equipment to maintain,

---

[288] Numbers 1:50-51.
[289] Ezekiel 40-44.

and huge event-activities to support. There will be implements to cleanse, structures to adorn and maintain, many animals to tend; food products to prepare; and all on a lavish and gigantic scale.

To these Levitical duties will be added new services related to the Prince and the center of world government from whence He will reign. The Levites will therefore administer and facilitate a vast array of functions for both the Temple and City. Clearly, there will be plenty of need for their labors; and clearly, it is not by accident that they are located between the City and Priestly-Temple regions.

We are told that at least the bulk of the Levite families chosen to live in this region (while others live in dedicated cities throughout Israel) will enjoy a permanent residence[290] in the Sacred District. We have also seen evidence of additional Levites, extracted from each tribe, residing here on a rotational basis. Furthermore, gentiles called to minister as Levites will be sprinkled throughout. In all cases, the homes here are for that tribe's permanent use.

Given their proximity to and involvement with the Temple's services and the Prince's activities, these Levite citizens of Zion will have diverse roles involving perhaps distinctive clothing, specific schedules, and regular procedures. In all this responsibility though, they will have received great blessing and honor; so there will also be great joy. We can expect these servants of the Lord to be just as joyful as their City-dwelling compatriots to the south, though perhaps in a quieter manner. For, understanding the setting and activity, the atmosphere will emphasize holiness. Counterbalancing the boisterous multi-national nature of the City, this region will reflect the ongoing service and reverent dedication to God's Presence that will once more reside among His people.

We see evidences of all these things as we continue on the main central highway from Jerusalem toward the Temple. Our walk is about 3.26 miles (5.24 kilometers) in ground distance, but with an uphill slope that is perhaps quite steep on the average. At last, we come to the northern border of the Levitical region, and the southern border of the Priestly.

Priestly Regional Purposes

From the Levite's dwellings we now pass through the Priestly area, the most holy of the Sacred District's three main regions. Here are the communities of an even more specific subgroup, descended from a priest who was faithful to

---

[290] As seen Ezekiel 48:14, these residences are mainly not "rotating" ones in which certain families come in for a limited amount of time, and later hand the residence over to the next group. Instead, they appear to be permanent residences for the families involved.

Chapter 6: Inhabitants and Borders

Messiah's "father," King David. Thanks to that ancestor, Zadok, these will be honored with the highest roles of Temple service.

Our final leg of this second uphill climb is short, traversing roughly half the width of the Priestly Region, specifically 4,750 LC[291] or 1.5 miles / 2.5 kilometers. Given the proximity to the Temple peak, this may well be the steepest section of our hike. As we continue upward, we are certainly reaching the highest elevation in this section of Israel, with grand vistas to witness.

In regards to roles, much of what has been said for the Levitical region can also be applied here, for the priests were, and will be, of the tribe of Levi[292]. However, a deeper layer of holiness applies to this northernmost region:

> *This is the law of the temple:* **All the surrounding area on top of the mountain will be most holy.** *Such is the law of the temple.*
> *Ezekiel 43:12, NIV*

> *It will be a special gift to them* [the priests] *from the sacred portion of the land,* **a most holy portion**, *bordering the territory of the Levites* [to the south].
> *Ezekiel 48:12, NIV*

Holiness has indeed been a driving factor in our progression. Area by area, as we journey closer to the Temple, the holiness of the land has increased as we near the apex of God's Mountain. In the prior "expedition" of the Approaching Country, we saw a similar telescopic phenomenon in the "chosen-ness" and holiness of the land: from country, to province, to Sacred District. We see it continue though the Sacred District, as we move upwards from the City toward the peak of God's Mountain. Taken together, the progression of holiness, dedication and gifting might be described as follows:

- All the nations of the world, from which one country is extracted for God's purposes:
  - The Holy Land of Israel, from among whose tribal provinces is granted:
    - The Prince's province, from which the central land is given as:
      - The Sacred District in general, wherein the southernmost section is granted for:
        - The City; and then, moving uphill:
          - The Levitical area; and finally, surrounding the peak:

---

[291] I.e., half the width of the Priestly Region (10,000 LC / 2), less half the width of the Temple area (500 LC / 2) = 4,750 LC.

[292] With certain prophesied Gentile exceptions, as discussed earlier. However, the priests will still be considered as Levites (Ezekiel 40:46, 43:19, 44:15; Isaiah 66:21).

- The Priestly area, which surrounds the most holy area of all:
  - The Temple, set upon the top of God's Mountain.

Correspondingly, the people serving God's holy purposes become more focused on, and selected for, those heightened positions. Israel was chosen from all nations; the tribe of Levi was selected from all Israel's tribes; and the priestly clans were selected from all Levi's clans. And now, a further distillation occurs. As the Lord declared through Ezekiel, only a certain strain of the Levitical bloodline will dwell in this northern sub-district and serve as priests of the Lord's Temple in this time: descendents of Zadok. This series of refinements for priestly qualification might be summarized as follows:

- Israel (the chosen priest-nation – e.g., Exodus 19:5b-6)
  - Levi (the chosen priest-tribe – e.g., Numbers 3:12-13, Joshua 18:7)
    - Aaron (the first priest – e..g, Exodus 29:9)
      - Phineas (chosen for his zeal for God – Numbers 25:10-13)
        - Zadok

Zadok was a priest in King David's day, one who stood by that king and served the Lord through thick and thin. When David was fully proclaimed as king of Israel, that event included the anointing of Zadok as foremost priest[293]. When David fled Jerusalem because of his son Absalom's attempted overthrow, Zadok stood with the king[294]. In this time to come, wherein the *Son* of David rules over all the earth, the fidelity of David's friend, the faithful priest Zadok, is honored in the priestly continuum by way of Zadok's progeny.

We have seen reasons why this strictly genetic population will be expanded, and therefore why this entire region[295] will be needed for their dwellings. As for specific duties, will the priests have plenty to do? Yes indeed! Per Ezekiel, they will need to fulfill the many and huge functions required by the awesome Temple that is to come.

---

[293] 1 Chronicles 29:22.
[294] 2 Samuel 15.
[295] Because of the Temple area, the land here belonging to the priests will be *slightly* less than that for the Levites, but only very slightly. Levitical area: 25,000 LC x 10,000 LC = 250,000,000 sq LC. Priestly area is the same, but the 500x500 LC of the Temple is subtracted, leaving 249,750,00, or 99.9% of the Levitical.

Chapter 6: Inhabitants and Borders 147

> *But the priests, who are Levites and descendants of Zadok and who faithfully carried out the duties of my sanctuary when the Israelites went astray from me, are to come near to minister before me;* **they are to stand before me to offer sacrifices of fat and blood***, declares the Sovereign LORD. 16* **They alone are to enter my sanctuary; they alone are to come near my table to minister before me and perform my service.**
> *Ezekiel 44:15-16, NIV*

Reading further in Ezekiel, we see that these duties are numerous, clearly requiring many, many priests. Whether these duties do or do not involve animal sacrifice[296], there will be much work to do. In the weekly cycles culminating in Sabbath observances, annual cycles involving the major feast periods, and all manner of personal, tribal and international pilgrimages here, there will be no shortage of need for priestly assistance in honoring God Most High.

These men, with their families, will need to live directly adjacent the Temple they will serve.

> *The special portion you are to offer to the LORD will be 25,000 cubits long and 10,000 cubits wide. 10* **This will be the sacred portion for the priests.** *It will be 25,000 cubits long on the north side, 10,000 cubits wide on the west side, 10,000 cubits wide on the east side and 25,000 cubits long on the south side. In the center of it will be the sanctuary of the LORD. 11 This will be for the consecrated priests, the Zadokites, who were faithful in serving me and did not go astray as the Levites did when the Israelites went astray. 12* **It will be a special gift to them from the sacred portion of the land, a most holy portion***, bordering the territory of the Levites.*
> *Ezekiel 48:9-12, NIV*

By the way, this need for nearness is a confirmation of the Temple's central location within the Priestly region, for it minimizes travel for all priests between the Temple and their homes.

We will now conclude our second uphill climb. As we continue through this southern half of the Priestly region and approach the Temple grounds, we notice differences with the Levitical region downhill. There is much activity relating to Temple rituals and events, performed by people often wearing specially-designed garments. Levites are here too, bringing food and other items, caring for facility and equipment, and performing numerous other supportive roles. The priests are the ones performing the actual rituals though, as described

---

[296] Whether or not animal sacrifice will be present in the Millennial period is a multi-faceted topic beyond the scope of our journey here. Suffice it to say that though there is Scriptural evidence on both sides of that argument, a decision on the matter is not critical to our present expedition.

by God, through Moses, long ago. Amongst them we perhaps see some that were born of other nations, now serving alongside their Israelite brethren as full-fledged priests of Almighty God.

Throughout all is a most holy atmosphere, stronger and loftier than in any other place in the world. This is the apex of God's holy Mountain to come; and in all activities here, for all that come here, holiness will reign. For His Name, His special Presence, will indeed dwell in this place.

Distinctive Divisions

Our cities grow and morph in every way possible, with geography and trade being among the primary drivers. Citizens can generally move around within our cities as they wish and can afford. If one has the money to do so, one can move to an alternate area entirely. If one has a lot of money, coastlines and terrain and rivers can be altered, dramatically changing the city's contours and appearance.

But here, things are different: for the special Presence of the Lord Almighty will dwell here as well, as will the great King. According to the prophecies we have seen, the layout will not be randomly dictated by geography and commerce, but instead be arranged according to God's specific purposes. So for the citizens here, and places of their dwellings, the boundaries are likewise fixed and clearly defined.

Because of the precision with which the Word defines these regions, and in view of the differing nature and purposes of the distinct populations involved, we should expect that actual architectural features will demarcate one region from another. So as we climb once more from the City to the Temple, let's turn our focus to these physical constructions.

City to Levitical Border

For all its glory, and even though it is contained within the Sacred District[297], the City itself will not be considered part of the most sacred-holy area of the Mountain. It is considered "common" by comparison, because it will be a place of normal human city activity.

---

[297] The City is still a part of the "holy oblation" of land that is 25,000 LC square: Ezekiel 48:20.

Chapter 6: Inhabitants and Borders

> *And the remainder, 5,000 cubits in width and 25,000 in length, shall be for* **common** *[Hebrew: chol[298]]* **use for the city***, for dwellings and for open spaces; and the city shall be in its midst.*
> *Ezekiel 48:15, NASB*

In contrast will be the regions to the north, home to those called for dedicated service toward God. Compared to those holy purposes, the City will be considered "common," or secular. The priests will be explicitly commanded to *"teach my people the difference between the holy and profane, and cause them to discern between the unclean and the clean"* (Ezekiel 44:23). The border between the City and the Levitical region will therefore provide a big object lesson for such "teaching," in that there will most likely be a very substantial wall here.

This border is carefully laid out in Scripture; we have mapped it and examined it in several ways. But now, we can appreciate it as an actual wall, strong and unavoidable. Here are some additional reasons to expect this to be a physical and significant boundary.

- ☐ The precision of the borders' prophecy demands equally precise and readily observable marking to confirm the fulfillment and to give proper glory to God Who defined them in ancient times.

- ☐ The presence of a substantial border underscores God's holiness, and the necessary separation from regular-secular daily human activity. Further elaboration of this physical border would simply accentuate His greater holiness.

- ☐ The Levites will have special rules. For example, they will not be permitted to sell their land (in the central region), and will have important regulations about intermixing the offerings from their farms[299]. Dwellers in the City will not have these strictures, making clear land demarcation, for these and similar matters, practically mandatory.

- ☐ A lack of such physical borders would potentially get City dwellers into trouble by accidentally encroaching into the sacred region belonging to the Levites. For example, by extending one's field into

---

[298] From Hebrew *chalal* (Strong's OT:2490). Similar to the Arabic *halal*, the Hebrew *chalal* (in this context at least) apparently refers to permissible everyday practices. The KJV rendering of this word here, "profane," is an overstatement of the idea of common or secular, for the coming Jerusalem will be the center of Messiah's government and described elsewhere as holy.
[299] Ezekiel 48:14.

where is mustn't be, allowing livestock to trespass and interbreed, etc. Likewise, the Levites dwelling in the central section need to have clear boundaries for where their homes, gardens, public spaces, event areas, and so forth, can (and cannot) be located. In other words, "good fences make good neighbors."

For reasons such as these we should expect there to be a significant, and beautiful, wall between the City and the holy[300] Levitical region. Where highways pass through, such as those associated with the three northern City gates, we can expect corresponding gates in the border wall to be present. These openings will likely stand directly opposite the City gates mentioned, because only 250 Long Cubits (143 yards, 131 meters) separate them.

Levitical to Priestly Border

Continuing northward, we move through the entirety of the Levitical region. Eventually, on the north side of that, we come to the border between Levites and priests. Will there be any special definition to this line between them? Apparently so.

> *And this oblation of the **land** that is offered shall be unto them a thing **most holy by the border of the Levites**. 13 And over against the border of the priests the Levites shall have five and twenty thousand in length, and ten thousand in breadth: all the length shall be five and twenty thousand, and the breadth ten thousand. Ezekiel 48:12-13, KJV*

So even though both these northern regions are holy, the northernmost Priestly region is, in comparison to the Levitical one, a particularly special "oblation" (offering) to God, a region "most holy."

We again see that there are levels of holiness within the Sacred District. As mentioned earlier, as we move uphill to the Temple, we move from holy to *more* holy. To briefly recap:

- ☐ The entire Sacred District is holy (including the City).

- ☐ But, the northern regions belonging to Levites and priests is especially holy, in comparison with Jerusalem (it being a place of "common" everyday activities).

---

[300] This Levitical area is described as "holy unto the Lord" in Ezekiel 48:14.

- However, the Priestly region is "most holy," in comparison with the Levitical region.

This shows a progression of dedicated to *more* dedicated. In fact, the Biblical term "holy" means just that: dedicated and set aside for God's use[301]. So instead of a stark contrast of really unholy vs. really holy, there is an overarching sense of holiness everywhere here. But within this holy setting of the Sacred District there are successive levels of God's Mountain, each increasingly given over to His Presence and purposes.

We can therefore expect that there will be a substantial demarcation in this border as well. Building on the reasons brought up for the City-to-Levite border, here are some reasons for this next physical boundary.

- Same argument of prophesied border precision coming to fulfillment.

- Same argument of underscoring God's holiness, but here increased to the next level.

- Same argument of the Levites being under strict rules of land use and offerings, now in comparison with priest's lands. There is a good possibility that the priests (being Levites) will be under similar or even heightened land use rules.

- Same argument of non-encroachment and "good fences."

- There are huge differences in the roles of priests and Levites, as shown from the earliest times and as reinforced by Ezekiel. Though we will not engage those factors here, it is easily seen that food, cleanliness, apparel, and many other matters are involved in these role distinctions. Keeping related activities separate would be helped immensely by a clear boundary that is not easily or accidentally encroached.

The regions of the priests and Levites will reflect such differences, almost assuredly necessitating a strong, clear and physical border between. The outworking will most likely be a distinct wall, strong and visually impressive.

---

[301] *Qodesh* (ko'-desh), hallowed, consecrated, dedicated. See Strong's OT:6944.

Priestly to Temple Border

In this last stretch, we climb approximately half the width of the Priestly region, slightly more than a mile and a half as the dove flies. Again, we can expect this last leg to be a steep one. As we reach the peak we come to the Temple grounds, clearly the most Holy area of the entire Sacred District.

> *This is the law of the house;* **Upon the top of the mountain the whole limit thereof round about shall be most holy.** *Behold, this is the law of the house.*
> Ezekiel 43:12, KJV

Continuing the progression of holiness, recall that the Priestly region was said to be "most holy" in comparison to the Levitical district. Now, the Temple area is "most holy" in comparison to the Priestly area. This is made quite clear in the following verse:

> *So he measured the area on all four sides. It* [the Temple grounds] *had a wall around it, five hundred cubits long and five hundred cubits wide,* **to separate the holy from the common.**
> Ezekiel 42:20, NIV

Again, we would never say that the Priestly area surrounding the Temple was "common," for God has said that it will be "most holy." But, in comparison with the Temple grounds, it is: for the area of the Temple will be all that much *more* holy.

Will that final border be a physical one? Yes, and emphatically! For Ezekiel tells us in great detail of the mighty walls[302] and gates[303] defining this border.

Surrounding Border

Along with all the above, we should acknowledge the outer borders of the Sacred District. To the north will lay the province of Judah; to the south, that of Benjamin. And to east and west, the Sacred District will border on the Prince's lands. With the internal borders just discussed, and for much the same reasoning, we can expect these external ones to be physically identifiable, socially purposeful, and spiritually meaningful.

---

[302] E.g., Ezekiel 42:20.
[303] E.g., Ezekiel 40:6ff.

Border Summary

Some walls of the Sacred District *are* described in Scripture: the wall surrounding the City, and especially that surrounding the Temple. If we take Ezekiel's descriptions of, say, the Temple gates as any indication, we would not be surprised if the remainder of the Sacred District's walls were equally impressive and beautiful. How much so? We can only guess. But as to the arrangement of these primary borders, the following illustration serves as a recap[304].

Figure 20: Main Borders of the Sacred District

Once again, this is only a schematic view. The designs of these walls reside in the mind of the Prince-King; and He will decide how they should be

---

[304] The illustration includes a hint of "boundary stones," indicating the border of the Prince's land (to east and west) with the tribal provinces to north and south. Tribal provinces bordering the Prince's will likely have some visual demarcation. Note that like the borders involved here, boundary stones are exemplary of things not to be moved or trifled with (Job 24:2, Hosea 5:10).

constructed. For now, we can anticipate them to involve height, thickness, materials, color; foundations, cornices, moldings and artistic embellishment.

The architecture will span great stretches of undulating terrain and cross at least three major rivers. It will therefore require bridges or huge culverts to allow the rivers to pass through. Because of Jerusalem's historical precedent, towers may well be present, especially at corners. Gates will definitely be needed, because of all the major pathways penetrating at different places. All these details will be subject to the art, knowledge and wisdom of our coming King, the carpenter who will here greatly surpass Solomon in His building.

Working together, these walls, gates and other architectural elements of the Sacred District will dramatize God's reaching out to us. Within the City, the distinction of its secular nature is evident in its border with the Levitical region. But thanks to the Anointed (that is, *mashiach* or *messiah*) Lamb, who now reigns as Anointed King, and with His throne within the City, we have a passageway to the Father.

As we walk uphill from City to Temple, the borders progressively declare increasing sacredness, heightened dedication. As the elevation grows, there is greater exaltation of Almighty God. Nearing the Father's Presence, with each gateway, we see His invitation to us, His offer of His own Being for us, His desire for communion with us.

This is why, in Ezekiel's prophecies, the Prince figures so highly in ceremonies involving the main Temple gate, the eastern one facing the sunrise[305]. God-made-flesh, Emmanuel, is that Prince. And indeed, He is the gate for us all.

---

[305] Ezekiel 46.

Chapter 7: Royal Thoroughfares

"And I will make all my mountains a way, and my highways shall be exalted."
Isaiah 49:11, KJV

Go through, go through the gates; prepare ye the way of the people; cast up, cast up the highway; gather out the stones; lift up a standard for the people.
Isaiah 62:10, KJV

"Then they shall bring all your brethren from all the nations as a grain offering to the LORD, on horses, in chariots, in litters, on mules, and on camels, to My holy mountain Jerusalem," says the LORD...
Isaiah 66:20a, NASB

Preparing the Way

Highway in the Wilderness

While reading in Isaiah we sometimes encounter interesting roads and highways that have never yet existed, but instead appear to be present during the Lord's coming reign. For example,

> *A voice of one calling: "In the desert prepare the way for the LORD; make straight in the wilderness a highway for our God.*
> Isaiah 40:3, NIV

Now, we know that to *"prepare the way for the Lord"* is a metaphor for readying our hearts and minds for the Holy Spirit's work. This was certainly true with John the Baptist's ministry, which was said to accomplish, at least in this spiritual sense, Isaiah's words[306]. However, the final fulfillment of this "highway" in the "wilderness" is not limited to a symbolic outworking. In fact, this same theme keeps coming up in ways specifically associated with real future events, places and transportation needs, such as in these verses:

> *See, I am doing a new thing! Now it springs up; do you not perceive it? I am making a way in the desert and streams in the wasteland.*
> Isaiah 43:19, NIV

> *I will turn all my mountains into roads, and my highways will be raised up. 12 See, they will come from afar — some from the north, some from the west, some from the region of Aswan."*
> Isaiah 49:11-12, NIV

As we virtually stand at the peak of God's Mountain, per Ezekiel's lead[307], taking in the tremendous view of the surrounding territory, we can look down and see some of these prophesied "ways" coming from afar. In this chapter we will take the opportunity to examine these future thoroughfares. For while the metaphor of a "path" or "way" to God, through His Son, holds firm for all eternity, there will be a time when the outworking becomes tangible, and serves as the factual symbol to the greater truth. The highways involved will be quite

---

[306] Matthew 3:3, Mark 1:3, Luke 3:4.
[307] Ezekiel 42:15-20.

real; and their convergence will indeed be upon the holy places of God, where His Presence dwells.

Practical Necessities

Let us first consider the volume of traffic involved when Messiah actually rules from His throne in Jerusalem. We have seen that multitudes of families will have permanent residences within the walls of the Sacred District. We can expect them to have activities similar to those we are familiar with, such as going to and from places of work, shopping, education and leisure. On any given day, at least all but the Sabbath, there will be a lot of travel for these purposes, within and between all regions of the Sacred District and beyond. And, on the Sabbath and special holy days, there will be the greatest need for travel: worship of the Lord, with the Temple area receiving the great focus. We can consider all this part of the "regular" motions of residents within the Sacred District. And to this regular flow of local citizens, we will now begin adding.

Next are the great waves of pilgrims from all nations coming to worship the Lord at His holy mountain and to participate in other events taking place within Jerusalem, the Prince's lands, or the tribal provinces.

> *"Also the **foreigners** who join themselves to the Lord, To minister to Him, and to love the name of the Lord, To be His servants, every one who keeps from profaning the sabbath, And holds fast My covenant; 7* **Even those I will bring to My holy mountain, and make them joyful in My house of prayer.** *Their burnt offerings and their sacrifices will be acceptable on My altar; For* **My house will be called a house of prayer for all the peoples."**
> Isaiah 56:6-7, NASB

> *This is what the Lord Almighty says: "In those days ten men from all languages and nations will take firm hold of one Jew by the hem of his robe and say, 'Let us go with you, because we have heard that God is with you.' "*
> Zechariah 8:23, NIV

It is interesting that this travel will not be solely pedestrian, but also animal-borne and vehicular. For example:

> *"Then they shall bring all your brethren from all the nations as a grain offering to the LORD, on **horses**, in **chariots**, in **litters**, on **mules**, and on **camels**, to **My holy mountain Jerusalem**," says the LORD, "just as the sons of Israel bring their grain offering in a clean vessel to the house of the LORD.*
> Isaiah 66:20, NASB

We don't know if those "chariots" will be powered by animals or machines or something else, because the technology of the coming time will be of the Lord's wise determination. Regardless, the point here is that with this enormous additional flow of pedestrian, animal and vehicular traffic toward Jerusalem, things simply must be organized and adequately facilitated. In this new Garden of Eden, many carefully landscaped and maintained spaces will require protection from accidental destruction. Residences, farms and pasturelands will need provisions for their preservation. Local facilities, such as civic gathering places and restored historical architecture, will necessitate orderly means of access.

A strategic system of traffic conduits therefore appears mandatory, for safeguarding of property as well as helping people get to where they need to go. When we look at the orderly nature of prophesied architecture of Temple, City and District[308], it practically (and literally) goes without saying that the access routes serving them will be just as well arranged.

For all these reasons, we can anticipate a well-planned network of highways within the Sacred District's borders, and perhaps extending beyond them. Though the traffic volume will be high, the stopping points many and the settings sometimes delicate or private, we can know that the overall system will be up to the task.

The Implicit Network

Not just one, but several kinds of highway will be present in Millennial Jerusalem, the larger Sacred District, and environs beyond. In this section we will explore this network of avenues within Israel's future borders.

City Streets

We will begin with the City, and the main arteries entering it. Future Jerusalem will have a four-square set of surrounding walls, each wall having three gates each.

> **And these are the goings out of the city on the north side**... *31* **three gates northward;** *one gate of Reuben, one gate of Judah, one gate of Levi. 32 And* **at the east side**... **three gates;** *and one gate of Joseph, one gate of Benjamin, one gate of Dan. 33 And* **at the south side**... **three gates;** *one*

---

[308] Seen throughout Ezekiel 40-48.

*gate of Simeon, one gate of Issachar, one gate of Zebulun. 34 **At the west side… three gates**; one gate of Gad, one gate of Asher, one gate of Naphtali. Ezekiel 48:30 -34, fragments, KJV*

All these gates are for the "goings out of the city" (v30), meaning that roads are associated with each of these twelve gates. This strongly implies a rectilinear series of highways converging on the City, and thereby forming a regular grid once they extend inside the gates.

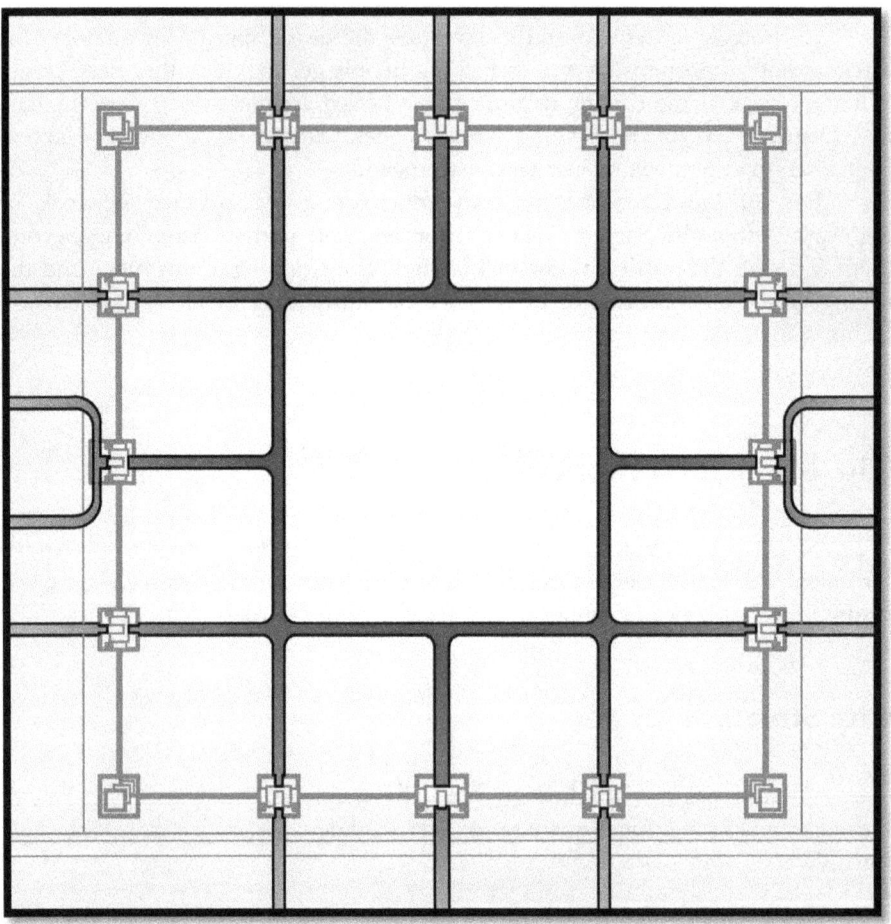

Figure 21: Internal City Highways

In the above figure the twelve gates are arranged along their respective sides, such that wall sections of equal length are the result. Since the four walls

Chapter 7: Royal Thoroughfares

are equal in length[309], equal gate spacing seems indicated as well. And though the actual design is obviously in the Lord's hands, the above diagram incorporates a few additional assumptions worth pointing out.

- ☐ The highway for each gate proceeds directly inward, perpendicular to its respective wall and parallel with its neighboring two gate highways.

- ☐ The center region (and environs of Mount Moriah) is a hugely important site[310], and is therefore shown as clear of highways and regular traffic.

- ☐ The east and west highways are split (for reasons we will examine).

- ☐ Each corner of the City wall is shown with a tower[311].

The result of this "grid" of internal highways is a ring of twelve City "blocks." These distinct sectors may well correspond with one of twelve tribes inhabiting each of them, perhaps the same tribe whose name is on an adjacent gate. This would be similar to the arrangement described in the Exodus encampment[312]. In fact, future Jerusalem is also called "the camp," a term clearly associating the City with the ancient Exodus arrangement.

> *And they went up on the breadth of the earth, and compassed* **the camp of the saints** *about, and* **the beloved city**: *and fire came down from God out of heaven, and devoured them.*
> Revelation 20:9, KJV

In the wilderness camp, the twelve tribes camped three on each side (East, South, North, and West). And though the tribe's positions are different here, the basic layout (especially in view of the gate names) is identical. Note also that the wilderness camp kept the center area clear for the Levites and, at the *very* center, the Tabernacle. Here as well, the center square is preserved as a special place: not for the Temple (which is northward, up at the peak of God's Mountain), but for some other important reason. Though we are not told what that reason is, we might guess that it has much to do with the site of Mount Moriah, and the "foundation stone" of Solomon's Temple.

---

[309] Ezekiel 48:15b-16.
[310] As discussed in The Approaching Country, and here in Chapter 3.
[311] Corner towers are shown, as fitting the often-expressed Scriptural idea of Zion and/or Jerusalem being a "citadel" or "fortress" for God's people.
[312] Numbers 2.

Radiant Roads

The internal streets of Millennial Jerusalem, being driven by the positioning of the twelve gates, connect with roads *outside* those City walls as well. Where do those twelve highways go? In what directions do they point?

The Prince will be the Master Planner[313], and one option He will have is that the twelve gate-roads each go directly forward in their four respective cardinal directions. The result would be like four three-lane highways going North, East, South and West, but with a lot of space in between their three "lanes" as they extend from each gate. Or, perhaps the street threesomes merge into four larger highways, each proceeding in the four cardinal directions.

Still, the presence of twelve City gates might argue against such a rigid four-direction highway system, for if the twelve gate-roads merely became four highways outside the City, it would be more practical for there to be only four City gates, one per wall and side and direction. But that is not what is prophesied. Twelve distinct gates will serve the City, with the implication of twelve distinct avenues of access. Indeed, people will not always be travelling along a due west, east, north or south axis, but also in directions somewhere in between. So, a different option at the Prince's disposal would be that the twelve gate-highways *evenly radiate* from Jerusalem, each in one-twelfth of the compass, that is, thirty degrees apart. Or, something approximating that.

Though such a radial highway arrangement isn't a prophesied thing, there is a symbolic argument in that people coming from all directions (that is, from all nations) will stream to the Lord's Mountain and City. Of the many examples of this point, here are three.

> *Go through, go through the gates; prepare ye the way of the people;* **cast up, cast up the highway;** *gather out the stones;* **lift up a standard for the people.** *11 Behold,* **the Lord hath proclaimed unto the end of the world,** *Say ye to the daughter of Zion, Behold, thy salvation cometh; behold, his reward is with him, and his work before him. 12 And they shall call them, The holy people, The redeemed of the Lord: and* **thou shalt be called, Sought out, A city not forsaken.**
> Isaiah 62:10-12, KJV

> *At that time* **they will call Jerusalem The Throne of the LORD,** *and* **all nations will gather in Jerusalem** *to honor the name of the* **LORD.** *No longer will they follow the stubbornness of their evil hearts.*
> Jeremiah 3:17, NIV

---

[313] In addition to the Temple, Solomon designed many cities and great facilities. But with the Prince, one "greater than Solomon" (Matthew 12:42; Luke 11:31) will be creating the designs and ordering the construction of things discussed here.

> *Who will not fear you, O Lord, and bring glory to your name? For you alone are holy.* ***All nations will come and worship before you****, for your righteous acts have been revealed.*
> Revelation 15:4, NIV

These verses show the City to be the future focus of global transportation, the destination of pilgrimage of all peoples. Beyond this general point, there is a further geometric argument for the future "centrality" of Jerusalem:

> *This is what the Sovereign LORD says: This is Jerusalem, which I have set in the* ***center of the nations, with countries all around her****.*
> Ezekiel 5:5, NIV

If people of the entire world are to converge on Jerusalem, and if Jerusalem is to be the spiritual and political center of all nations, a twelve-direction (vs. four-direction) radiating pattern for her major access routes seems like a good idea. The twelve gates support such a design approach, and it would better serve the needs of omnidirectional traffic patterns. More importantly, it would greatly emphasize, by design, Jerusalem as the City *"set in the center of the nations"* by the Lord Almighty. On the practical side, a radiating arrangement better serves the many travelers to and from adjacent sections of the Sacred District, the Prince's Province, and the neighboring tribal provinces of Judah and Benjamin.

Again, the Prince is in charge of these design matters. But for the reasons stated above, a radial arrangement for the City's twelve extending highways will be followed in the subsequent explorations.

Encircling Arteries

A third form of road to consider is that of "ring roads" or, as they are often described for major cities today, "beltways." Their little brothers are "traffic circles." This kind of circular road allows numerous routes to converge on a focal area, such as a monument or a city. At the same time, traffic can circulate along the circumference between all points of entry and exit, allowing complete freedom of where to come in and get out. The center area is preserved from undue traffic, while still being accessible from all directions. Similar traffic needs will exist in the Sacred District: central key areas having access from numerous directions, with circulation required amongst all points.

There are several obvious opportunities for these, and we will start inside the City, where a small ring road was illustrated just prior. The natural grid of the City's internal highways preserves the central area, Mount Moriah, from regular daily traffic flow with a four-square highway encircling it. This miniature "beltway" would be accessible by all twelve gate highways, providing needed circulation for all residents of the City and visitors to it. At the same time it permits access for anyone wishing to go to the center region (vs. to another tribe's "block," or out though one of the gates), all in an orderly fashion.

There is precedent for this arrangement, if you can take for "precedent" a *future* architectural outworking: the coming Temple, for which we have our next instance of a ring road. The coming House of God will also have gates in its boundary walls in the main cardinal directions (East, North and South, though not to the west[314]). And Ezekiel was readily walked around these walls and gates[315], indicating that such a ring road will connect the Temple's gate avenues on its outer perimeter.

There are good reasons for this square highway around the Temple area's walls, in view of the traffic moving <u>around</u> it. Here are some examples.

- ☐ Worshippers from north and south, wishing to access the north and south Temple gates (note that the east gate is permanently closed, because *"the Lord, the God of Israel, hath entered it* [316]*"*).

- ☐ Priests and Levites traveling between various areas of the Priestly region, when tasks do not require their presence within the Temple grounds.

- ☐ Pilgrims, citizens and merchants, from north of the Sacred District, needing to access Jerusalem.

These sorts of travel do not go into the Temple area, but must go around it. They strongly argue that a route *around* the Temple area will be well provided for, and this may very well have been the road Ezekiel walked when describing the outer walls and gates. The Temple walls will *"separate the holy from the common"* (Ezekiel 42:20b, NIV), and will surely have ample means designed for traffic to and from their gates at some times, and bypassing them entirely at others.

For similar reasons, a third and much larger ring road will most likely encircle the City proper, linking all its gates on its outer perimeter. And just like the ring road of the Temple, there are many reasons for this one, for there are certain kinds of traffic motion that do not require entry into the City, only *around* it. For example:

---

[314] Ezekiel 40.
[315] Ezekiel 42:16-20.
[316] Ezekiel 44:1-2.

Chapter 7: Royal Thoroughfares 165

- Pilgrims, residents and merchants coming from north or south, needing to get to the specific City sector adjacent to one of its twelve gates.

- Someone within the city wanting to get to another sector, but finding the outer highway to be a shorter path (for a neighboring sector) or a less congested route.

- Residents and others within the City wanting to access various parts of the surrounding outer margin of park / pasture land.

- People inside the City needing to visit various parts of the farmlands lying to east and west of the City.

- Pilgrims, residents and merchants approaching the City from south, but needing to go the Levitical or Priestly regions, the Temple area, the Prince's lands, or the tribal province of Judah, and therefore bypass the City entirely.

All these are reasons for having a well-designed outer perimeter avenue for Jerusalem as a whole. There is in fact confirmation of exactly this, in view of the numerous processions around the City that will take place:

> **_Walk about Zion, go around her,_** _count her towers, 13 consider well her ramparts, view her citadels, that you may tell of them to the next generation. 14_ **For this God is our God for ever and ever; he will be our guide even to the end.**
> Psalms 48:12-14, NIV

With all the people, from all countries, making pilgrimage to the beloved and focal City of the King, many will wish to take these verses as a command and perform this very walk. Perhaps millions, over time, will have this objective in mind. Surely these "walkabouts" will be provided for, by the coming Designer-Creator-King; and surely, there will therefore be some form of ring road around Jerusalem.

There is a fourth and much larger [317] ring road to be considered, circumscribing the entire Sacred District on our map. The prior chapter's discussion argued for distinct boundary walls around the District as a whole, and for notable gateways at numerous points along them. All these structures must

---

[317] As addressed in Chapter 2 and elsewhere: 8.15 miles (25,000 LC, 13.1 km) to a side, or 32.6 miles (52.4 km) in circumference.

be strong and impressive enough for their practical and symbolic tasks, and remain so for a thousand years. Though Ezekiel did not describe it, there will almost surely be an impressive perimeter road, outboard of these surrounding walls and gates of the Sacred District. Reasons for this outermost ring road are similar to the others we have explored, with the following examples showing the need for it, that is, the need to go around the Sacred District.

- ☐ People journeying between Judah's province (and points north) and Benjamin's province (and points south), not needing to enter the Sacred District.

- ☐ People journeying between the Prince's lands east and west of the Sacred District, not needing to enter the Sacred District.

- ☐ People wishing to interpret "Zion" in Psalms 48:12-14 (cited above) as the whole Sacred District and the Mountain of God, and therefore make the 32.6 mile (52.4 km) procession around its entirety.

Again, Ezekiel does not describe such an encircling thoroughfare for the Sacred District. But for practical reasons such as these, and prophetic implications cited elsewhere, we should anticipate its presence in one form or another. *"For God is not a God of disorder but of peace"* (1 Corinthians 14:33, NIV).

Princely Promenades

A fourth category of highway relates to Messiah, and *His* special access to areas of *His* special concern. From Ezekiel, it is clear that the Prince will often travel to and between:

- ☐ His Father's "House" (the Temple)
- ☐ His regnal City (Jerusalem)
- ☐ His lands (to east and west of the Sacred District)

A haphazard or difficult route would not be appropriate for such royal journeys and processions. Instead we should expect a very special series of roads for He who will govern the world in glory, strength and wisdom. The idea of "red carpet" comes to mind, with all the adornment (in landscaping, masonry, civil engineering, decoration, etc.) the Prince deems fitting. But though we don't know the aesthetic details, we can certainly anticipate these special highways to be *even* and *straight*.

He led them by a straight way to a city where they could settle.
Psalms 107:7, NIV

I guide you in the way of wisdom and lead you along straight paths.
Proverbs 4:11, NIV

In the desert prepare the way for the LORD; **make straight in the wilderness a highway for our God.**
Isaiah 40:3b, NIV

Though loaded with beautiful symbolism, these and other verses uphold the physical idea of "straightness" for the ideal road, *especially* in reference to our Creator and God in the coming Day. When Emmanuel reigns here, walks here, and literally leads people on His roads here, it will be on actual avenues made very straight, botanically sumptuous and (arguably) very beautiful in their own right. People of all nations will recite verses such as these in praise of He who literally leads them here.

This coming King will indeed travel. He will have His own vast lands, to either side of the Sacred District. Yet He will rule from their central point, in Jerusalem. A highway between these regions is a foregone conclusion; and the suggested radial arrangement of roads from Jerusalem provides these routes. We will return to that point in the summary of these highway subsystems.

We also know that the Prince will have frequent and most holy activities within the Temple area. From Ezekiel, we get a glimpse of how frequent these travels will be.

*It will be the duty of the **prince** to provide the burnt offerings, grain offerings and drink offerings at the **festivals, the New Moons and the Sabbaths** — at all the appointed feasts of the house of Israel. He will provide the sin offerings, grain offerings, burnt offerings and fellowship offerings to make atonement for the house of Israel.*
Ezekiel 45:17, NIV

*In the first month on the fourteenth day you are to observe the **Passover**, a feast lasting **seven days**, during which you shall eat bread made without yeast. 22 On that day the **prince** is to provide a bull as a sin offering for himself and for all the people of the land. 23 Every day during the **seven days** of the Feast **he** is to provide seven bulls and seven rams without defect as a burnt offering to the LORD, and a male goat for a sin offering.*
Ezekiel 45:21-23, NIV

> *On the **Sabbaths** and **New Moons** the people of the land are to worship in the presence of the LORD at the entrance to that gateway. 4 The burnt offering the **prince** brings to the LORD on the **Sabbath** day is to be six male lambs and a ram, all without defect.*
> *Ezekiel 46:3-4, NIV*[318]

Indeed,

> *The prince is to be among them, going in when they go in and going out when they go out.*
> *Ezekiel 46:10, NIV*

In addition to this frequent travel of the Prince and His retinue and followers, there will also be many other people moving between His province and the Sacred District. Throughout His eastern and western lands the Prince will potentially have palaces, colleges, public gardens, guest residences and other establishments[319]. These will be frequented by their respective participants and staff members, perhaps on a daily basis. Many people will travel between these facilities in the eastern and western portions of the Prince's province and Jerusalem, other parts of the Sacred District, or to points north or south. All of this traffic will necessitate adequate roadways.

In view of all the above, we can expect there to be royal highways fit for a King, communicating with His lands and adequate for all His glorious purposes.

Scenic Highways

In Chapters 4 and 5 we explored the three main prophesied rivers of the Sacred District. And though there may well be additional ones[320], these are the

---

[318] The huge subject of sacrifice during the Millennial era is not something we can adequately investigate here. Clearly, Jesus' personal sacrifice as the Lamb of God remains the only atonement for our sins, with First Testament animal sacrifices being only foretelling and emblematic of Him (e.g., Hebrews 10). If animal sacrifices exist in the Millennial era, they will serve the same purpose, though in retrospect: memorial and emblematic. Also, we do not know what the exact rituals may be in that time, or what changes may be enacted by Messiah. For example, drink and grain offerings may be the prominent ones, if He so decides. Again, this is a large topic; and the point here is that the Lord Jesus, "the Prince," will frequently travel to and from the Temple grounds, just as Ezekiel describes.

[319] We examined some of these potential establishments in Chapter 7 of The Approaching Country.

[320] At the time of the Lord's return and victory, *"streams of water will flow on every high mountain and every lofty hill"* (Isaiah 30:25b, NIV), at least within Israel. But, other than the

three singled out in Scripture: the rivers arising from Jerusalem and running to east and west; and the Temple River, exuding life and growing in strength as it travels east. These rivers will be significant, and will therefore impact our highways quite a bit.

Jerusalem's "twin rivers" will travel through the large farmlands lying on either side of the City, flowing the length of those areas (10,000 LC, 3.26 miles, 5.24 kilometers) and beyond. To facilitate north-to-south travel within these farmlands there will need to be bridges (and lesser roads) crossing these rivers along their courses.

People will also need to travel from Jerusalem toward the east and west, and the rivers flowing from the City provide a natural path – on both their northern and southern banks – for those roads. When people take these roads beside Jerusalem's rivers, some might recall a prophecy uttered over two millennia ago:

> *Thus saith the Lord of hosts;* **Behold, I will save my people from the east country, and from the west country;** *8 And I will bring them, and they shall dwell in the midst of Jerusalem: and they shall be my people, and I will be their God, in truth and in righteousness.*
> *Zechariah 8:7-8, KJV*

Travelers here will witness some of the most marvelous scenes in tomorrow's Jerusalem, set as the jewel in the Lord's coming "Eden." They will walk through the great farmlands of the City, witnessing firsthand crops flourishing without "thorns" or "thistles," or the need for hard effort to raise them[321]. Strolling along these twin rivers, on both their northern and southern banks, people like you and me will see such wonders and praise our Creator in new ways.

This scenic opportunity, with an avenue on either side of the river to enjoy it, will be especially present for the Temple River. Its arrangement with the eastward highway from the Temple likewise suggests a highway running along both its banks.

All three rivers remind us of the eternal River of Life which will also follow this same pattern: a mighty river, with a thoroughfare on either of its banks, all set amidst botanical wonders. With that ultimate thoroughfare, we get an interesting clue for those in the coming Sacred District: its avenues along both its banks will be considered a single (though split) highway, with the River flowing down the center.

---

three rivers discussed, we don't know which of those other streams will remain as steady watercourses through the Millennial period.

[321] Genesis 3:17, in view of that curse being lifted as has been discussed elsewhere.

> *Then the angel showed me the river of the water of life, as clear as crystal, flowing from the throne of God and of the Lamb 2* **down the middle of the great street of the city.** *On each side of the river stood the tree of life, bearing twelve crops of fruit, yielding its fruit every month. And the leaves of the tree are for the healing of the nations.*
> Revelation 22:1-2, NIV

From many prophesied perspectives (discussed in Chapter 5), the Temple River is hugely analogous to the ultimate River that will forever flow from the City-Temple of God Almighty. Thanks to this eternal River-Road pattern, we now have this clue: a highway will exist, running along both banks of the Temple River as it flows eastward and through the Prince's eastern lands. Though split by the river running between, it will still be considered as a single highway.

This riverside dual highway will be important for the Prince's access to His eastern lands. It will also be vital for people needing access to the leaves and fruit of the miraculous healing trees growing along the River's banks – exactly as portrayed for the eternal River of Life and its divided highway. Since these leaves and fruit are for general use in food and medicine[322], the dual highway will not be a mere pair of footpaths, but be heavily used by people of all nations. However, as all others in this coming network, these river-roadways will be designed for the task, and beautiful to see.

An Overall Network

Each of these kinds of potential thoroughfares can be plotted onto the prophesied map of the Sacred District, in an at least schematic manner. The reality will surely differ: highways from the City gates may not be strictly radial; the rivers (with their avenues beside them) may not run absolutely straight; and so forth. We won't know the map's details until the King lays them out for all to see. That said, we can build a diagram from what we are told and can infer, and see that there will indeed be not just one or two roads involved, but an entire and organized network of avenues designed for varying purposes and volumes of future travelers.

Many lesser streets and "byways" will surely be involved, and an inspired artist might well incorporate them in a portrayal of these lands. For these diagrammatic depictions though, will stick with the major highways being discussed.

---

[322] Ezekiel 47:12.

Chapter 7: Royal Thoroughfares 171

Figure 22: Sacred District Highway Network

At the heart of the network lies Jerusalem (to the lower left) with its internal ring road around Mount Moriah, internal grid of streets between its gates, external ring road and parkway around its walls, and twelve radial roads extending outward. The City's eastward and westward radial highways are split, following their respective rivers along both banks. To the south are five highways into the "right hand" and most honored province of Benjamin, following different trajectories. To the north are two going through the Levitical region and into the Prince's Province; and two traversing both Levitical and Priestly regions before entering Judah's province.

The center northward road from the City travels to the greater focus which is, of course, the Father's "House" at the summit of His Mountain. At that juncture the north-south highway branches around the Temple grounds, forming a smaller ring road there, and then continues north to the province of Judah. On the west side of the Temple, though there is no gate there, an avenue branches from its ring road to the western half of the Prince's Province. To the east, the highway from the Temple's eastern gate splits to either side of the

Temple River, heading to the Prince's eastern lands. When the River turns south at the Jordan River and continues to the "Eastern" Sea, one or both of these eastward roads may follow and do the same.

Around the overall Sacred District and outside its walls is our largest ring road. Intersecting this will be the various highways radiating from City and Temple, which will ultimately reach all tribal provinces to north and south. From highways such as these, all nations will be reached by the avenues of the Lord.

We should take one more look at a particular highway from Jerusalem, the one heading directly to the Temple peak. From different perspectives (in Chapter 6) we have virtually "hiked" this avenue from Jerusalem's Judah Gate to the Temple's southern gate. We should notice also that this is the procession route the Prince will generally take when going from His City to His Father's House. Taking that as a clue, there is something more behind this particular and central stretch of highway, something very important for us to grasp; and it has much to do with the Prince's royal travels here, along this very path.

The Royal Highway

We've just explored a network of avenues within the Sacred District. But there will also be a larger system that connects the Sacred District with lands far beyond, an international highway arrangement that is explicitly prophesied to converge upon God's Mountain.

Foreseen Avenues

Countless people of all nations, people just like you and me, will make repeated pilgrimages to Jerusalem in the Day of the Lord. Here are just a few examples of this massive and ongoing phenomenon in the Day of the Lord's reign.

> *The kings of Tarshish and of the isles shall bring presents: the kings of Sheba and Seba shall offer gifts. 11 Yea, **all kings shall fall down before him: all nations shall serve him**... 17 His name shall endure for ever: his name shall be continued as long as the sun: and men shall be blessed in him: all nations shall call him blessed.*
> *Psalms 72:10-11,17, KJV*

> *<u>All nations</u> whom thou hast made **shall come** and worship before thee, O Lord; and shall glorify thy name.*
> Psalms 86:9, KJV

> *This is what the Lord Almighty says: "In those days ten **men from all languages and nations** will take firm hold of one Jew by the hem of his robe and say, **'Let us go with you, because we have heard that God is with you.'** "*
> Zechariah 8:23, NIV

> *And it shall come to pass in the last days, that **the mountain of the Lord's house** shall be established in the top of the mountains, and shall be exalted above the hills; and **<u>all nations shall flow unto it</u>**. 3 And **many people** shall go and say, **Come ye, and let us go up to the mountain of the Lord, to the house of the God of Jacob;** and he will teach us of his ways, and we will walk in his paths: for out of Zion shall go forth the law, and the word of the Lord from Jerusalem.*
> Isaiah 2:2-3, KJV

> *For I know their works and their thoughts: it shall come, that **I will gather <u>all nations and tongues</u>;** and they shall <u>come</u>, and see my glory.*
> Isaiah 66:18, KJV

Time after time, the Word declares to us that people from *all* nations will travel to Jerusalem, come before the Lord, witness His glory, and worship Him. These are astounding things that will truly come to pass on this Earth. When it does, there will be an enormous need for pretty serious roads leading to Jerusalem and God's Mountain.

Some might reasonably opine that these trips will be infrequent for most people, like a pilgrimage once or twice in a lifetime; and maybe that kind of travel could be staged throughout the year. That would keep the flow to and from the Sacred District to a manageable minimum, impressive though it would still be. But it's not like that. As declared via Zechariah, all who obey the Lord will make these journeys on an *annual* basis. Not only that, but they will do so *at the same time of every year*!

> *Then the **survivors from all the nations** that have attacked Jerusalem **will go up year after year to worship the King, the Lord Almighty, and to celebrate the Feast of Tabernacles.** 17 If any of the peoples of the earth do not go up to Jerusalem to worship the King, the Lord Almighty, they will have no rain. 18 If the Egyptian people do not go up and take part, they will have no rain. The Lord will bring on them the plague he inflicts on the nations that do not go up to **celebrate the Feast of Tabernacles.** 19 This will be the punishment of*

*Egypt and the punishment of all the nations that do not go up to **celebrate the Feast of Tabernacles.***
Zechariah 14:16-19, NIV

Three times in the above passage, the Feast of Tabernacles is singled out as the required time for all peoples to come to Jerusalem in the coming "Day" when the Lord is King of this world[323]. That would be a staggering volume of traffic by any estimation. For this massive influx to work at all, perhaps it is because the global population is reduced by this time; or, perhaps only a representative attendance is involved for each nation; or, perhaps some other factor we are not yet aware of is in play. But whatever the final count is for travelers to the Feast of Tabernacles[324], it will be a huge number. Yes, there will be a continual flow to and from God's Mountain throughout the year; but that particular season will see an incalculable increase.

If not properly provided for, the sheer numbers of people would bring great damage to properties within Israel's tribal lands. Via random and accidental trampling at the least, the traffic would take a destructive toll on farms, villages, infrastructure, and so forth. Fortunately, we are assured that provision will be made for this. Two major international arteries will indeed converge on the Sacred District from north and south, having passed through the various provinces of Israel, yet originating from regions far beyond. The prophet Isaiah seems the one most tasked with conveying this information to us, and we will begin with these few hints from him.

*The voice of him that crieth in the wilderness, Prepare ye the way of the LORD, **make straight in the desert a highway for our God.** 4 Every valley shall be exalted, and every mountain and hill shall be made low: and the crooked shall be made straight, and the rough places plain: 5 And the glory of the LORD shall be revealed, and all flesh shall see it together: for the mouth of the LORD hath spoken it.*
Isaiah 40:3-5, KJV

Though the fulfillment of these verses began with Jesus' first coming[325], their ultimate unfolding is set in the time of His literal reign over the Earth. As

---

[323] Certain "feasts of the Lord" remain mandatory in this present age (e.g., Leviticus 23:4 & context). For an excellent examination into the vitality and prophetic importance of these feasts, see Howard & Rosenthal. In the Millennial period, some or all of these feasts may continue to be celebrated for Israel and those who wish to join in. But for *all* peoples of the world, it is clear from the cited passage that the Feast of Tabernacles remains the mandatory and annual gathering event before the Lord Almighty.

[324] We must permit the additional ideas of maritime and even aviatic means of travel here. Even so, their final approaches to the Sacred District are almost surely to be by road.

[325] E.g., Matthew 3:1-3.

Chapter 7: Royal Thoroughfares

the above verses describe, that comes *after* massive alterations in terrain have been performed, and *after* Messiah's visible glory has been revealed to all peoples. So while there remains incalculable symbolic-spiritual value in this passage, the face-value prophetic facts remain firm, their fulfillment awaiting only God's timing. Specifically,

- There will be a physical highway upon which the Lord makes processions as King.

- This highway will extend even through distant desert regions.

- Much preparation of the roadbed will be necessary[326], involving lowering of high places, straightening the route, and generally smoothing things out.

- The result is an unmistakable "highway for our God," no doubt leading towards His City and Temple. Messiah-King will use this literal roadway; and when He does, bystanders will witness His great glory as He passes by.

Much of this is confirmed in another of Isaiah's prophecies:

> *Go through, go through the gates;* **prepare ye the way of the people; cast up, cast up the highway; gather out the stones; lift up a standard for the people.** *11 Behold, the LORD hath proclaimed unto the end of the world, Say ye to the daughter of Zion, Behold, thy salvation cometh; behold, his reward is with him, and his work before him. 12 And they shall call them, The holy people, The redeemed of the LORD: and thou shalt be called, Sought out, A city not forsaken.*
> Isaiah 62:10-12, KJV

The Lord-Redeemer is He that brings salvation to His people; and it is in honor of Him that "the highway" will be built, with an additional result being Jerusalem's comfort and glorification. At the same time, the highway is described not only in terms of the coming King who will be using it: it is also called *"the way of the people."* The highway in view here is therefore not exclusive to the King's usage: rather, all His people will, quite literally, walk in His "ways," the avenues belonging to Him.

---

[326] Corresponding with the fact of the Sacred District's being comparatively "smoothed" in general, though greatly uplifted at its peak.

We can see in these verses certain activities described for those involved in the development of this royal highway.

- ☐ They will leave the city (going through the gates) and proceed to places of excavation and construction.

- ☐ They will clear away boulders and other debris and build up the raised roadbed of the highway.

- ☐ They will place banners along the way.

- ☐ They will construct the highway so that it is "cast up," that is, with a roadbed raised above the surrounding grounds.

People of all nations, engineers, designers, masons, artists, laborers, foremen, signalers, landscapers, and so forth, will heed the call to build this highway, even as they will be involved with building Jerusalem's walls [327]. Subsequently, all peoples wishing to visit the King's City and pray at the House of God will see the King's welcoming banners as they walk these beautiful roadways. Upon glimpsing the Prince-King as He makes procession to either the Temple or His City, or anywhere else, visitors will be awestruck with His glorious grandeur, and with all He will have designed and built.

From these same passages we see a consistent theme for these highways. They will not be mere paths or randomly swerving roads between craggy obstructions and immovable boulders; nor will they simply follow the meanderings of riverbeds or goat paths. Instead, and in spite of the (presently) wild regions traversed, they will be straight, by design; and they will be raised above their surroundings – that is, *"exalted."*

> And **_I will make all my mountains a way_**, and **_my highways shall be exalted_**. *12 Behold, these shall come from far: and, lo, these from the north and from the west; and these from the land of Sinim. 13 Sing, O heavens; and be joyful, O earth; and break forth into singing, O mountains: for the LORD hath comforted his people, and will have mercy upon his afflicted.*
> *Isaiah 49:11-13, KJV*

Taking all this into account, we can know that a major highway to Jerusalem will be developed in the coming Day of the Lord's reign. It will be physically elevated ("raised," "exalted", "cast up") above its surrounding terrain. By the way, this is common practice even in our day, the purpose being to keep

---

[327] Isaiah 60:10.

the highway well drained and never submerged. And though extending at times through what are now desert and wilderness regions, the Lord's highway will remain comparatively level, straight, and smooth. Again, this would be analogous to our major highways today.

The difference here is that, though capable of being so, this will not be a high-speed motorway like we are familiar with. Pedestrian traffic will be plentiful here, as will also be conveyance on animals and in animal-drawn vehicles[328]. Yet even with the increased volumes of international pilgrimage for the Feast of Tabernacles, and even though the traffic will move more slowly than we are used to, the design of this highway will be sufficient. It will be broad enough, and have appropriate markings, way stations, landscaping and other features, to be safe and pleasant for all concerned.

Again, the highway will be used by people from all nations; and its very presence will bring ongoing comfort to the Lord's "first-born" people, Israel. With its architecture and embellishments, it will be fit for a King. Indeed, when King Yeshua travels upon them, these avenues of His building will further honor His own glorious appearance.

North-South Route

Now let's discuss the actual route, and comparing it with a well-known historical basis. In ancient Biblical times the main international avenues reaching Jerusalem were from north and south, simply because of difficulties with the other two cardinal directions. To the east were (and are) the high plateaus of Edom-Moab-Ammon (now Jordan), and to the west is the Mediterranean Sea. This leaves north and south for distant travel opportunities.

Here are two examples from Biblical military history. When Egypt (lying to the west and south) attacked, they first travelled eastward across the Sinai region, but then entered Israel from the south. On the opposite end, when Assyria (lying to the north and east) invaded, they first journeyed westward across the Fertile Crescent, and then came down into Israel from the north.

This basic ancient pattern of north-south access to Palestine is echoed in the "King's Highway," a well-known and major roadway from very ancient times. This was the highway which Israel was barred from using while on her original Exodus journey. Here is a description of it.

> A second route of importance that intersected the land of promise is known in the Old Testament as the King's Highway (Num 20:17; 21:22) and outside the Bible as the Sultan's highway or Trajan's highway (Via

---

[328] Isaiah 66:20-21.

Nova Traiana). It was the emperor Trajan who converted this route from a track into a bona fide road in the second century AD. This passageway stretched from the head of the Red Sea at Ezion-geber and essentially rode the watershed of Edom and Moab, past the cities of Bozrah, Kir-haresheth, Dibon and Heshbon, before coming to Amman. It made its way from Amman across the Gilead and Bashan plateaus to Damascus, where it joined the Great Trunk Road[329].

In the original "exodus" (exit) from Egypt and slavery, this north-south "King's Highway" was indeed the main road[330] to Philistia[331], but the Edomites and Amorites denied the Israelites use of it. But, with the *coming* Royal Highway, it will be just the opposite: under ownership of Israel's ultimate King, not only will Israel proper have full access, but so will the greater "Israel" of all God's covenant-children. No Edomites or Amorites, literally or figuratively, will bar the way.

But how will this next "King's Highway" be situated? Will its route correspond with the one of old? Not necessarily, for there seems to be a lack of prophetic connection between the two. In fact, there would be a symbolic truism in the *rejection* of the ancient King's Highway as the route of the coming King's, in that an entirely new course might better convey His dominion over all the world's kings, past, present and future. Further, that road of the past was not (as things turned out) God's intended route for ancient Israel anyway. And, it was not located entirely in Israel, but mostly within the territory of her enemy-neighbors.

Is there an alternate route that suits things for the coming "Day"? Indeed there is, and we have recently seen a big clue:

> And ***I will make all my mountains <u>a way</u>, and my highways shall be exalted.***
> *Isaiah 49:11, KJV*

So we see that God's mountains will become the basis, the foundation, for an important and raised set of "ways" and "*highways*." Which mountains are we talking about though? The answer is in the word "*my*." The mountains of Israel are specifically said to be owned by the Lord[332], mountains contained within the

---

[329] Beitzel, Barry J. "As the Land Prepared By God." <u>The Moody Atlas of Bible Lands</u>, Chicago, IL, Moody Publishers, Inc, 2000.
[330] Numbers 20:17-21, 21:21-23.
[331] From whence we get the word "Palestine."
[332] Isaiah 14:25, 65:9; Ezekiel 38:21.

Chapter 7: Royal Thoroughfares

land He likewise explicitly owns[333]. Though *"The earth is the Lord's, and everything in it"* (Psalms 24:1a, NIV), this land and its mountains are His special property.

Thanks to Isaiah, we now have the clue we need. And if any single particular peak is owned by God, it is obviously Mount Zion, the Mountain of God, the place of our current expedition. And that Mountain is connected to others. Palestine, to the west of the Jordan River, has a central geological "spine" that runs through Israel's original lands. Contained within promised and prophesied Israel, this ridge lies upon God's mountains. Isaiah declares that these very mountains will be made the "ways" upon which His *"highways shall be exalted."*

By contrast, the ancient King's Highway avoided Israel, running along the plateaus east of the Jordan River and through the modern country of Jordan. Isaiah's version though remains atop the mountains (literally) owned by God, that is, those running through His Land. Unlike the ancient thoroughfare which came nowhere near Jerusalem[334], this new one will come directly to *the* Mountain of God, from north and south; it will access the Lord's City directly, welcoming all His people.

By the time the new King's Highway is built, terrain will certainly have changed in the events of the King's revealing (that is, the "apocalypse"); for example, Zion will have been made "chief of the mountains." After things settle down, the route will be laid out, smoothed, and "made straight," following the path Isaiah prophesied. But in advance of all that, the present-day ridge atop God's mountains certainly suggests an approximate route.

---

[333] Leviticus 25:23.
[334] See Beitzel, Map 19: "Roads of Palestine."

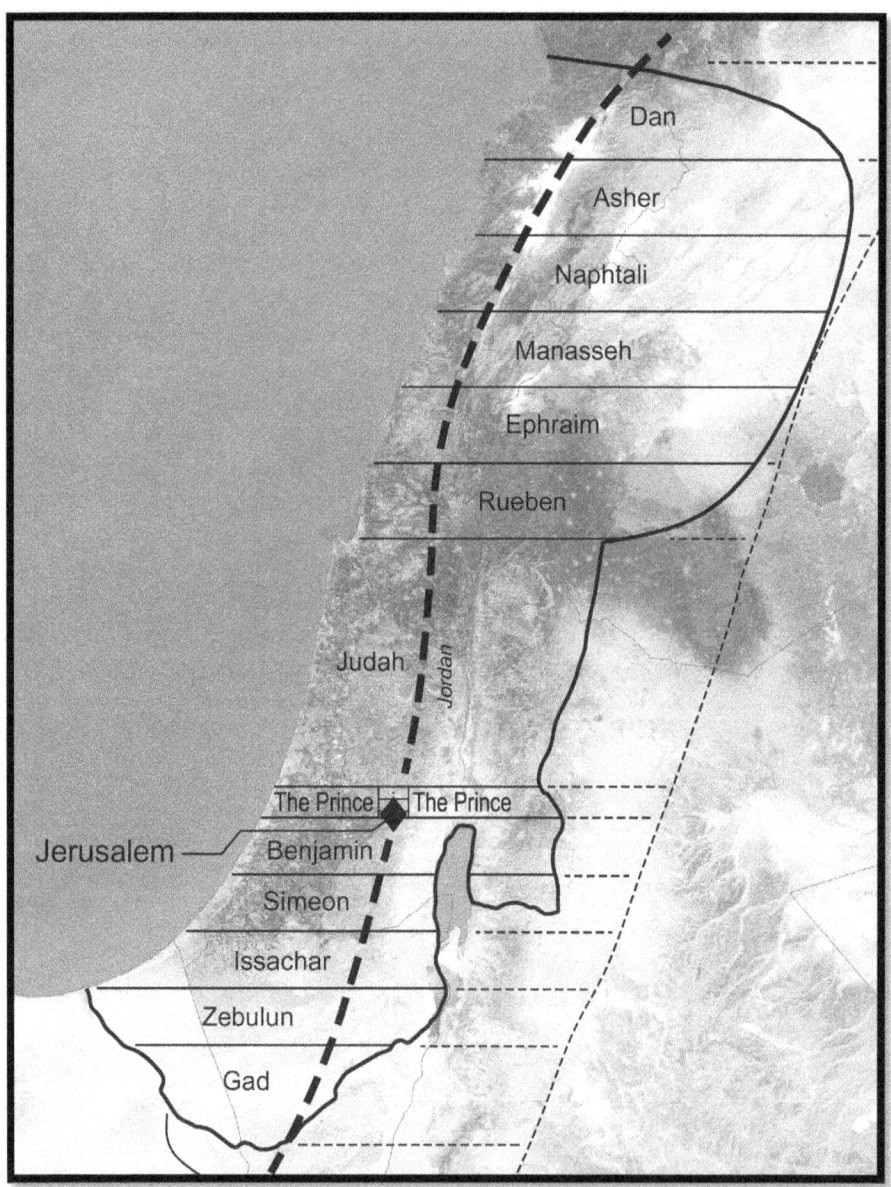

Figure 23: Central Mountain Ridge

Chapter 7: Royal Thoroughfares

The above map of Palestine[335] shows a thick dashed line following this mountain ridge, essentially a rough tracing of the region's continental divide. Due to the geography involved, it travels from north and south. Due to the high elevation, in view of passages we have explored before[336], there will be no shortage of water features along the way.

Though an unremarkable geological feature for most people today, the ridge upon God's mountains will be hugely important in the future. For no matter what the final plotting, or shape of the mountains involved, this highway will convey royal processions such as have never been seen, and eager pilgrimages in numbers never imagined. Unlike as in ancient events, these avenues will be possessed by God's people; unlike the ancient route, they will ride upon *His* mountains, in *His* land.

Many questions remain though. How wide will the highway be? What specific provisions will be made for rest and refreshment? How will the architecture and engineering and art and landscaping of the highway appear? What historical sites will be preserved and available in the tribal provinces, along the way? But such things are in the Lord's purview, and remain things we can't even imagine at this time. For not all things are prophesied; and He keeps many wonderful surprises in store.

> *"No eye has seen, no ear has heard, no mind has conceived what God has prepared for those who love him"*
> *1 Corinthians 2:9b, NIV (quoting Isaiah 64:4)*

Returning again to pilgrimages to Jerusalem and the Temple, and the roads facilitating them, we can appreciate further details. With Jerusalem sitting astride this same mountain ridge, the royal highway will pass directly through the City – accepting and hosting the vast flow of people, of all nations, just as prophesied.

Anticipating this extraordinary traffic from north and south, we should expect that the avenues through the Sacred District, in these particular directions, will be especially wide.

---

[335] Background image of all Palestine geographic maps here are from the NASA satellite image file "Middle East," February 17 2003, Jacques Descloitres, MODIS Rapid Response Team, NASA/GSFC, 4 January 2008, <http://visibleearth.nasa.gov/view.php?id=65114>. Graphic overlays by author, with borders developed as described in The Approaching Country.
[336] E.g., Isaiah 30:25.

Figure 24: Sacred District and the Kings Highway

For these reasons, this diagram shows the central north-to-south highway as wider than the others. Though only God sees the actual picture, we can appreciate that this route through the Sacred District will connect all nations to City and Temple, and be therefore broad enough to do so. At the same time, we can also see that the ring-roads around the Temple, the City, and the Sacred District as a whole, will need adequate breadth as well.

Far Origins

The ancient version of the King's Highway bent southwestward to Egypt and northeastward toward Assyria (Modern Iraq). And though the future King's Highway will follow a different route within Israel along "God's mountains," it is interesting to realize that it will likewise reach those particular countries. Again it is Isaiah who gives the details:

Chapter 7: Royal Thoroughfares

> *And **there shall be an highway for the remnant of his people**, which shall be left, from Assyria; like as it was to Israel in the day that he came up out of the land of Egypt.*
> Isaiah 11:16, KJV

Once more, a highway will serve Israelites coming from a place of prior captivity, a "remnant" of God's people living into the coming age. The highway will originate from the eastern realms of modern Iraq (ancient Assyria), bending southward as it enters Israel and heads toward Jerusalem. It is likened to that of the original Exodus, perhaps because of its capacity for traffic (probably in the millions[337]), or because of the Lord's similar facilitation to come, or for some other connection we don't know about yet. Regardless, the highway will be a significant one, and from Jerusalem it will reach northward and eastward across the Fertile Crescent.

The above verse hints at a highway from Egypt as well, in referencing the original Exodus journey. And in fact, the brand-new highway will facilitate a greater second "exodus." For in this very context, and as seen many related passages, the establishment of the King's reign coincides with His gathering of His people from *all* regions and nations.

> *And it shall come to pass in that day, that the Lord shall set his hand again the second time to recover the remnant of his people, which shall be left, from **Assyria**, and from **Egypt**, and from Pathros, and from Cush, and from Elam, and from Shinar, and from Hamath, and from the islands of the sea.*
> Isaiah 11:11, KJV

The final "exodus" will not, however, be only by pedestrian means, for to "*recover*" people from those "*islands*," boats will clearly be involved. But for people arriving from Egypt (and points south and west), and also from Assyria (and points north and east), land-based avenues to Jerusalem from north and south are obvious.

Now, one might consider this gathering of "*the remnant of His people*" to be a one-time thing, soon after Yeshua's return and victory. However, Isaiah leaves no doubt that this highway and its traffic, with its particular origins in both Egypt and Assyria, will be permanent phenomena:

> ***In that day shall there be a highway out of Egypt to Assyria***, *and the Assyrian shall come into Egypt, and the Egyptian into Assyria, and the Egyptians shall serve with the Assyrians. 24 In that day shall **Israel be the third with***

---

[337] The census at Mt Sinai (Numbers 1) enumerated 603,550 Israelite males able to go to war. The overall population, including women, children, elderly and disabled, was far greater than that.

> *Egypt and with Assyria, even a blessing in the midst of the land: 25 Whom the LORD of hosts shall bless, saying,* **Blessed be Egypt my people, and Assyria the work of my hands, and Israel mine inheritance.**
> Isaiah 19:23-25, KJV

With Zion-Jerusalem as the focus of the royal highway system, these two primary origins of Egypt and Assyria are kept in the forefront. The routes will follow a north-south trajectory while within Israel, following the peaks of God's mountains. But outside Israel, the northbound part will bend eastward into Assyria, while the southbound leg will proceed westward toward Egypt.

Let's appreciate the significance of what Isaiah is saying. There were mainly two nation-empires that held Israel captive in First Testament times: Egypt at first, and Assyria-Babylonia[338] near the other end of that chronology. When Messiah rules the Earth, one might expect prophecies about severe punishment, even obliteration, of those two enemy-nations. But we see something very different: forgiveness, and even welcoming. We see that, during Yeshua's reign, descendents of those ancient enemies will be invited into Israel as participants in holy covenantal worship with them[339]. We see that long after the "remnant" of Israel is gathered, many people from Egypt and Assyria will, in ongoing fashion, travel to Israel in peace and as friends.

> <u>*In that day*</u> *shall Israel be the third with Egypt and with Assyria, even a blessing in the midst of the land: 25 Whom the Lord of hosts shall bless, saying,* **Blessed be Egypt my people, and Assyria the work of my hands, and Israel mine inheritance.**
> Isaiah 19:24-25, KJV

What a wonderful sign that will be, when the Prince of Peace reigns! "The land" will embrace Egypt, Israel and Assyria – with Israel *"in the midst of the land"* as a specially blessed portion. So for all these pilgrimages we have been discussing, everyone involved will see this mighty witness to not only God's

---

[338] The Babylonian empire is closely related to the Assyrian: it came right after, and conquered, Assyria; and it engulfed Assyria's territory. From some perspectives, the Babylonian empire was the continuum of the Assyrian. However, from certain prophetic viewpoints, a distinction must be made with the *city* of Babylon (vs. the entire empire it controlled). It was the place of mankind's original confusion (Genesis 11), was the eager destroyer of First Testament Jerusalem under Nebuchadnezzar (e.g., Daniel 1-7), and will have murderous intent on God's people in the future (Revelation 18). Babylon proper is therefore denied any Millennial-era reconstitution in the prophecies (e.g., Isaiah 14; Revelation 18). By contrast, Assyria as a nation survives and flourishes in Messiah's day, though in clear submission to the coming King of Israel.

[339] See Isaiah 19:18-22 for a vivid depiction of such, regarding Egypt.

great mercy, but also His faithfulness and ability to heal and transform. He can heal and transform people; and He can heal and transform entire nations. That will be an undeniable message to people walking this great highway.

With this great north-south highway travel, we can see that the historical tables will be turned. Instead of being the oppressed captive, Israel and Jerusalem will connect directly with, and be honored by, the descendants of those people who did them the earliest harm. And paradoxically, these early enemies will be Israel's close associates in Messiah's day. All this is but one example of the works of the Prince of Peace, the wisdom of the King of kings who comes soon to our realm.

Though Israel, Egypt and Assyria are specifically named as travelers by Isaiah, does that mean other nations will be excluded? Of course not! Huge branches to the highway will surely be present, reaching surrounding countries and continents: for this is the point of Isaiah 11:11. Whether those branches will be considered part of the royal highway network is a decision for the coming King. If the overall system involves maritime "highways" and ports, or even air routes and travel means, those decisions are also up to the Lord. But the main land routes to Egypt and Assyria, extending from God's mountaintop "ways" and to points far beyond, will be there, revealing Prince's magnificent design. And people of all nations will walk upon them.

A Peek at the Paths

We have seen Scriptures that speak of the "ways" of the Lord: symbolic "paths" of our spiritual walk with Him today, referring simultaneously to *physical* paths in His coming terrestrial Kingdom. If we were to literally see those material avenues and the features accompanying them, what sorts of things might we observe?

The Main Event

As far as highways go here, the central roads to and between Jerusalem and the Temple will be, by far, the most "exalted" ones. Here will be processions of King Yeshua; here will be untold millions of pilgrims, especially for the Feast of Tabernacles. From north and south, this will be a raised roadway, proceeding straightly and evenly through regions once considered wilderness and, within Israel's borders, along the heights of God's mountains as it nears the Sacred District. The architecture and landscaping will be fit for not only *a* king, but *The* King: the "King of Glory". Seeing Him make procession upon His "way," and

Jerusalem's mighty gates opening at His approach, will be truly spectacular to witness.

> *Lift up your heads, O ye* **gates**; *and be ye lift up, ye everlasting* **doors**; *and the* **King of glory** *shall come in. 8 Who is this* **King of glory**? *The Lord strong and mighty, the Lord mighty in battle. 9 Lift up your heads, O ye* **gates**; *even lift them up, ye everlasting* **doors**; *and the* **King of glory** *shall come in. 10 Who is this* **King of glory**? **The Lord of hosts, he is the King of glory.** *Selah.*
> Psalms 24:7-10, KJV

To visualize the details, we will have to wait. But whether directly witnessing these events on Earth, or indirectly from Heaven, we shall indeed see them come to pass. For though the "revelation" will be here in this realm, *all* mankind will still witness the coming King's glory.

> *Every valley shall be raised up, every mountain and hill made low; the rough ground shall become level, the rugged places a plain. 5 And* **the glory of the Lord will be revealed, and <u>all mankind together will see it</u>.** *For the mouth of the Lord has spoken.*
> Isaiah 40:4-5, NIV, quoted in Luke 3:5-6

Since this is so, "all mankind" includes those on Earth, and, of course, all those in Heaven at the time[340]. One way or another then, when we observe the unfolding of these matters, this central highway will be a place of focus for all of us, and a place where the Lord's glory will be greatly manifested for *all* to see.

Evident Artistry

In addition to the central highway we have seen evidence for many other avenues, a complete network in fact. Beyond the roads though, several related features have also been touched on in this chapter. We can be sure though that the Lord's highways will not be barren, ugly or plain, but instead wonderfully designed in regards to civil engineering, architecture, landscaping, art, and other disciplines. So in this final section in our exploration of the Lord's coming highways, let's permit ourselves a peek at a few details that seem to be implied.

---

[340] For the ongoing fact of humans in Heaven witnessing events on Earth, see Hebrews 12:1ff.

Chapter 7: Royal Thoroughfares

Take civil engineering for example. We have seen that the north-south central highway will be particularly wide, with ring roads present for the Temple and City. We have also discussed the roads radiating from the City's gates, and those beside the three main rivers.

Just from those facts, we can see many engineering issues coming into play.

- Drainage culverts will allow lesser streams to pass beneath the main causeway.

- Proper surveying and grading of the broad roadbed will ensure the prophesied geometry.

- Railings, perhaps masonry, will prevent people falling from elevated portions.

- Expanded sections may facilitate rest areas. Walls along either side may, in some portions, protect the privacy of residents.

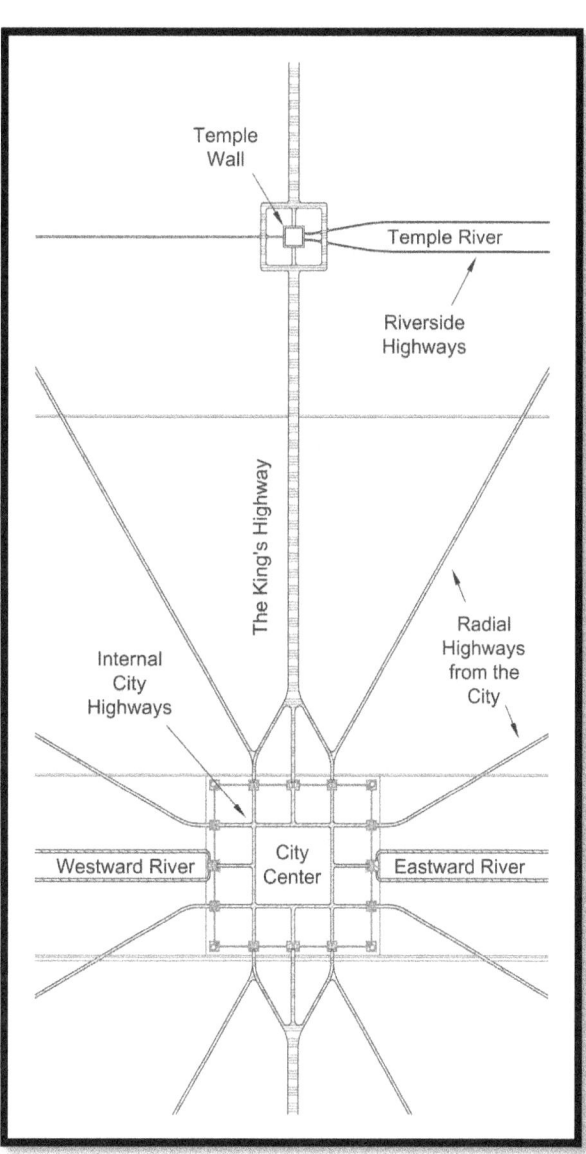

Figure 25: Sacred District Central Highway

☐ Entryways in the walls or parapets and ramps from the causeway would permit access to surrounding residential areas.

☐ Stairs and ramps (vs. only stairs, or only ramps) may alternate, perhaps with ramps bypassing the stairways for those requiring gentler means of access.[341]

If we also consider the aesthetic elements overlaid upon all this, we might see decorated pavers and tiles, mosaics, murals; ornate work in stone, wood and metal; structures for large banners[342], with huge fabric artwork flowing from them; planters and arbors for all kinds of plants and trees; and lighting devices of various forms for night time excursions.

If we mentally accommodate related social and recreational elements, we might further observe entire arboretums; places for animals of all sorts to live and be interacted with[343]; provision for displays or galleries of numerous forms of art; opportunities for musical and other performance; eating establishments and rest areas of many and beautiful designs.

The passages we have read do not depict the details of these features. On the other hand, this hasn't been an exhaustive Scriptural analysis of what those details might be; and a studious effort would surely produce more information along these lines. Regardless, when we see these things come into being, we should not be surprised at their extent and grandeur. One detail though that we can be sure of is the embellishing presence of precious metals everywhere: for gold and silver will be more than plentiful[344]. Yet even this abundance of precious material will only declare that the Word and Wisdom of the Lord are more precious than all of it[345].

Breathtaking Bridges

Things get even more interesting when we consider the additional architecture and engineering involved where the prophesied rivers interact with the prophesied highways. We have discussed the three major rivers of Millennial

---

[341] Though health and longevity will be the norm (e.g., Isaiah 65:20), there is still the potential of injury. Hence, the need for healing leaves of the trees growing beside the Temple River (Ezekiel 47:12).

[342] E.g., Psalms 20:2, 60:4; Isaiah 11:12, 18:3; Zechariah 9:16.

[343] E.g., Isaiah 11:6-9.

[344] E.g., Isaiah 60:6,9,17; Zechariah 14:14. Compare with Solomon's situation, e.g., 2 Chronicles 1:15; 1 Kings 10:21.

[345] E.g., Psalms 19:10, 119:72; Proverbs 8:19.

Zion and seen them to be noteworthy ones, and no mere creeks. Their courses will be sometimes dramatic, with the Temple River making a great drop in elevation over a fairly short distance, involving perhaps deep chasms along the way. We have also discussed the major roadways that must span these rivers. The Lord's highways will need to cross their valleys, yet presumably remain comparatively "straight" and even as they do so. All this means that bridges are involved[346] for at least some of the Sacred District avenues here.

Given the breadth of the rivers (especially the one from the Temple), the spans may sometimes be quite long. Given the traffic volume involved, the width and strength requirements will certainly be great. If crossing deep gorges, tall piers that arise from within the river may be necessary. Either that or the bridges must launch from one abutment to the far-off other one, and be self-supporting along their entire length. In view of such issues, these will not be insignificant engineering feats; and the bridges of the Lord's highways will not be inconsequential structures.

What materials will be used? Only stone? Or will steel and/or other more modern materials be used? We are not informed of these details. But whatever their composition these bridges will be noteworthy in their design and grand in their embellishment. As with the Lord's highways leading to them, there will be aesthetic treatment in numerous forms: banners, coloration, trim & moldings, lighting, detailing of all kinds. Like the highways they convey, these bridges will be gorgeous, fit for the King of kings who will walk upon them.

Exquisite Entries

In the last chapter we discussed the significant walls composing the major borders within the Sacred District and around it. Our highways here will intersect these borders of the Sacred District, requiring openings through their walls. These penetrations could be very impressive, involving massive gateway structures.

Evidence of future Zion's gateways abounds in the Psalms, where a number of praise-texts can only have their ultimate actualization during Messiah's coming reign and with certain gateways therein. Here are some examples, beginning with a passage just cited that bears repeating.

> *Lift up your heads, O you **gates**; be lifted up, you ancient **doors**, that the **King of glory** may come in. 8 Who is this **King of glory**? The Lord strong and*

---

[346] Since the three (eastward & westward) rivers originate in the Sacred District, they will not intersect the main north-south central highway (except perhaps in the case of ring roads). The bridge discussion here mainly applies therefore to the lesser and outer routes that must traverse these watercourses.

*mighty, the **Lord** mighty in battle. 9 Lift up your heads, O you **gates**; lift them up, you ancient **doors**, that the **King of glory** may come in. 10 Who is he, this **King of glory**? The Lord Almighty — he is the **King of glory**.*
Psalms 24:7-10, NIV

*Open for me the **gates** of righteousness; I will enter and give thanks to the Lord. 20 This is the **gate of the Lord** through which the righteous may enter. 21 I will give you thanks, for you answered me;* **you have become my salvation***. 22* **The stone the builders rejected has become the capstone***; 23 the Lord has done this, and it is marvelous in our eyes. 24 This is the day the Lord has made; let us rejoice and be glad in it.*
Psalms 118:19-24, NIV

I rejoiced with those who said to me, **"Let us go to the house of the Lord."** *2 Our feet are standing in your **gates**, O Jerusalem... 5* **There the thrones for judgment stand, the thrones of the house of David.**
Psalms 122:1-2,5, NIV

*Extol the Lord, O Jerusalem; praise your God, O Zion, 13 for he strengthens the bars of your **gates** and blesses your people within you. 14* **He grants peace to your borders** *and satisfies you with the finest of wheat. 15 He sends his command to the earth; his word runs swiftly.*
Psalms 147:12-15, NIV

Without a doubt, very visible (and even monumental) portals will be present in Jerusalem's walls and those of the Sacred District in general. If we need an example of massive gateway structures here, we need look no further than Ezekiel 40. And though these gates of the Temple will have their own special and most holy purposes and functionality, those of the City and Sacred District will have the far greater traffic flow. So while the Temple gates will have ornate and unique designs as prophesied, the others will have their own special attributes based on their position and function. For example, many of the Sacred Districts non-Temple gates will be remarkable for their sheer size: they'll have to continually let a lot of people through.

Let's talk about the physical integrity of these doorways. The usual and primary purpose of a gate is not to be ornamental, but to effectively block unauthorized entry and defend against outsiders. And indeed, the truly massive gates of the coming Temple will have that capability: for in addition to being ornamental, they will also be fully operable[347]. An example of their potency is specifically seen in those of Jerusalem (and therefore Mount Zion as a whole). For at the very end of the Millennial period the Lord's last enemies will gather

---

[347] Ezekiel 44:1-2; 46:1, 12.

around the City, yet be prevented entry up until the point of their being vanquished [348]. So these gates of Zion are not mere aesthetic trimmings around apertures in the border walls. They are structures having huge defensive integrity, involving enormous and quite functional doors.

Even so, the gateways of the City will mostly have an opposite purpose throughout the Millennium: not of excluding, but of welcoming. The overwhelming sense in the prophetic Psalms such as those cited above is of people gathering in celebration of and to their Lord. His gates will be profound and spectacular landmarks that these pilgrims, people like you and I, will finally pass through after their long journeys. The mighty doorways of the Lord will declare the boundaries of God's special precincts, and do so with a thrilling welcome to all that enter. And at the same time, they will remind everyone that our coming King, the Son of God and Lamb of God, is our passageway to the Father.

> *Therefore Jesus said again, "I tell you the truth,* **I am the gate** *for the sheep. 8 All who ever came before me were thieves and robbers, but the sheep did not listen to them. 9* **I am the gate**; *whoever enters through me will be saved. He will come in and go out, and find pasture.*
> John 10:7-9, NIV

Stalwart Sentinels

We have read many Bible passages, especially in the Psalms, that describe God as our stronghold, citadel and fortress. Such verses reveal His absolute strength that simultaneously loves us, envelopes us and defends us, provided that we come near. The ultimate expression of that idea is eternal Zion, where the City-bride is made one with the fortress-God[349], spiritually, socially and even architecturally. Before that time though, this world will see the coming Mountain, House, and City of the Lord as the great physical analogy to that ongoing reality. Here too will be the protective-fortress theme, evidenced in Ezekiel's description of the Temple walls and gates, and likewise in other prophecies regarding Jerusalem and God's Mountain in general.

> **Let mount Zion rejoice**, *let the daughters of Judah be glad, because of thy judgments. 12* **Walk about Zion, and go round about her: tell the towers thereof.** *13 Mark ye well her* **bulwarks**, *consider her palaces; that ye*

---

[348] Revelation 20:9.
[349] Revelation 21-22.

> *may tell it to the generation following. 14 For this God is our God for ever and ever: he will be our guide even unto death.*
> *Psalms 48:11-14, KJV*

> *And I will make her that halted a remnant, and her that was cast far off a strong nation: and the* **Lord shall reign over them in mount Zion from henceforth, even for ever.** *8 And* **thou, O tower of the flock, the strong hold of the daughter of Zion,** *unto thee shall it come, even the first dominion; the kingdom shall come to the daughter of Jerusalem.*
> *Micah 4:7-8, KJV*

In verses such as these, the City and the Sacred District as a whole are likened to a stronghold. This is not surprising, since Jerusalem, from its very beginning, was considered a fortress-city[350]. Under David's and Solomon's building projects, Jerusalem became much more fortified with many towers along its walls. When the "Son of David" who is "greater than Solomon" arrives as King, Jerusalem will again become the "tower of the flock," as Micah prophesied. As the Psalmist declared, the City will have numerous towers and bulwarks that people will enthusiastically discuss.

For any fortress-like structure, high vantage points from which to observe surrounding areas are, of course, part of the architecture. With the magnificent and citadel-like venue we are exploring, towers are all the more anticipated. As discussed for gateways though, they will not primarily serve defensive purposes – though they will almost certainly do so at the very end of the Lord's 1,000-year reign[351]. There is, however, another purpose for these towers though: for the observation of worshippers of all nations, as they come from afar on the King's highways.

> *How beautiful on the mountains are the feet of those who bring good news, who proclaim peace, who bring good tidings, who proclaim salvation, who say to Zion,* **"Your God reigns!"** *8 Listen!* **Your watchmen lift up their voices; together they shout for joy.** *When the LORD returns to Zion, they will see it with their own eyes. 9 Burst into songs of joy together, you ruins of Jerusalem, for the LORD has comforted his people, he has redeemed Jerusalem.*
> *Isaiah 52:7-9, NIV*

From towers along the walls of coming Zion, watchmen will be on duty, witnessing and welcoming the ongoing flow of arriving pilgrims. The towers,

---

[350] 2 Samuel 5:7; 1 Chronicles 11:5.
[351] Again, the practical defensive capabilities of these architectural towers will likely be involved in the defense against the final rebellion of "Gog," in the closing events of the Millennial period (Revelation 20:7-9).

along with the gates, will stand as massive monuments of the Lord's welcome to all peoples and nations, to tribes, families and individuals.

What do we know about the towers? As with other architectural features of Jerusalem and greater Zion, we are not told very much. However, we can try to connect at least a few dots.

- For structural purposes, we can anticipate towers to be present at corners of major walls, e.g., for those bounding Jerusalem and the Sacred District. Corners provide both the reinforcement that high walls need, and the most obvious opportunities for large and high observation platforms.

- For observational and further structural purposes, we might also anticipate numerous towers along each exterior wall of the Sacred District (which is 100,000 LC, 32.6 miles, 52.4 km in circumference).

- The gateway structures may well be towers in themselves. Their architecture must reinforce the wall to either side of the opening, thereby providing the same opportunity as corner areas for supporting heightened platforms. Note that the Temple gates are particularly deep (in the direction of entry). If that style is an indicator, the upper floors of such towering structures would be impressively adequate, having large observation decks.

We don't know about the appearance of the towers, but decoration with banners seams anticipated in several passages we have seen. We can also expect that brilliant illumination will emanate from both towers and gates, symbolizing the fact that this is the City full of divine light[352], the home of the Light of the World[353].

Again, we do not know the specifics. But like the highways and other architecture in the Sacred District, the Lord will ensure that His towers will be lovely to look upon by all who come to His City and Mountain. By banner and light, by art and architecture, people will be astounded at how wonderful the towers of the Lord will be. And as the psalmist said, visitors will talk about these towers long after seeing them.

---

[352] 1 Kings 11:36; Matthew 5:14.
[353] E.g., John 8:12; 9:5; 12:46.

Portraying the Implied

As indicated at the beginning of this section, the walls, bridges, gates and towers of the Sacred District are not explicitly spelled out, nor always even demanded, by Scripture for the Millennial era. *But*, other factors that *are* clearly prophesied seem to necessitate them or at least imply their existence. So for the sake of completeness of our expedition, the following figures are put forward for purposes of discussion.

Figure 26: Implied Features of Roads and Walls

How does one illustrate such things? It is an impossible task: only the Lord knows the reality of it all, and He is keeping almost all the details as a series of wonderful surprises for His people. So we cannot know right now how tall the walls and gates will be[354]; how numerous the towers; how lengthy the bridges;

---

[354] In the following figures, vertical scales of features have been exaggerated to help them stand out against the landscape. Windows and other design details have been added for interest, and should be considered only for their value in that respect.

Chapter 7: Royal Thoroughfares   195

how broad the roads; and so on. Such designs are firmly in the loving hands of the coming Prince of Peace, whose desire it is to delight His people[355].

For our discussions here, rough diagrams must suffice. In these figures, gates have been added at all intersections between the major highways and borders we have discussed[356]. Four bridges have been illustrated: three for the outer ring road, and one for where the radial road from Jerusalem heads northeast, over the Temple River. Tower groups have been shown at ends of bridges, at gateways, and at corners of the Sacred District's outer walls. Lastly, the Prince's lands, east and west of the Sacred District, have been demarcated from tribal provinces to north and south with lines of large pillars.

Figure 27: Towers, Gates & Bridges

---

[355] See 1 Corinthians 2:9 (quoting Isaiah 64:4).
[356] Gates belonging to the City and Temple will assuredly be present, but have not been the focus here. They are therefore not indicated in these figures.

When the Lord builds His capitol City, its visible wonders will surely make prior depictions pale in comparison. That said, we can, and should, hang on to what *has* been declared to us. We can try to dimly appreciate, based on what we have been told by our Creator, the *coming reality* of His great Mountain and its highways, walls, gates and towers.

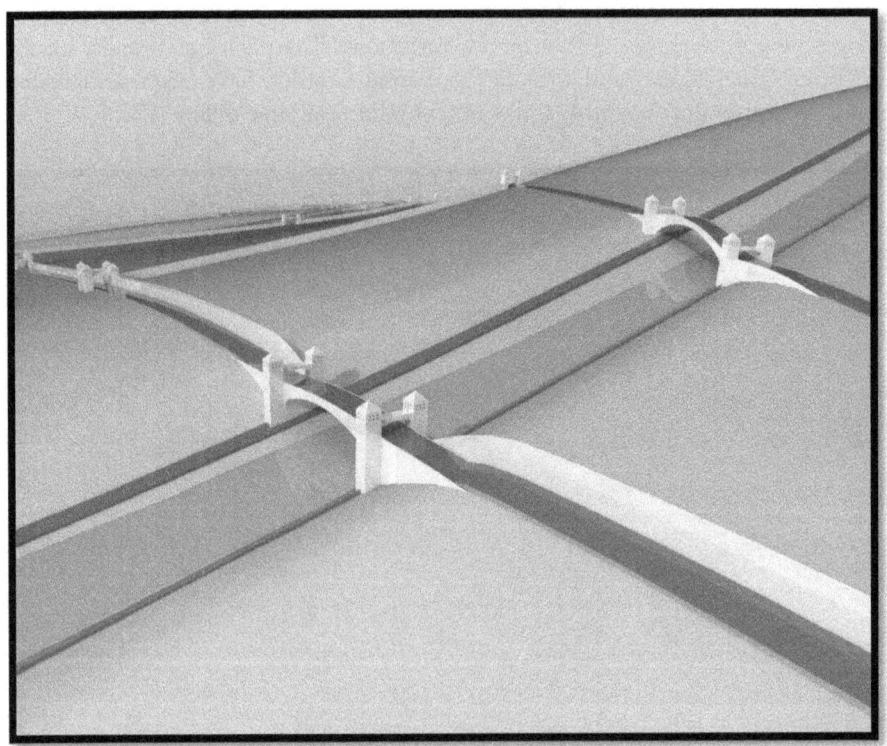

Figure 28: Towers, Gates & Bridges (cont'd)

It would take a whole chapter to list everything else that *might* be illustrated here, especially in view of this region being the answer to Eden's glories, on the other end of the Biblical timeline. Artists might explore such matters further, obtaining far better results than the diagrams presented here. But for the purposes of our expedition, we will have to be satisfied with the knowledge that, in a Day soon to come, practically *everyone* will know about these things. Practically *everyone* will have seen these realities on the horizon.

Chapter 8: Tiara of Towns

This is what the LORD says... of the towns of Judah, 'They shall be built,' and of their ruins, 'I will restore them,'
Isaiah 44:24a & 26b, NIV

Your people will rebuild the ancient ruins and will raise up the age-old foundations; you will be called Repairer of Broken Walls, Restorer of Streets with Dwellings.
Isaiah 58:12, NIV

I will bring back my exiled people Israel; they will rebuild the ruined cities and live in them. They will plant vineyards and drink their wine; they will make gardens and eat their fruit. I will plant Israel in their own land, never again to be uprooted from the land I have given them," says the LORD your God.
Amos 9:14-15, NIV

Further Renewals

We'll go once again to the peak of God's Mountain, to a place just outside the Temple's outer southern gate. Standing on or near the porch there, as Ezekiel did almost two and a half millennia ago, we can imagine looking downward and southward toward Jerusalem to come. Our view includes the marvelous highways around and within the Sacred District, especially the one coming up from the City. We also cannot help but notice the vast throngs of people using this concourse, with all their shouting and singing, their color and motion. In a real sense, by faith in God's Word, we are virtual participants with those multitudes flowing to and around this most holy area.

In addition to the City, the Temple, and rivers, roads, walls and other things we have explored, we can envision another kind of feature: certain towns which the Sacred District will enfold. In this chapter we'll take the opportunity to visit these towns, and investigate how their stories will blend with the greater drama of this Mountain.

Restorations Foreseen

The premise in this chapter is that certain Biblical cities, in whole or in part, now sometimes in ruins or perhaps buried entirely, will be "resurrected" and rebuilt in a coming time. Looking down from the Temple area, we would see such ancient towns, freshly restored and full of life.

For evidence, what follows is a number of prophetic statements that bear on this very matter. True, portions of some have had preliminary fulfillment in history[357]. But for the full impact of the prophecies, a Messianic context appears to be in view[358]. So please read the underlined phrases carefully for support of that point. Also, notice the phrases highlighted in bold type, for they describe this rebuilding of ruins to come.

> *I have swept away your offenses like a cloud, your sins like the morning mist... 23 Sing for joy, O heavens, for the LORD has done this; shout aloud, O earth beneath. Burst into song, you mountains, you forests and all your trees, for the LORD <u>has redeemed Jacob, he displays his glory in Israel</u>. 24 "This is what the LORD says... 26 <u>who carries out the words of his servants and fulfills the predictions of his</u>*

---

[357] E.g., with the Jews' return from the Babylonian captivity.
[358] Either explicitly (via direct statement) or implicitly (e.g., the results or contexts are complete, enduring, inviolable).

messengers, who says of Jerusalem, 'It shall be inhabited,' of **the towns of Judah, 'They shall be built,' and of their ruins , 'I will restore them,'** "
Isaiah 44:22a, 23b-24a, 26, NIV

The LORD will surely comfort Zion and **will look with compassion on all her ruins**; *he will make her deserts like Eden, her wastelands like the garden of the LORD. Joy and gladness will be found in her, thanksgiving and the sound of singing. 4 "Listen to me, my people; hear me, my nation: The law will go out from me; my justice will become a light to the nations.*
Isaiah 51:3-4, NIV

The LORD will guide you always; he will satisfy your needs in a sun-scorched land and will strengthen your frame. You will be like a well-watered garden, like a spring whose waters never fail. **12 Your people will rebuild the ancient ruins and will raise up the age-old foundations; you will be called Repairer of Broken Walls, Restorer of Streets with Dwellings.**
Isaiah 58:11-12, NIV

"The Redeemer will come to Zion, to those in Jacob who repent of their sins," declares the LORD. 60:1 "Arise, shine, for your light has come, and the glory of the LORD rises upon you. 2 See, darkness covers the earth and thick darkness is over the peoples, but the LORD rises upon you and his glory appears over you. 3 Nations will come to your light, and kings to the brightness of your dawn... 10 **"Foreigners will rebuild your walls**, *and their kings will serve you. Though in anger I struck you, in favor I will show you compassion.*
Isaiah 59:20, 60:1-3,10, NIV

'But I will restore you to health and heal your wounds,' declares the LORD, 'because you are called an outcast, Zion for whom no one cares.' 18 This is what the LORD says: **'I will restore the fortunes of Jacob's tents and have compassion on his dwellings; the city will be rebuilt on her ruins, and the palace will stand in its proper place.'**
Jeremiah 30:17-18, NIV

But you, O mountains of Israel, will produce branches and fruit for my people Israel, for they will soon come home. 9 I am concerned for you and will look on you with favor; you will be plowed and sown, 10 and I will multiply the number of people upon you, even the whole house of Israel. **The towns will be inhabited and the ruins rebuilt.** *11 I will increase the number of men and animals upon you, and they will be fruitful and become numerous. I will settle people on you as in the past and will make you prosper more than before. Then you will know that I am the LORD. 12 I will cause people, my people Israel, to walk upon you. They will*

possess you, and you will be their inheritance; you will never again deprive them of their children.
Ezekiel 36:8-12, NIV

This is what the Sovereign LORD says: On the day I cleanse you from all your sins, I will resettle your towns, and **the ruins will be rebuilt.** *34 The desolate land will be cultivated instead of lying desolate in the sight of all who pass through it. 35 They will say, "This land that was laid waste has become like the garden of Eden;* **the cities that were lying in ruins, desolate and destroyed, are now fortified and inhabited."** *36 Then the nations around you that remain will know that* **I the LORD have rebuilt what was destroyed** *and have replanted what was desolate. I the LORD have spoken, and I will do it.*
Ezekiel 36:33-36, NIV

"In that day I will restore David's fallen tent. **I will repair its broken places, restore its ruins, and build it as it used to be***, 12 so that they may possess the remnant of Edom and all the nations that bear my name," declares the LORD, who will do these things. 13 "The days are coming," declares the LORD, "when the reaper will be overtaken by the plowman and the planter by the one treading grapes. New wine will drip from the mountains and flow from all the hills. 14 I will bring back my exiled people Israel;* **they will rebuild the ruined cities and live in them.** *They will plant vineyards and drink their wine; they will make gardens and eat their fruit. 15 I will plant Israel in their own land, never again to be uprooted from the land I have given them," says the LORD your God.*
Amos 9:11-15, NIV

'After this I will return and rebuild David's fallen tent. **Its ruins I will rebuild, and I will restore it***, 17 that the remnant of men may seek the Lord, and all the Gentiles who bear my name, says the Lord, who does these things' 18 that have been known for ages.*
Acts 15:16-18, NIV

So many passages speak to this matter! And each demonstrates that certain Biblical sites will be rebuilt and restored. Let's walk through a few key lessons we can take away from these verses.

- ☐ Though the name 'Zion' embraces the City chosen by God, it also applies to the entire Mountain of God upon whose southern slope that City will reside. When the Lord causes Zion's ruins to be restored, the application is not only to Jerusalem proper, but also to the Sacred District as a whole. We can consider God's Mountain as the epicenter of prophesied restorations.

☐ Though the towns of ancient Judah receive special attention, let's remember that the larger kingdom of Judah included the lands of Benjamin as well[359]. Since ancient Jerusalem was located between the territories of Judah and Benjamin, both those provinces were greatly affected by Zion's activities. In the future, both provinces will again border Zion, and again be impacted by events of God's Mountain. This larger region comprised of the Sacred District, the Prince's Province, and the provinces of Benjamin and Judah, will therefore see many ruins restored.

☐ This phenomenon will, however, apply throughout the land of Israel. Especially in view of Ezekiel 36:10, we can anticipate a widespread rejuvenation of certain ancient cities all through the country, to some noticeable degree.

There will be a great contrast between these restored towns and the relatively huge new constructions. In Ezekiel 40-48, the walls and gates of Jerusalem and the Temple are given great attention. But now, in addition to all those new facilities, we see that actual ruins will be unearthed and regenerated. So we should consider the totality of coming architecture here in that dual sense: new-plus-resurrected.

Again, the differences will be dramatic. Regarding the Temple, City and Sacred District, we are told of straight walls laid out in squares, with regular patterns of gates. But with the restored ruins, we would see walls meandering with the terrain and rivers, having gate and tower positions driven by a host of varying factors. So it is interesting that, in this very context when the Kingdom of Heaven is fully deployed on this Earth, the coming King said this:

> *He said to them, "Therefore every **teacher** of the law who has been instructed about the **kingdom of heaven** is like the owner of a house **who brings out of his storeroom new treasures as well as old**."*
> *Matthew 13:47, NIV*

Jesus is the great Teacher who will indeed bring forth "new treasures as well as old," in many ways including the very visible form of architecture. He will do so throughout His kingdom, with a prophesied emphasis that increases as one nears Zion. Similar to the foretold crescendo of holiness and dedication, this pattern of rejuvenated ruins can be described as follows:

---

[359] After the split of Israel into northern and southern kingdoms, only the territories of Judah and Benjamin remained under the Davidic rule (e.g., 1 Kings 12), with the name "Judah" applying to this "remnant" kingdom of the two tribes. Restoration of "David's fallen tent" therefore involves both Judah and Benjamin.

- ☐ Involves Israel as a whole
- ☐ Emphasize for the provinces of Judah and Benjamin
- ☐ Implicitly includes the Prince's Province (being the lands of the coming King, and flanked by Judah and Benjamin)
- ☐ Zion / God's Mountain as a whole
- ☐ The City, Jerusalem

Some architectural art will be completely new; but some will be brought forth and restored, just as the King described, and to His glory. In that day, each of these walls, gates, foundations, pools, columns, and streets will be a meaningful, visible and tactile demonstration of God's faithfulness and sovereignty. The innumerable details will each be an exclamation point to His healing and comforting work within His "firstborn" nation, and to all people in covenant with Him.

Ruins Preserved

This coming "day" will certainly be exciting for anyone having even the least appreciation of Biblical history or archeology, for they will be able to connect events in the Bible with architecture they can physically experience. For as we can see, the prophecies do not involve a mere dusting off of crumbled stone and brick we might see today, but a rebuilding of what stood when the Biblical stories took place, at least to some appreciable degree.

But how could this happen? After all, the landscape has seen devastating ruination in wars ancient, contemporary, and all points between. Erosion has taken a great toll, especially with brick structures. Then there are fire, earthquakes, floods, and the natural breakdown of wood and metal materials over the millennia. Add to this the ever-present extraction of handy building materials from the rubble, combined with the confusion of subsequent construction. Add to everything not only modern-day bombs and missile strikes, but also the war-related activities, and massive tectonic events, of Revelation 16.

In view of such destruction, many sites are now practically vaporized: reduced to sand, ashes or smoke long blown away. Their stones are no more, their bricks particles of clay. So again, how might the prophesied restorations come about? The first answer is that a lot of enthusiastic human labor will be employed, for Jerusalem at least: *"foreigners will rebuild your walls"* (Isaiah 60:10).

But that does not appear to be the complete answer. If an ancient site has been completely annihilated, along with its foundations and roads, how can it be surveyed for its newly-rebuilt architecture? Where is its location in the first place? Even if the foundations are there, which period of time are they from? Even if one is able to determine foundations of Biblical import, how tall would the walls be? How many stories to the building? Of what placement and design should the doors and windows be? How would the building be roofed, painted, decorated? How would the grounds be laid out, with their trees and other plants? Clearly, questions would abound for any team of restorers, no matter how well armed with enthusiasm, talent, funds, and authorization. There needs to be something further.

So, for the question of how the prophesied restorations might come about, the second answer is *divine guidance*. The Lord and King, He who remains "greater than Solomon," will be on the scene and in charge of the program. Whether He directs the rebuilding directly or via His captains, the necessary and detailed knowledge will be there. The perfection of recreation is only limited to His insight into the facts, which is infinite: for Immanuel, "God with us," is one with the Father. Technically, the Creator could recreate, say, the ancient city of Shiloh (where the Tabernacle once stood), down to the last block, brick, beam, nail, and bit of fabric; and do so for any given time He wishes. That would be an easy thing for God to do: He spoke this planet into being and He could do the same for the ancient Shiloh, or any place else.

Between this extreme, and that of the completely unaided work force, there is a third element to consider. Of course there will be human involvement; and of course there will be divine guidance. But a face-value reading of the prophecies is this: that a certain amount of divine preservation is also at work. Evidently, the Lord will have *preserved certain ruins and artifacts* from the deep past, *keeping them to be revealed* in His own timing.

If these things were easy to find, they would have been unearthed already. So we are here considering things that await discovery, in the hidden "storeroom" perhaps hinted at by Jesus. Indeed, God can easily keep things secret from mankind if He wishes, and reveal them when He sees fit.

> *I will go before you and will level the mountains; I will break down gates of bronze and cut through bars of iron. 3* **I will give you the treasures of darkness, riches stored in secret places, so that you may know that I am the Lord, the God of Israel,** *who summons you by name.*
> Isaiah 45:2-3, NIV

This uncovering (which is what "discovery" means) of *"treasures of darkness"* will bring hidden things to the light of day. Since this will happen when Messiah *"shall build my city"* (Isaiah 45:13b), we can anticipate that some of these *"riches stored in secret places"* will include archeological ones. New discoveries along those lines will surely abound.

All this uncovering will most likely be assisted by related tectonic events also prophesied. Those that cause the Mountain of God to be physically lifted and "exalted," for example, may very well be a major factor in raising hidden

Chapter 8: Tiara of Towns

architecture and artifacts to the surface. Rather than causing further destruction, God will use certain earthquakes for His purposes. For the ruins to be restored are not faked, such as we do in our theme parks, shopping malls or other venues. No, these architectural resurrections will be genuine, having solid archeological basis that is yet to fully emerge.

> *This is what the LORD says: "Only if the heavens above can be measured and the foundations of the earth below be searched out will I reject all the descendants of Israel because of all they have done," declares the LORD. 38 "The days are coming," declares the LORD,* **"when this city will be rebuilt for me from the Tower of Hananel to the Corner Gate.** *39 The measuring line will stretch from there straight to the hill of Gareb and then turn to Goah. 40 The whole valley where dead bodies and ashes are thrown, and all the terraces out to the Kidron Valley on the east as far as the corner of the Horse Gate, will be holy to the LORD.* **The city will never again be uprooted or demolished."**
> Jeremiah 31:37-40, NIV

> *The whole land, from Geba to Rimmon, south of Jerusalem, will become like the Arabah [i.e., smooth, like the Jordan valley plain].* **But Jerusalem will be raised up and remain in its place**, *from the Benjamin Gate to the site of the First Gate, to the* **Corner Gate**, *and from the* **Tower of Hananel** *to the royal winepresses. 11* **It will be inhabited; never again will it be destroyed. Jerusalem will be secure.**
> Zechariah 14:10-11, NIV

Here we have explicit examples of ruins that are raised and restored in the time to come: the "corner gate" and the "tower of Hananel." Also, "Horse Gate," "Benjamin Gate," "First Gate," and so on. These were major stone structures in ancient times. Though not clearly understood now, they will be restored when these Words of God are fulfilled sometime soon.

From these verses we can confirm that tectonic activity <u>will</u> indeed be involved in the "resurrections" of at least Jerusalem's ruins, for "*Jerusalem* [as a whole] *will be <u>raised up</u>*" simultaneously. Likewise, the Mountain of God will arise just after (or during) the greatest series of earthquakes ever experienced by humankind[360]. All this activity seems therefore linked. And the events causing Jerusalem's exposure of ruins apparently applies to other cities residing upon God's Mountain and surrounding regions.

In view of all these actions, let's pause to admire God's unique and mighty hand at work here. Even right now, He has been preserving certain ancient structures for two or three millennia. In His timing, and by His sheer power, they will physically emerge as tangible elements in tomorrow's landscapes.

---

[360] See Revelation 16:18.

Though the ancient features are fragile, He will lift them from the ground; while many layers of soil and debris fall away, His invisible hand will protect the artifacts and architecture for His purposes. What an awesome thing to witness!

The Creator will have at His discretion the massive forces by which He created the world in the first place, by which He made the mountains. Having preserved, and while still preserving, He will remove the overburdening soils and layers of the ages, while raising great stretches of landscape, and lowering or smoothing other terrain. And after this work is complete, and after exposing anew these historical works of man, He will allow people of many nations to participate in the reconstruction, instructing them perfectly in their joyful work.

In such ways, God will cause these buildings, walls and cities of Israel to "live" anew. And all will testify to His faithfulness and patience, His omnipotence and sovereignty, and His abiding wisdom and love. Truly, our God is an awesome God.

Candidate Sites

What sites will be involved in all this rebuilding? In addition to Jerusalem, which ancient cities will be rebuilt? Though we are not told exactly, we know the phenomenon is to be widespread throughout Israel, at least as anciently bounded. True, those borders fluctuated over time, with their greatest extent being prophesied by Moses and Ezekiel, and applicable in the Millennial period[361]. But even with the much reduced borders of Israel's Northern and Southern Kingdoms in mind[362], a huge amount of real estate is involved, containing many hundreds of sites. Either way, all Biblical towns and cities of Israel are candidates for reconstruction.

Of these, one particular kind of site may be particularly suited to restoration: those covered by a mound. This is because many such towns have been long-inhabited from ancient times, resulting in a mound, or *tel*, from many layers of occupation. This Hebrew word *tel*[363] remains in use in or day, and is reflected in modern place-names. For example, the name of the ancient city (and mound) of Gibeah is *Tel el-Ful*. Since the ancient sites had good geographic reasons for their locations, such as a high vantage point, a broad place near a body of water, a river crossing or a major crossroads, modern cities are often nearby for the same geographic benefits. For example, modern *Tel Aviv-Yafo* is situated against the ancient site of *Jaffa* (or *Joppa*).

---

[361] As discussed in detail in The Approaching Country, chapters 2-3.
[362] For example, borders as seen by the declaring prophets, Isaiah, Jeremiah and (young) Ezekiel, in the 700-589 B.C. time frame.
[363] Strong's OT:8510, *tel*, meaning heap or mound.

Such tel-sites often remain, in part or in whole, blanketed by their centuries of overburden, with the earlier buried structures and artifacts sometimes more intact than if left exposed. So it may well be that God will have used these layers of debris and soil as a protective cover, to be removed when He says so.

Whether so covered or not, there are many candidate sites in Israel, and perhaps many will be reconstructed. But, we must limit things in our discussion here. And per the charter of our expedition, we will stick to the environs of God's Mountain to come, and the candidates within it.

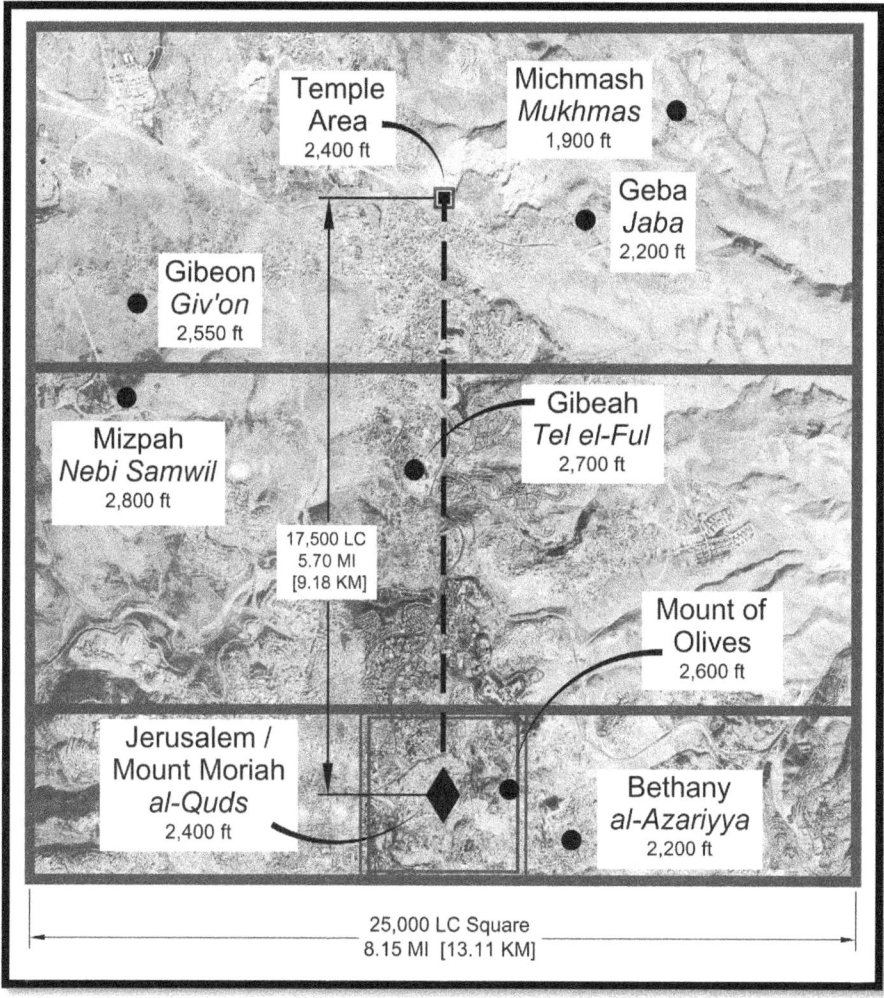

Figure 29: Ancient Sites within the Sacred District

Their positions can be located upon present-day terrain as illustrated in the above figure, with Jerusalem in the south and the Temple due north[364]. When such long-gone cities are "resurrected," when the *tels* of ancient Israel fully give up their secrets and contents, when many additional structures and artifacts are revealed, and the Lord explains everything, what stories might be told?

Far in advance of that rebuilding, we can listen to those stories, and get a sense of how they will resound in Messiah's Day. So as we said at the beginning of this chapter, if we could stand near the peak God's Mountain and gaze downward and southward upon the landscape, yes, we would see many things we've already talked about. But we would also see towns such as these – though in a reconstituted form, and very full of life. So let's take one more journey up the coming Mountain of God, exploring potential residential hubs around its sacred peak, and hearing the ancient echoes of what people will again talk about.

Jerusalem's Neighbors

Of all the ancient cities being restored here, clearly the most important is *the* City, Jerusalem. That topic is far too big for this expedition, and deserves a study-journey all its own. But we will here explore other towns nearby; and the nearest neighbor of Jerusalem, Bethany[365], will be the first on our itinerary of ancient towns within the Sacred District.

This won't be a history lesson or present-day travelogue. Instead, we will explore each town's Biblical significance, as if we were visiting its restored ruins in the Lord's Day ahead of us. In the light of His overwhelming victory at the time of His coming, we can ask ourselves certain questions beforehand: When a particular town's ruins are restored, what might we interpret from them? When inhabited once more, what messages will that town uniquely convey?

For possible answers we can examine two main sources: the *meaning* of the town's ancient Biblical name, and the *story* connecting the town with God's overarching story of redemption.

---

[364] Background image ©2007 DigitalGlobe™ via GoogleEarth™, 18 November 2007, <http://www.google.com/earth/index.html>. Multiple images stitched together, and overlaying graphics applied, by the author. As the ancient cities were originally known (and often named) for their elevation ("Hill," "High Place"), the position dots here are centered on present-day topographic high points. Historical positions may have varied somewhat, due to excavations and earthquakes since then.

[365] The following figures for Sacred District towns are intended for diagrammatic purposes only, not for explicit shape and dimension. Boundaries of the towns are arbitrary, with terracing only intended to convey a sense of the surrounding terrain discussed in prior chapters. A northward-pointing arrow is included in each for reference.

Bethany: House of Living

What is special about the name "Bethany"? The Hebrew syllable "*beth*," as you may know, refers to "house" of something. It prefixes many Biblical place names, and also those of many synagogues and other Jewish institutions or organizations to this day. However, the "*any*" suffix is subject to scholarly debate. Depending on the Bible dictionary used, "Bethany" might translate to "house of figs," or "house of unripe figs," or even "house of dates[366]." For argument's sake though, we will settle on "figs," in a general sense.

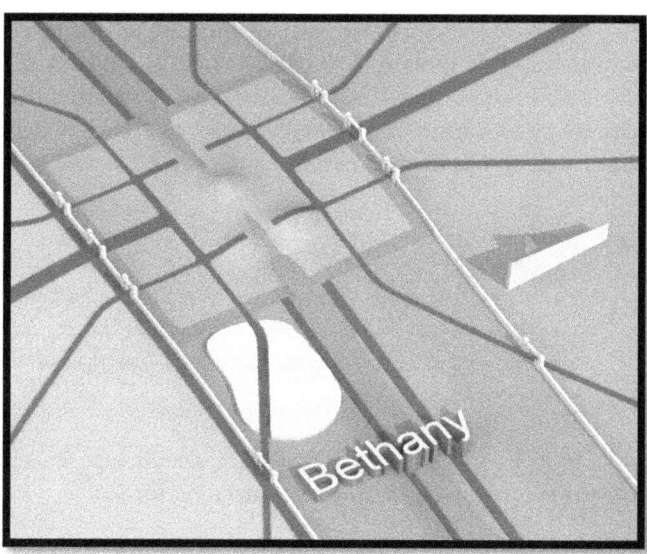

Figure 30: Bethany

There is more significance in this particular fruit than might at first meet the eye. Today, figs are not a staple food in most western cultures. But in Biblical times, figs *were* a staple. Indeed, to have a fig tree on one's own property (along with a grapevine from which to create wine) was proverbial for a truly God-blessed and comfortable life[367]. So the city named *beth-any* invokes the thoughts of rich blessing and pleasant living.

One might consider that the "House - of - Figs" name is merely coincidental, and therefore irrelevant. But, not so. In the coming age when Eden is again on Earth, any town here named for special fruitfulness is in very good shape. In fact, we can prove that Bethany will explode in botanical abundance, for it stands unique in the entire world: it is the only ancient Biblical city that will be contained within the farmlands of coming Jerusalem.

---

[366] Some scholars have said that the meaning of "Bethany" is "house of affliction" or "house of song": see Hitchcock's Bible Names Dictionary. However, the preponderance of interpretations reviewed by this author point towards "house of" things related to *figs*.
[367] E.g., 1 Kings 4:25; 2 Kings 18:31; Isaiah 34:4, 36:16; Joel 1:12, 2:22; Micah 4:4; Haggai 2:19; Zechariah 3:10.

> *"The remaining area, 5,000 cubits wide and 25,000 cubits long, will be for the common use of the city, for houses and for pastureland. The city will be in the center of it..."*
> *Ezekiel 48:15, NIV*

This ancient town will therefore be a true highlight of the farmlands east of the Lord's capitol City, and a place of His special natural blessings.

In addition to the agricultural message though, there is another way to detect the import of this place: through the Biblical events that happened here. This little town, situated just east of the City where Jesus ministered most, was also the home of three of His closest friends: Lazarus, Martha and Mary. These were relationships that Jesus Himself held as profoundly important. When He rules from Jerusalem, and when people recall what happened right here, the stories will convey deep meaning. One example is that the Lord *never* forgets His friends.

> *Greater love has no one than this, that he lay down his life for his friends. 14 You are my friends if you do what I command. 15 I no longer call you servants, because a servant does not know his master's business. Instead, I have called you friends, for everything that I learned from my Father I have made known to you.*
> *John 15:13-15, NIV*

It is in the context of deepest friendship that the idea and place of Bethany take on its perhaps fullest meaning for us.

> *Jesus loved Martha and her sister and Lazarus.*
> *John 11:5, NIV*

You are familiar with the story where Jesus wept for Lazarus, and then caused him to arise back to life – one of the most powerful miracles recorded in the Bible. So profound is the story that it echoes to this very day: for the modern place-name for Bethany is *al-Azariyya* (or *el-Azariyeh*), from *Lazariyeh*, meaning "place of Lazarus[368]."

Since long ago, this alternate modern name for the town of Bethany has preserved two things. First, it recalls the deep friendship that Jesus had with *Lazarus*; and second, it recalls the great miracle Jesus accomplished in raising that friend from the dead.

When Yeshua reigns and Bethany's ruins are restored, when Jerusalem's new river flows nearby, and people of all nations come to visit, what might be

---

[368] Easton, Matthew G. Easton's Bible Dictionary, Nashville, TN, Thomas Nelson Publishers, 1897.

the story most told of this little town? Will the area be primarily a sign and centerpiece of the Lord's blessing, an agricultural jewel set amidst His wonderful Garden? Will the figs it produces symbolize the culmination of His promises of blessing? Or will the town mainly bear witness to the Lord's faithfulness toward all those He loves? Will the restored ruins of Lazarus' home declare Jesus' victory over death, not only for Himself, but for all His friends?

I suspect all these meanings will be evident, as one walks through this resurrected and rejuvenated city. In the mean time, we can think of *Bethany* as both a name and place that speaks renewal, prosperity, and friendship in life to come, by the Lord's great power, and because of His love.

Gibeah: A Statement of Sovereignty

The next town on our tour is Gibeah, which is distinguished in its marvelous position in the Sacred District: directly between future Jerusalem and the Temple area. Practically at the midpoint of that key stretch of the Lord's highway, it is also fairly central within the Levitical region. When anyone, including the coming King, journeys from the City's northern Judah Gate toward the Temple, he or she will pass through this ancient city.

In our virtual uphill journeys so far, we would have definitely noticed this town if our feet were actually on the ground. Now, we can explore the place more closely. If Gibeah's ruins are to be restored as a testimony to God's faithfulness, with its consequence in His story comprehended, what might we

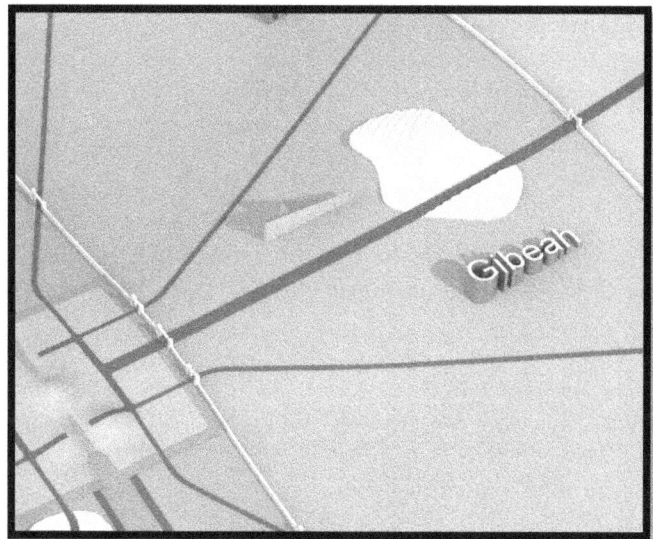

Figure 31: Gibeah

know in advance? What might be the stories told of this town, directly located as it will be on the processional axis between God's earthly focal points?

One early story about Gibeah is certainly not a happy one, for the ancient town was the scene of one of the Bible's most horrific recorded incidents of human atrocity and consequent judgment[369]. We'll not here go into that depraved situation and the slaughter of many thousands of Israelites that resulted. But we can point out the staggering contrast: what was a place of one of the lowest points in Israel's history will be elevated to a place of great honor. This is but one more example of God's grace and mercy, displayed in a clear physical manner for all to see.

On a happier note, Gibeah later became known as the home of Israel's very first king, Saul[370]. But before that king came to power, this place was also known as "Gibeah [the hill] of God," having numerous prophets in the area[371]. When newly-chosen Saul came to this place, a strong (though temporary) prophetic capacity came upon him[372]. So the first king of Israel became a prophet, right here; and Saul made it his home, the place becoming known thereafter as "Gibeah of Saul[373]." Now, please notice something important in this story. These remarkable prophesying events were summed up as "signs" to be conducted by Saul and the prophets and musicians there at the time[374]. But what were these "signs" pointing toward? They were surely not signs of God's pleasure with making Saul king[375]. But here and now, we finally have a perfect answer. People will once again have a king over Israel, and see Him prophesying right here in Gibeah – though righteously, permanently and wisely, completely unlike the ungodly first king. Israel's *final* King-Prophet, Jesus, will walk through this ancient site. When these ruins are restored, our Lord and Messiah will stand among them and speak ("prophesy") the very Words of God – for He is Immanuel, *God With Us*[376]. *He* is ultimately the sign that the first king was made to point toward, here in Gibeah.

But we are not done; there are additional stories that we should consider for Gibeah here. As you know, that initial kingship with Saul had massive issues. Though he was Israel's first, it was a monarch demanded by the people in a way that was evil[377]. Saul continually disobeyed the Lord, and his coronation was later

---

[369] See Judges 19-21, where almost the entire tribe of Benjamin was wiped out due to flagrant and awful sins. See Hosea 9:9 & 10:9 for the longevity of these consequences and their memories.

[370] 1 Samuel 10:26, 15:34, 22:6.

[371] 1 Samuel 10:5.

[372] 1 Samuel 10:5, 10.

[373] 1 Samuel 11:4, 15:34; 2 Samuel 21:6; Isaiah 10:29.

[374] 1 Samuel 10:7.

[375] Israel's demand for a king was against God's will (e.g., 1 Samuel 12:17-20), and God later regretted choosing Saul for the role (1 Samuel 15:35).

[376] Isaiah 7:14.

[377] 1 Samuel 12:17-20.

Chapter 8: Tiara of Towns

deeply regretted by God the Father[378]. However, there came a remedy. It was David that the Lord would choose, over Saul. It is therefore the *Son* of David Who will reign supreme over Gibeah, over Israel, and over all the world. When the Son of David walks from His City to the Temple of His Father, He will pass through restored Gibeah in ultimate triumph. It will be a victory not merely over Saul in the past, but over every king or queen refusing submission to our Maker, the Lord God Almighty. In wisdom, yet with undeniable firmness, the coming King will rule over all other kings. For as David prophesied of his coming descendent,

> *I will proclaim the decree of the Lord: He said to me, "You are my Son; today I have become your Father. 8 Ask of me, and I will make the nations your inheritance, the ends of the earth your possession. 9 You will rule them with an iron scepter; you will dash them to pieces like pottery." 10 Therefore, you kings, be wise; be warned, you rulers of the earth. 11 Serve the Lord with fear and rejoice with trembling. 12 Kiss the Son, lest he be angry and you be destroyed in your way, for his wrath can flare up in a moment. Blessed are all who take refuge in him.*
> Psalms 2:7-12, NIV[379]

At all levels then, there will be a final end to the phrase "Gibeah of Saul." Messiah's physical forebear, David, was chosen by God the Father over the popular contestant of the day; and this town named for Saul will now belong to the Son. The "hill" of Saul, *Gib'ah Sha'uwl*, will now belong to Jesus: *Gib'ah Yeshuwa'*. David, through his Son, will overwhelmingly prevail.

One last story relates to the priesthood, and the term "the messiah" (*ha mashiach*), meaning "the anointed." This title applies in two Biblical ways: anointed priest, and anointed king. We've seen Gibeah's importance from the kingly perspective. For the other kind of anointing, Gibeah was also the burial place of the first high priest after Aaron, Eleazar[380]. Jesus-Yeshua is the final High Priest[381], and thus the ultimate descendent of Aaron, the concluding *anointed* priest. In being the Son of David, He is also the concluding *anointed* King. Gibeah has meaning in both these senses: burial place of Israel's first high priest born into that office, and prophetic anointing place of Israel's first king. From both perspectives, in both His roles, *ha mashiach*, "the anointed," the *Messiah*, will walk through the resurrected ruins of Gibeah.

Such are the messages that will hit those walking through Gibeah's restored gates, past its walls, over its streets. People just like you and I, in a time soon to come, will touch real architecture that shouts the truth of the Prince,

---

[378] 1 Samuel 15:11.
[379] See also Revelation 12:5, 19:15.
[380] Joshua 24:33.
[381] Hebrews 8,9.

who reigns even now. For He is the *final* High Priest, fulfilling and completing the role of Aaron; He is the *final* King, fulfilling and completing the role of David. There is no other High Priest or High King but Him, nor will there ever be.

Mizpah: Watchtower-Ruler

Moving north and west, the next town we come to is Mizpah. Like Gibeah, it also lies within the Levitical region, though near its north-western border with the Priestly region (see the figure for Gibeon below).

The town is closely associated with Samuel, the last of the Judges and one of the foremost prophets of Scripture. Mizpah was the place from which Samuel led the Israelites as "Judge," and where he directed them in requests made to the Lord. By God's grace, Samuel led the people from Mizpah in a successful victory over the Philistines[382]. Mizpah is also the traditional place of Samuel's (final[383]) burial, with his name still present in the place-name that survives to this day: *Neby Samuel* (or *Nebi Samwil*), that is, the "tomb of Samuel."

As with all these towns, much more can be gained with further study of Mizpah's history[384]. Taken at face value though, the place firmly represents one of the greatest leaders and prophets of Israel. With Samuel, and the body of Biblical passages he figures in, we have ample discussion areas and pondering points for anybody visiting Mizpah's restored ruins in Messiah's coming Day.

But there will be an additional layer for such visitors to ponder. The word *mizpah* has its own significance, for it means "watchtower[385]." And as a matter of fact, it is one of the highest points in all the Sacred District, at least as its terrain stands today. Like Gibeah ("hill"), the word and name of *Mizpah* re-emphasizes to us the idea of a geographically high vantage point.

If the Lord decides to make this area smooth and level, to make this high place low, that is up to Him, and always with perfect and wonderful purpose. But if He decides to leave Mizpah relatively elevated, the visual message would also be clear to observers. For its very name would continue to convey the idea of "watchtower," its higher altitude upon the God's Mountain reminding all of His leadership and Voice through the prophets.

As pointed out before, watchtower-*Mizpah* is closely associated with one of the greatest human "towers" of the Bible, Samuel. That leader and prophet,

---

[382] 1 Samuel 7.
[383] Per tradition, Samuel's bones were moved here from his home town of Ramah just to the north-east.
[384] E.g., Joshua 18:26; Judges 20:1,3; 21:1,5,8; 1 Samuel 7:5ff; 1 Kings 15:22; 2 Kings 25:23; 2 Chronicles 16:6.
[385] Strong's OT:4708.

shepherding the young nation of Israel through its transition to monarchy, prefigures the coming and greatest leader and Prophet of all. Samuel was judge, priest and prophet of Israel, and his authoritative anointing of Saul was the beginning of Israel's story of kings. But the coming King-Priest-Prophet, Yeshua, is the glorious conclusion of that ministry. In Jesus, Samuel's mission is completed; and of the Son of David, it will forever continue to be said:

> *For you have been my refuge, a strong tower against the foe.*
> *Psalms 61:3, NIV*

The town of Mizpah may well inspire people to consider this verse anew, in the day when the ultimate *"mizpah,"* our King and Savior, our living "refuge" and "tower," reigns over all the earth. Mizpah may be a small town. But of all the restored high places of the Sacred District, it may be a very special one from which to sing such praises to the Lord.

Temple Neighbors

We've explored Jerusalem's city-neighbors which may well be restored in the coming Day. Now it's time to do the same for ancient cities neighboring the coming Temple, and hear what stories they might have to tell.

Gibeon: Forerunner to Glory & Rule

From Mizpah we make a short walk north, just across the border between the Levitical and Priestly regions, to the next key locale: Gibeon. You will notice that 'Gibeon' sounds very much like 'Gibeah,' which we have already talked about, but the two are quite different places. Let's examine what makes Gibeon stand apart, and explore its unique traits.

Trait 1: Place of Priestly Dwellings

Gibeon was one of the original priestly cities of the First Testament [386]. When the lands were being divided up among the tribes, this town was selected from the tribe of Benjamin and dedicated to Aaron's descendents. This is significant, for as a city originally declared a home for priests, Gibeon will fully reside within the Priestly region of the Sacred District.

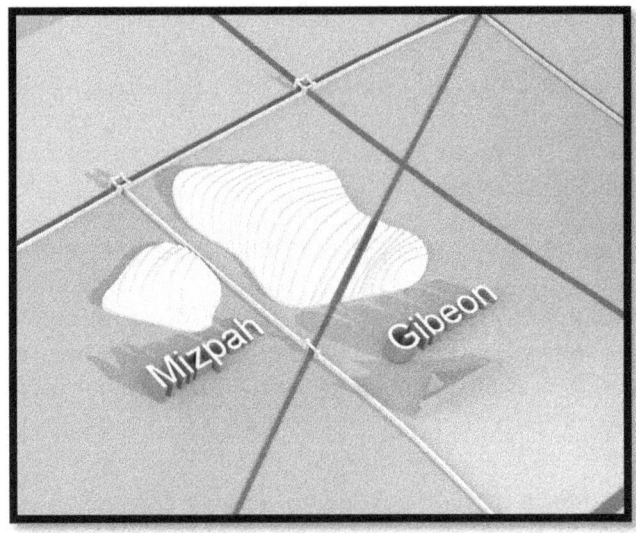

Figure 32: Mizpah and Gibeon

When Gibeon's ruins are restored, they will therefore be a loud reminder of the original priesthood that God defined and developed under Moses and Joshua; they will affirm God's faithfulness over history, and declare the conclusion of His promises. The restored city will demonstrate to all that these events of the Millennial Day are a completion of divine plans and purposes commenced long, long ago.

Trait 2: Last Place of the Tabernacle

Gibeon has the distinction of being the last site of the Tabernacle of the Lord, resulting in this city's being known as "the great high place[387]" of worship. This honored was bestowed just prior to establishment of Solomon's Temple[388]. When the Ark of the Covenant was brought from Gibeon to the just-completed Temple in Jerusalem, the Tabernacle's equipment and furnishings were brought as well[389], but afterward, ceased to be mentioned.

---

[386] Joshua 21:13-19.
[387] 1 Kings 3:4.
[388] 2 Chronicles 1:3.
[389] 1 Kings 8:4.

Thus the portable Tabernacle gave way to the permanent and magnificent Temple built by Solomon, the former holy location giving way to a far more significant place. Historical Gibeon is therefore an early example of turnover in the site of God's "House" from one holy site to a better one. That is, as final place of the Tabernacle, Gibeon bowed to the more lasting and superior site of God's choosing, that of Mount Moriah, within Jerusalem. Likewise, the coming Temple will be far more grand than Solomon's, and also receive a new location – this time, north of Jerusalem, as described by Ezekiel and seen in our maps.

In the restoration of its ruins during Messiah's reign, perhaps the Lord will use Gibeon once again as an object lesson in transitioning from the formative to the permanent. Perhaps in the resurrected walls and gates, He will also cause the last site of the Tabernacle to be reconstructed, a physical reminder of the story from ancient Tabernacle to ancient Temple. But whether He chooses to or not, in Gibeon people will uniquely perceive just how purposeful each step of God's immutable Plan has been, in His creation of an eternal people for Himself.

Trait 3: Place of Princely Vision

As ancient Gibeon gave way to Mount Moriah and the Temple, another momentous change was taking place: David's kingdom was about to be surpassed in glory under the reign of his son, Solomon. There was a pivotal event in this additional transition, when the Lord appeared to the newly-crowned Solomon. God blessed him with unequaled wisdom and unprecedented "riches and honor" amongst all kings throughout his lifetime[390]. With this divine blessing of wisdom and wealth, Solomon was enabled to construct the holy Temple and undertake many other spectacular projects. Where did this dream, appearance and blessing happen? Did it happen in Jerusalem, on the new Temple site? No. It took place right here in this ancient city of priests, here where the foreshadowing Tabernacle still stood: in Gibeon.

In Messiah's day an identical form of exaltation will transpire, but in a massively surpassing way. Both Gibeon *and* Mount Moriah will bow to the new northerly location of the Temple and the far greater glory it will radiate. As magnificent as Solomon's kingdom was, it will likewise give way to the exceeding glory of Messiah's dominion. At the center of both phenomena is the coming King, Jesus, who said:

> *The Queen of the South... from the ends of the earth to listen to Solomon's wisdom,* **and now one greater than Solomon is here.**
> Matthew 12:42, portions, NIV; also Luke 11:31.

---

[390] 1 Kings 3:5-15; 2 Chronicles 1:1-12.

People visiting tomorrow's Gibeon will surely be reminded of Solomon's divine enablement, in the unique and powerful vision he witnessed in this place. But they will also consider the much greater fact, that *"now one greater than Solomon is here."* When the coming Prince speaks from Gibeon, it will be with God's own wisdom. And everyone who hears will be blessed.

Trait 4: Place of Time's Stopping

If none of the above events had taken place, Gibeon would still stand out as a unique place in the entire Earth. Right here, a certain spiritual-natural event occurred that has never happened in any other place or time.

Picture the following. During Israel's initial conquest of the Holy Land under Joshua's leadership, there came a pivotal battle. This was against the various Amorite kings, their forces newly joined against Israel in a powerful federation. In the heat of this decisive conflict, Joshua prayed the following:

> *On the day the LORD gave the Amorites over to Israel, Joshua said to the LORD in the presence of Israel:* **"O sun, stand still over Gibeon**, *O moon, over the Valley of Aijalon." 13 So the sun stood still, and the moon stopped, till the nation avenged itself on its enemies, as it is written in the Book of Jashar.* **The sun stopped in the middle of the sky and delayed going down about a full day.**
> *Joshua 10:12-13, NIV*

So amazing was this incident that the Bible goes on to tell us:

> <u>There has never been a day like it before or since, a day when the LORD listened to a man.</u> *Surely the LORD was fighting for Israel!*
> *Joshua 10:14, NIV*

How this event happened, we don't know. If it was a local or global phenomenon, we aren't explicitly told. We do know though that time essentially "stood still" for one day here, in a manner never happening before or since. God uniquely honored this unprecedented command, and its observed effects happened right here: in Gibeon, and the area around it.

In this story, let's notice another telling fact. Not only does Solomon serve as emblematic for Messiah to come, but also Joshua: for he was the great warrior-leader that led His people to the Promised Land. In fact, the name *Yeshua* (from whence we get the name 'Jesus') is the very same name, meaning, "The Lord is Deliverer." We look forward to Yeshua-Jesus coming in concluding fulfillment of that saving role which is, like Joshua's, declared in His very name.

When the ultimate "Joshua" comes, many natural wonders will also occur, events to which analogues of the past will bear testimony. For example, in this ancient battle of Joshua's, it was God who slew the enemies of His people – with hailstones[391]. And in the events of Yeshua's coming, God will again deliver hailstones upon His enemies, but on a far larger scale[392]. Thus the ancient miracle is sometimes like a prophecy in itself.

As for the massive and truly unique miracle of time standing still, will Jesus-Joshua perform a similar action during the final battle of this age? Will He command the sun and moon to stop in their courses? Will other foreseen phenomena, such as "stars" falling from the sky[393], be attributable to such a cessation of the Earth's rotation? We can't know for certain now, because we have not been told. But when the ultimate Joshua comes, and *"the Lord Saves"* comes as warrior-Lord to save His people, it seems clear that the sky-events of Gibeon will be overwhelmingly echoed and answered.

As an ongoing reminder of such mighty events both ancient and future, Gibeon will signal the majesty, power and glory of the God and Savior before whom all nature and mankind must bow. When in this ancient town, one will contemplate historical Joshua, his commanding the sun to "stand still," that God agreed, and that He also defeated Joshua's enemies. In the Day to come, when walking the streets of restored Gibeon, people will be reminded of He who made the sun in the first place, the Lord who has been Savior of His people all along, and who now has taken His throne as King over all His creation.

Trait 5: Place of Foreign Participation

This last feature of Gibeon's is not as spectacular in the physical miracle sense. It is a more down to earth trait; yet it remains a vital one, especially for those of us who are not "natural" Jews. With our Jewish brothers and sisters in Messiah, we indeed share a "blessed hope[394]" in He who is named *"the Lord Saves."* Our coming King, Jesus-Joshua, was Himself born a Jew, of the tribe of Judah. Yet for all "gentiles," Gibeon has a very powerful story to tell in regards to direct inclusion in His dominion. Here is a summary of the story's main points.

---

[391] Joshua 10:11.
[392] Ezekiel 38:22; Revelation 16:21.
[393] Revelation 6:13. That is, space junk orbiting our planet today, if it all fell and burned in re-entry, might very well look like a vast number of "shooting stars."
[394] Titus 2:13.

- In the early times of the original conquest of Canaan, Israel, under Joshua's leadership, intended to destroy the Canaanite inhabitants of Gibeon per the Lord's command[395].

- Seeing what had been done to the Canaanite cities of Jericho and Ai, the fearful Gibeonites tricked Joshua by disguising themselves as people from a distant land, a people who would not therefore be under God's ban on treaties between Israelites and Canaanites[396].

- The terms suggested by the supposedly foreign Gibeonites involved their becoming servants of Israel. That treaty was made; but the deception was soon found out. Because of the ruse, the Gibeonites were indeed "cursed" by Joshua, and made servants to Israel – not only to serve the community at large, but *especially for serving the purposes of the Tabernacle* (specifically as woodcutters and water carriers)[397].

- Despite the Gibeonites' trickery, the treaty was legally binding in God's eyes. So when surrounding enemy Canaanites sought revenge on their prior ally, Gibeon cried out for help. And Israel came to Gibeon's rescue!

- This amazing irony of warfare and loyalty happened on the very day discussed just prior: the day when the sun and moon stood still. This unique day not only concluded the Israelite victory, but did so in a way that protected certain non-Israelites in binding covenant relationship with them and their God[398].

In this ancient story, we have a very unlikely underdog: a town-full of Canaanite people who, in view of many Biblical examples that we don't need to pursue here, practiced hideous acts that were profoundly abominable to God. But, they got the message: *the real God is taking over.* By trickery, they legally joined themselves to Israel in a perpetual service to them and, specifically, to God Himself.

God honored that binding agreement. And though the Israelites were initially infuriated by the deception, they later went to the Gibeonite's defense with all their might. In that battle the Lord upheld the covenant with these

---

[395] E.g., Exodus 23:28.
[396] Joshua 9. Note that "Canaanites" was not an ethnic group, but a general term applying to the many non-Israelite peoples then living in Canaan (Palestine).
[397] Joshua 9:23.
[398] Joshua 10.

Chapter 8: Tiara of Towns

"foreigner-Israelites," even to the extent that certain laws of nature were overturned in the battle that defended them[399].

If we want another example of how serious God was about this contract with the gentiles of Gibeon, we can fast-forward about two hundred years. The Gibeonites still retained this important role of Tabernacle service. But in huge ignorance and misdirected zeal (for his own domination, not for God), King Saul attempted to annihilate these very people[400]. Because of this, with regard to the binding treaty with Gibeon and their long and faithful service, the Lord brought three years of punishing drought to the *entire* nation of Israel[401]. Later, King David met with the Gibeonite survivors and worked out the recompense for them: the handing over, and execution of, seven of Saul's sons.

These stories show how real and sometimes violent can be the clash between the forces of God's redemption and those of the Enemy's destruction. At the same time, these are visceral reminders of just how committed God is to those who willingly enter covenant relationship with Him. With the events of Gibeon as a profound harbinger, those of us who are Gentiles can read with renewed appreciation the following:

> *Therefore, remember that formerly you who are* **Gentiles by birth** *and called "uncircumcised" by those who call themselves "the circumcision" (that done in the body by the hands of men) — 12 remember that at that time you were separate from Christ,* **excluded from citizenship in Israel** *and* **foreigners** *to the covenants of the promise, without hope and without God in the world. 13* **But now in Christ Jesus you who once were far away have been brought near through the blood of Christ. 14** *For* **he himself is our peace, who has made the two one and has destroyed the barrier, the dividing wall of hostility***, 15 by abolishing in his flesh the law with its commandments and regulations. His purpose was to create in himself* **one new man out of the two***, thus making peace, 16 and in this one body to reconcile both of them to God through the cross, by which he put to death their hostility. 17* **He came and preached peace to you who were far away and peace to those who were near.** *18 For* **through him we both have access to the Father by one Spirit.**
> Ephesians 2:11-18, NIV

Hallelujah! All of us "foreigner" believers are made full citizens of Israel. And with Israel's natural citizens, we are together being made "one new man" through Jesus-Joshua. When the Lord Saves, He will therefore save the entirety of Israel, including all "Gibeonites" who have become members of that first-

---

[399] That is, the battle referred to prior when the sun "stood still."
[400] 2 Samuel 21:2.
[401] 2 Samuel 21:1.

chosen nation: Gentiles who have entered into covenant relationship with Him. He will fight mightily for each of us, and save us in that final conflict of this age.

Given the history of this little town of Gibeon, we might expect a particularly large contingent of foreigners living here, just as in Biblical days. As we have seen, Gibeon will again be a priestly city of those serving the Temple; and we have also seen that certain Gentiles will also be called as priests[402]. As with no other city on God's Mountain perhaps, future Gibeon may well embrace a broad racial blend. Whatever the mix ends up being though, future Gibeonites will share a fascinating history and meaningful service towards "the meeting place" of God. All these priests and their families, of various nationalities and cultures, living in or near the ancient ruins now restored, will have many things to talk about.

Gibeon to Geba: Dwellings of Priesthood

As mentioned, a special trait of Gibeon is that it was designated for priestly families when Israel originally came into the Promised Land. Within the Sacred District is one more town so assigned to *"descendants of Aaron"* in Biblical times: Geba.

> *And from the tribe of Benjamin they gave them* **Gibeon**, **Geba**...
> *Joshua 21:17a, NIV (also 1 Chronicles 6:60a)*

Flanking the Temple on east and west then are *two* ancient sites dedicated to the priestly servants of the Lord.

Remember that the priests were themselves selected from the tribe of Levi, a tribe that, as a whole, was selected and "purchased" from all Israel by the Lord[403]. Recall also that though the tribe of Levi remains one of the original twelve tribes of Jacob, it was extracted for special service to the Lord[404]. So instead of having an "inheritance" of a tribal territory[405], God chose to intermix His ministers throughout all the tribes of Israel. Instead of giving them a huge land allocation clustered around the Tabernacle and (later) Temple region, He dispersed the chosen tribe throughout the chosen nation, giving the Levites specifically deeded towns and pasturelands – such as Gibeon and Geba.

---

[402] E.g., Isaiah 66:19-21.
[403] Numbers 3:12-13, 8:14.
[404] Numbers 1:49-50.
[405] Numbers 26:62; Josh 13:14, 18:7.

From the perspective of this special role[406] for which the tribe of Levi was extracted, one can say that those chosen families were "sprinkled" throughout Israel[407], perhaps analogously to how all believers are like "salt" that sprinkled throughout the entire world now[408].

From the fact that Levi is not assigned a province in the Millennial period[409], we can infer that their role, and their "sprinkling" throughout Israel in dedicated cities, will be reconstituted in that Day to come. These twin priestly cities of Geba and Gibeon represent two of the Levitical cities to be restored and given to that tribe in Messiah's day[410]. We therefore have independent confirmation of Ezekiel's prophecy that this northernmost portion is intended for habitation by priests (who are themselves Levites).

When the ruins of Gibeon and Geba are rebuilt under Messiah's rule, they will therefore be doubly associated with service to God: first, in their original and *renewed* role as Levitical cities; and second, in their being bounded within the northern Priestly region of the Sacred District.

It is interesting also that between Gibeon and Geba is the location of the Temple to come. To

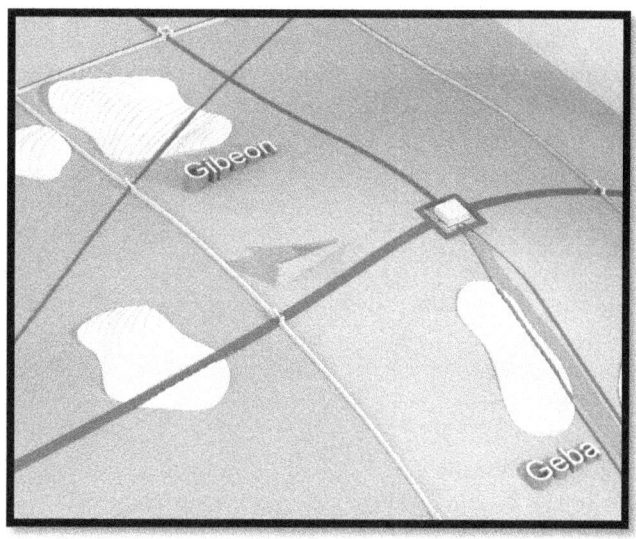

Figure 33: Gibeon to Geba

east and west of the Temple grounds, these resurrected towns will surely play prominent roles within the Priestly region of the Sacred District. Both will be home to many involved with Temple activities, where close proximity will be of

---

[406] Deuteronomy 10:8-9.
[407] Numbers 35:2-8.
[408] Matthew 5:13.
[409] As discussed in The Approaching Country.
[410] As the tribe of Levi is fully present in population (see Revelation 7:7), and in view of Levitical functions remaining in force (per Ezekiel), the ancient reconstitution of the Levitical city network is a straightforward explanation of why this tribe would not have a provincial territory allocated.

practical benefit. Further, these "twin" cities are natural foci for their respective east and west portions of the Priestly region, perhaps serving as centers of civic activity or logistical support of Temple provisioning on either side.

On a technical point, as mentioned in an earlier footnote, these diagrams roughly indicate where the ancient cities were, with shapes that are mere guesswork. When their ruins are unearthed and restored, the results will surely be much more detailed and interesting than what is illustrated here.

It is also important to understand that the restored walls and other architecture will first serve a memorial purpose, and not necessarily define the functional borders of the future towns. That is, future Geba and Gibeon may engulf quite large portions of the Priestly region, with their ancient ruins being smaller and specially preserved locales within each.

However arranged, Gibeon and Geba help us see that God's Temple will be literally surrounded by the dwelling places of those that serve Him. Ezekiel has shown that the homes of the priests and their families will reside throughout this northern subdivision. Yet with these two very ancient towns, and knowing now they will be restored (with homes, shops, walls, streets, etc.) for these very purposes, we gain a profound sense of the tangibility of these future residential surroundings.

Again, Gentiles will also be chosen to serve as Levites and priests here[411]. So while Levi was dispersed throughout Israel in ancient times, and as all believers are the "salt" of the entire Earth today, it is interesting that people from many nations will "sprinkle" the priestly population here!

Of course, the Lord will have many other non-priestly purposes for other believers, both Jew and Gentile. But no matter what those roles might be, or in what region of the world they will be enacted, all God's people will be welcomed into these precincts when they make pilgrimage. All will travel to this realm and joyfully participate [412] alongside those whose ministry revolves around the Temple, whose permanent residences are perhaps within Gibeon or Geba.

Whether in times ancient or present, the Lord's promises to Israel are inviolable[413], just as they are to all who are in relationship with Him through His Son[414]. Whether Jew or Gentile, and whatever our role in service to Him is, all in Messiah are assured:

> *...you will be for me a kingdom of priests and a holy nation...*
> Exodus 19:6b, NIV

---

[411] Isaiah 66:20-21.
[412] Zechariah 8:23.
[413] Romans 11:28b-29, NIV: *as far as election is concerned, they are loved on account of the patriarchs, for God's gifts and his call are irrevocable.*
[414] E.g., 2 Timothy 2:11-13.

> *But you are a chosen people, a royal priesthood, a holy nation, a people belonging to God, that you may declare the praises of him who called you out of darkness into his wonderful light.* **10 Once you were not a people, but now you are the people of God...**
> 1 Peter 2:9-10b, NIV

If any of these restored cities will speak to these mighty truths, surely the twin priest-cities of Gibeon and Geba, standing to either side of the Temple area, will do so. If we could touch their restored ruins, as people will in that Day to come, we would be touching proof of God's mighty plan, and how nothing was able to prevent its accomplishment.

Michmash: Hidden Cache

Geba will reside near the Temple River, on its southern side. If we were to cross that River, perhaps walking across a bridge over a deep chasm, we would find on the northern bank another ancient city: Michmash. In Hebrew, *Mikmac*[415] means 'hidden.' This ancient Biblical name is retained to this day, even in its Arabic place name: *Muchmas*. What mysteries are involved with this "hidden" place? Several.

Michmash wasn't a hugely significant town in the Biblical record. In fact, its very name implies relative insignificance when compared with towns named for their height (like Gibeah, Gibeon and Geba; more on that later). Michmash is infrequently referred to in the Bible; and when it is, not many major events of symbolic import jump out. There is an exception though. Long ago, when foretelling a vast invasion by enemies coming from the north[416], Isaiah said this:

> *...they store supplies at Micmash. 29 They go over the pass, and say, "We will camp overnight at Geba." Ramah trembles; Gibeah of Saul flees.*
> Isaiah 10:28b-29, NIV

In this rare specific referral to Michmash, we have a word play: the enemy is stashing their supplies in a place named for the idea of hiding or being hidden. In an initial fulfillment of this prophecy, the Assyrian army did indeed invade, and perhaps availed themselves of Michmash as a storage facility. But the attempt failed spectacularly[417], for the Angel of Lord destroyed that vast army

---

[415] Pronounced *mik-maws'*; Strong's OT:4363.
[416] A near-term interpretation of this prophecy relates to the Assyrian invasion of 701 BC; a far-term interpretation perhaps relates to the ultimate conflict between ungodly nations and Messiah to come, seen in Revelation 16:12-16 and elsewhere.
[417] Isaiah 36-37 (see also 2 Chronicles 32).

without any human assistance whatsoever. Here's another thing about the name *Michmash*. The word *mikmac* comes from the *kamac*[418], meaning "to store away" or "lay up in store." This root word *kamac* shows up only once in the entire Bible:

> *Is not this laid up in store [kamac] with me [God], and sealed up among my treasures? 35 To me belongeth vengeance, and recompence; their foot shall slide in due time: for the day of their calamity is at hand, and the things that shall come upon them make haste.*
> Deuteronomy 32:34-35, KJV

The above verses are part of the "Song of Moses" wherein the Lord Himself declares lasting victory over His enemies and those of His people, holding "in store" (*kamac*) for Himself certain *"treasures"* of *"vengeance and recompense."* One would not want to be on the receiving end of such "hidden" (*mikmac*) power, as the Assyrians were in 701 B.C. With that in mind, notice this interesting fact: that this same song will be sung by the Lord's people in the time immediately prior to the coming of our warrior-savior, Jesus-Joshua:

> *[They]* **sang the song of Moses** *the servant of God and the song of the Lamb: "Great and marvelous are your deeds, Lord God Almighty. Just and true are your ways, King of the ages."*
> Revelation 15:3, NIV

Just before that future singing of the Song of Moses, and similar to the ancient invasion, Jerusalem (and Israel as a whole) will again be threatened by an invading army. Yet the Lord's people will once more receive divine protection. Here are but a few proofs to that point, all set within the "apocalyptic" series of events:

> *On that day, when all the* **nations of the earth are gathered against her**, *I will make Jerusalem an immovable rock for all the nations. All who try to move it will injure themselves... 9 On that day* **I will set out to destroy all the nations that attack Jerusalem.**
> Zechariah 12:3 & 9, NIV

> **I will gather all the nations to Jerusalem to fight against it... 12** *This is the plague with which the LORD will strike all the nations that fought against Jerusalem...*
> Zechariah 14:2a, 12b, NIV

---

[418] Pronounced *kaw-mas*; Strong's OT:3657.

*Then the survivors from all **the nations that have attacked Jerusalem** will go up year after year to worship the King, the LORD Almighty, and to celebrate the Feast of Tabernacles.*
Zechariah 14:16, NIV

*And **when ye shall see Jerusalem compassed with armies**, then know that the desolation thereof is nigh.*
Luke 21:20, KJV

There are several takeaways in all this. Michmash, the "hidden" place, was once used to store and hide resources used in ancient times by the Lord's and Israel's enemies. In a time ahead, it may very well be used for the same purposes.

But the Lord had the upper hand then, and will also in the future. In the ancient past, when Assyria used this "hidden" place to stash their stores and munitions for their attack upon Jerusalem, the Lord Himself obliterated that army. In times ahead, another gathering of armies will attempt the same, though on a vastly larger scale. But once again, their human supplies – no matter where piled up, or how numerous, or how secret – will not stand against the Lord's *kamac*, that is, what *He* has stored up for *them*. Their hiding of weapons will be no match for God's *mikmac* stores of recompense, paying them what they will have earned.

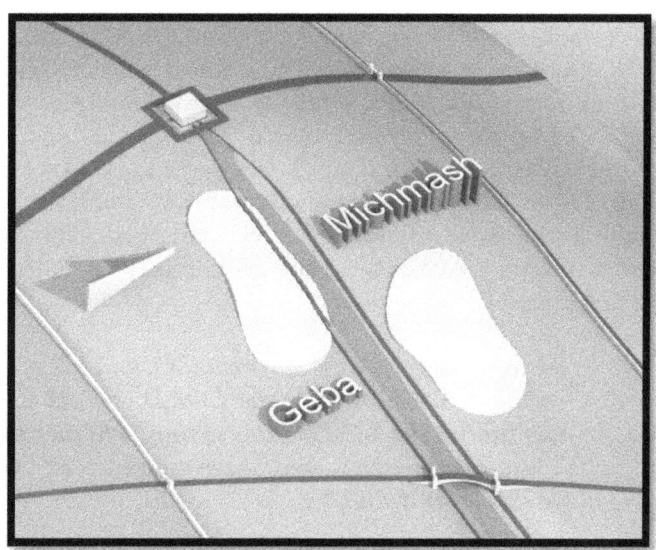

Figure 34: Geba and Michmash

So though Michmash is not Biblically great in an outward historical manner, its restoration and subtle meanings will not be lost to perceptive visitors in the Day of Messiah. The message will be clear: mankind may, for a time, hide away their energies and resources against the Lord and His people. But the overarching answer will be equally clear: that His sometimes hidden and always limitless energy and love will bring about salvation on the one hand, and *justice* on the other.

Geba & Michmash: Pillars of Grandeur

When viewed as a pair, the cities of Geba and Michmash share their own unique story. It involves one of the most astounding factual accounts in human history of God-inspired bravery and God-enabled victory, all in the face of apparent impossibility[419].

A deep, steep-walled valley exists between these two sites, both today and in ancient times. And though much eroded now, in Biblical days there were two steep and high cliffs on either side. This is the setting of our final stories about the Temple's neighboring cities.

Once upon a time, two lightly-armed men of Israel stood on the south side of this valley, while a heavily-armed contingent of the Philistine army encamped on the north side. One of the two men was Jonathan, son of Saul; and he dared to go up and attack that larger force. But Jonathan, best friend of King David, faced insurmountable odds in thinking he could take on the Philistine garrison atop the other cliff. Inspired with the Lord's overarching power though, Jonathan acted upon a sure foundation of faith. With his servant, Jonathan bravely took action:

> *Jonathan said to his young armor-bearer, "Come, let's go over to the outpost of those uncircumcised fellows. Perhaps* **the LORD will act in our behalf. Nothing can hinder the LORD from saving, whether by many or by few."** *7 "Do all that you have in mind," his armor-bearer said.* **"Go ahead; I am with you heart and soul."**
>
> *1 Samuel 14:6-7 NIV*

The story goes on to tell how Jonathan and his armor bearer attacked the far greater enemy forces, and had complete victory. The message for us is obvious: *"by many or by few,"* God can act with and through us; and He assuredly *will*, if we are "fighting" in line with His purposes. It doesn't matter how dark and thorny our present situation is, how big the enemy, how deep the chasm separating the position of fearful need from that of shining victory. Jonathan and his brave and trusting armor-bearer understood; and with their tremendous story, we are invited to bridge similar chasms in our lives today. Geba-Michmash is an excellent metaphor for these truths.

Back to geography. A chasm remains between Michmash and Geba, stemming from near Ramah and proceeding roughly eastward. Here's that scene as described in Jonathan's (and David's) time:

---

[419] 1 Samuel 14:1-15.

> *On each side of the pass that Jonathan intended to cross to reach the Philistine outpost was a cliff; one was called **Bozez**, and the other **Seneh**. 5 One cliff stood to the north toward **Micmash**, the other to the south toward **Geba**.*
> *1 Samuel 14:4-5, NIV*

Michmash and Geba, and the chasm that separates them, are places we can locate on a map. The following figure[420] shows the dividing valley running vertically, with the north-to-south direction running left to right. Erosion and earthquakes have occurred with this terrain over the intervening 3,000 years, and at least this author cannot pinpoint how those cliffs correspond with today's topographic features. But, we can get at least a general idea.

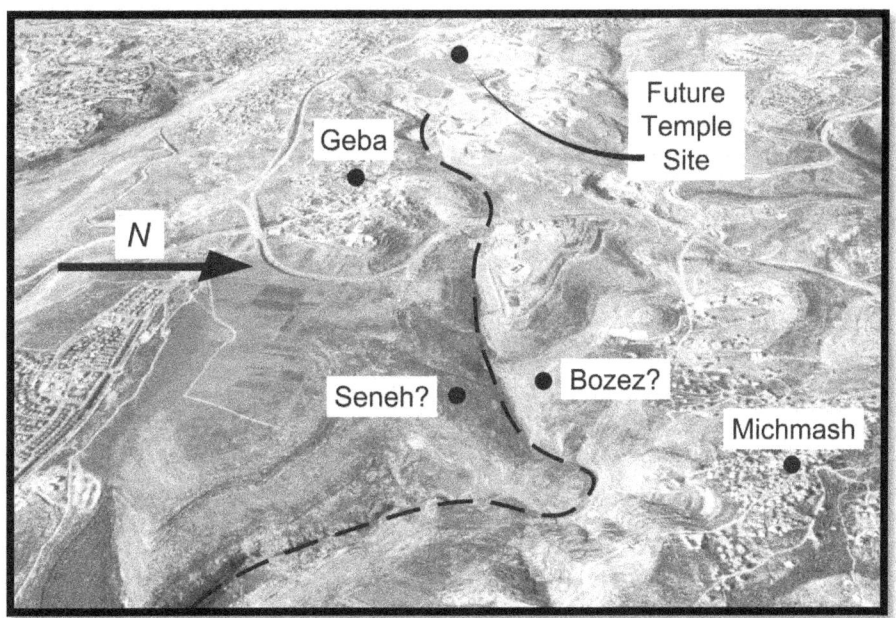

Figure 35: Seneh and Bozez, Looking East

With Jonathan's story we see an important link between these ancient cliffs on either side of the valley. On the south side was the one named *Seneh*, its name referring (literally) to the thorny acacia plants which grew in that vicinity. This was the place from which Jonathan yelled out his challenge to the Philistines – and knew that God would be with him.

---

[420] Background image ©2015 DigitalGlobe™ via GoogleEarth™, accessed 29 October 2015, <http://www.google.com/earth/index.html>. Overlaying graphics applied by author.

On the north side was the cliff named *Bozez*, a name that means "shining." It was the one that better caught the sun, while its twin, Seneh, remained in comparative shadow[421].

From the personal-faith-analogy viewpoint, yes, we prefer the *Bozez*, the bright and shining side of the story in all our conflicts. But the victory and story wouldn't be complete without the dark and thorny *Seneh* beforehand. For it is not our strengths and personal "weapons" that will ultimately win the day, but the Lord's power that is "stored" (*kamac*) and hidden (*mikmac*) on our behalf, even if hidden from our eyes. For as Jonathan said, *"Nothing can hinder the LORD from saving, whether by many or by few."*

There is another component of this story for us, and for those visiting the area in Messiah's day. These twin cliffs of Bozez and Seneh stood in ancient times as geological sentinels on either side of a great chasm. Now, we have seen that another east-west chasm will be present here in Messiah's day, originating from the same area – that is, from the peak upon which the Temple will stand, forming a great valley through which the mighty Temple River will flow.

The corresponding location of these valleys, ancient/present and the one in the future, is surely not a mere coincidence. After the great coming geological upheavals are completed, the "pillars" of Bozez and Seneh may well be present once more as pronounced features of the terrain. If so, these twin peaks will again testify to the Lord's enablement and protection of those who remain bravely faithful to Him.

But there is one final point of significance to add here. This literal geography to come takes on special meaning if we look back at Solomon's Temple, for which the Millennial Temple is the far-surpassing structure. In the former, two gigantic and lavishly decorative pillars stood to either side of its eastward-facing door. So important were these pillars that they were given names: one was *Jakin* ("he shall establish"), the other *Boaz* ("in it is strength"[422]). Why would the Bible make sure we know the names of those pillars of the Temple? And why would it do the same, indicating the names of those cliffs to either side of the river flowing eastward from the coming Temple? A likely answer is that *Seneh* and *Bozez* may well stand due east before the Temple's eastern gate[423], serving as two enormous and natural "pillars."

---

[421] Per the ISBE, topic of "Bozez":"It [Bozez] catches the sun during most of the day, while the southern cliff is in the shade. To this circumstance it may owe its name, 'shining.' 'The contrast is surprising and picturesque between the dark coal color of the south side, and the ruddy or tawny tints of the northern cliff, crowned with the gleaming white of the upper chalky strata. The picture is unchanged since the day when Jonathan looked over to the white camping ground of the Philistines, and Bozez must have then shone as brightly as it does now, in the full light of an eastern sun.' "

[422] 1 Kings 7:21; 2 Chronicles 3:17.

[423] The Biblical Temple is always oriented toward the east, not the north. In fact, that is the vector by which we refer to things eastward, that is, "oriental": "to orient [verb] was

The significance in these "cliff-pillars" would be two-fold: that the Lord works through and on behalf of those who act on faith in Him, in spite of the odds. This is what Jonathan was doing. But now we have a second meaning, in the Lord affirming to us that only in Him is strength, only in Him will our lives be firmly established. Thus in tomorrow's landscape, these twin cliffs of Bozez and Seneh may become the analogues to the twin Temple pillars of Boaz and Jakin, massive geological witnesses to the establishing strength of God Almighty.

If, in the future, we were to visit Geba or Michmash, we would find in them two ancient towns restored and very inhabited. If standing at Geba, we would see Michmash on the other side; and vice versa. Perhaps there will be a bridge between the two cliffs of Seneh and Bozez, or at a location nearby, and a main highway conveyed by it. Regardless, the peaks will stand to either side of the deep valley through which the Temple River will flow. Because of this River, boisterous greenery and life-giving trees will grow on either side. Especially perhaps for what was once dark and thorny *Seneh*, the horticultural transformation will be breathtaking.

When standing on one cliff or the other, people will grasp the profound meaning of the rock they stand upon, and the final meaning of these ancient high places. Only in the Lord will we gain final victory. Only in the Lord will we gain our strong foundation. Only in the Lord will we become ourselves a "pillar" for His eternal purposes[424].

A Threefold Exaltation

Triad of Heights

We have explored three towns surrounding the coming Temple site, and all of them are good "resurrection" candidates under Messiah's restorative work. Forming an almost cross-like pattern, these ancient cities have practically identical names: Geba to the east, Gibeah to the south, and Gibeon to the west.

The reason these places sound the same is because their names all derive from the same Hebrew word: *gibh`ah* (or *gib`ah*), meaning 'hill'[425]. Nowadays we don't usually see hills named simply "Hill." But in ancient Israel, that kind of

---

originally to make something face east (to the Orient), especially a church". Roget's New Millennium™ Thesaurus, First Edition (v 1.3.1). Lexico Publishing Group, LLC. 19 Nov. 2007.
[424] "*Him who overcomes I will make a **pillar** in the **temple** of my God*" (Revelation 3:12, NIV).
[425] From the ISBE, topic of "Hill": *gibh`ah*, from a root meaning "to be curved."

basic naming often took place. These three ancient towns therefore received a fairly pragmatic name meaning "hill" or "high place."

It is interesting though that this most basic naming ("hill") happened three times in the same small region of our exploration. Is there some significance to this? And is there some additional meaning to "hill" and "high place" here? Yes indeed, there is.

As a bit of background, consider the typical Biblical hills, in the period of time after the conquest of the Promised Land, but before the Exile[426]. Elevated places were important vantage points for military purposes. But generally speaking, during this monarchical period of the Israelites, "high places" were associated with one thing: idol-worship. The prior inhabitants, the Canaanites, had employed these heights for sacrifices to Baal and Ashteroth (a.k.a Ishtar, Astarte, Ashtoreth). The ever-present temptation for the Israelites was therefore to give in to these false deities of nature and honor them on the loftier patches of real estate.

Foreseeing such disastrous behavior, the Lord strongly warned His people to not follow such practices of the Canaanites[427]. Yet Solomon, the son of David and wisest man (except Jesus) who ever lived, disobeyed here. For on a hill east of Jerusalem (most likely the Mount of Olives), to satisfy some of his foreign wives, Solomon set up worship places for the gods of surrounding nations[428].

Things went decidedly downhill from there, to the point where *every* high place in Israel and Judah was utilized for idolatrous practices[429]. Israel came to a low point of practicing the same idolatry as the peoples they had "righteously" driven out. In those days, when a person in ancient Israel encountered a hill, it is a good bet that the place was employed for idol worship and its often despicable activities of sacrifice.

With all that as ancient background, let's shift gears and look forward to the Messianic era where we see three key places literally named "high place": Geba, Gibeah and Gibeon. Each has been associated with serious idolatry in the past. Yet the coming Temple will be at the center of these sites. When their ruins are restored, what additional messages might be proclaimed in this regard?

One clear meaning will be that the lofty Temple peak will stand as the *only* and *ultimate* place at which to honor the one true God; for all other "gods" are nothing. These three surrounding peaks, though places of false worship in the past, will therefore "bow" to the Mountain of God. Their idols will be forgotten in the brilliant light of The Almighty; their topographical *gibh`ah* will proclaim honor to the Chief of all Mountains.

---

[426] That is, before the Assyrian and Babylonian captivities.
[427] E.g., Deuteronomy 12:2.
[428] I Kings 11:4-8.
[429] E.g., 1 Kings 14:23; 2 Kings 17:11; Jeremiah 2:20, 3:5; Ezekiel 6:13.

Humbled and Cleansed

But there is more to it. The proximity of these ancient "high places" bears another clear message, proclaiming that the ancient idolatries will be utterly cleansed and forgotten.

> *"This is the covenant I will make with the house of Israel after that time,"* declares the LORD. *"**I will put my law in their minds and write it on their hearts.** I will be their God, and they will be my people. 34 No longer will a man teach his neighbor, or a man his brother, saying, 'Know the LORD,' because they will all know me, from the least of them to the greatest,"* declares the LORD. *"**For I will forgive their wickedness and will remember their sins no more.**"*
> Jeremiah 31:33-34, NIV

With Jeremiah's prophecy we see a coming time when even the thought of following after a false god will simply not occur in the hearts of His people. With the law (literally, *Torah*) written upon their hearts, the people of Messiah will worship the true God and Him alone, and in every place: even every "high place" such as Geba, Gibeah, and Gibeon.

As we have seen, these three towns will play practical roles for Levites and priests in Temple service. No longer stained with memories of ancient idolatry, these three *gibh`ah* will speak loudly of God's holiness and utter forgiveness, being major hubs of activities in His honor.

Let's talk about the general terrain involved with these three ancient hills and cities. It has been emphasized that certain prophecies underscore the idea of lofty elevation throughout the Sacred District, yet with the Temple at the apex:

> *In the **last days** the **mountain of the LORD's temple** will be established as **chief among the mountains**; it will be **raised above the hills** [gib`ah], and all nations will stream to it.*
> Isaiah 2:2 NIV (also Micah 4:1)

Recall also that "*Jerusalem will be raised up and remain in its place*[430]," and yet be lower in elevation than the ("very high mountain") peak upon which the Temple will reside [431]. So after all these divine actions of terra-forming are complete, and this arrangement is the result, what will have become of the three hills of Geba, Gibeon and Gibeah? Will they remain visible as distinct hills? We

---

[430] Zechariah 14:1b, NIV.
[431] Ezekiel 40:2.

have seen good symbolic messages arising if that becomes the case; yet there seems to be one clear prophecy saying otherwise:

> ***All the land shall be turned into a plain** from **Geba** to Rimmon south of Jerusalem. Jerusalem shall be raised up and inhabited in her place from Benjamin's Gate to the place of the First Gate and the Corner Gate, and from the Tower of Hananel to the king's winepresses.*
> Zechariah 14:10, NKJV

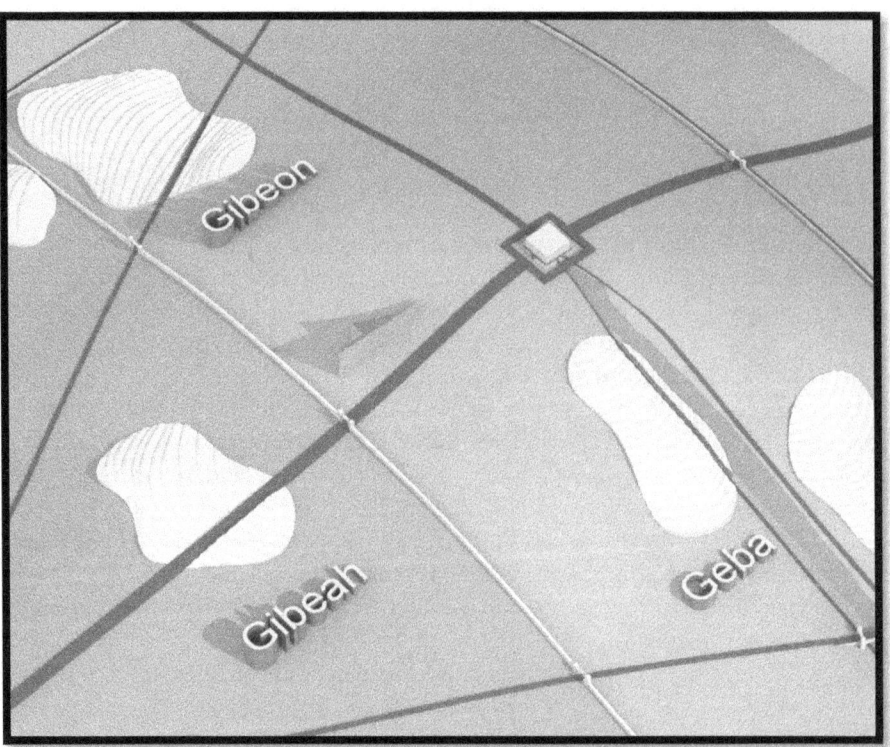

Figure 36: The Three Exaltations

With Geba as the cited example, all "high places" from here southward will be generally smoothed out. The three sites of Geba, Gibeon and Gibeah will therefore see their elevations comparatively lowered – that is, in comparison with the peak of the Mountain upon which they will reside – and their environs made like "a plain." Still, there is reason to anticipate some relative elevation to these sites, like humps on the larger mountainside, to set their *tels* apart from the surrounding landscape and otherwise identify where they were.

No matter what will be their final elevation though, all three of these high points named "Hill" will be "humbled" and made to geographically "bow" to the "Chief of the Mountains." Through Geba, Gibeon and Gibeah, all ancient "gods" worshipped on them, and by extension all others of the world and throughout all time, will bow to the One Almighty God. It is His mighty Temple that will stand high above all other "high places." And it is to the Lord alone that these ancient surrounding elevations, in their very names, will declare: *Exalted! Exalted! Exalted!*

The Defining Apex

As we sum things up, we should add to our list of Geba, Gibeon and Gibeah the town Mizpah, for its name means "tower" – clearly a term also denoting height. When their ruins are restored, these four ancient high places will probably not be very much higher than their immediate surroundings. If their elevation raises them somewhat above their environs, it will be to God's glory, toward purposes of His choosing. So in their time of "humbling," none of these place names will be bragging about the grand loftiness of their owners.

Still, these titles will continue to convey *height*, announcing the idea of loftiness: "hill," *gibh`ah*, or "tower," *mizpah*. If these names no longer illustrate their own cities, what will the repeated proclamation of loftiness refer to? What will their names describe, if not the cities themselves? Just this: the most exalted place on Earth to come, the holy summit of God's Mountain. These former "high places" will ascribe the meaning of their names to the sacred Mountaintop upon whose eastern, southern and western slopes they will reside.

Thus the Temple will have a "crown" of three hill-cities surrounding it, each declaring by their identity: Highest! Lofty! Exalted! In application to their new setting, these ancient names will shout: Highest is the Chief-Mountain of God! Lofty is the place of His dwelling! Exalted is our Lord God Almighty!

Mizpah will add her voice as well. For example: The Lord is *"my high tower, and my deliverer"*! (Psalms 144:2b, KJV). Standing on either side of the Temple River, the twin cliff-pillars of Seneh-Jakin and Bozez-Boaz may well arise anew to announce: He shall establish! In Him is strength! Also, let us not forget Michmash: In Him is hidden power! And Bethany: In Him is joyful life! All these places will declare the loftiness, sovereignty and love of the Lord Almighty.

From east, west and south, the ancient sites will declare His honor from all directions[432]. In their restored ruins, in their renewal of residences and vibrant life, in their very names, all these settings will uniquely shout their praises to our Lord. If we were standing near the Temple like Ezekiel did, we could look downward upon all of this. Foremost in our sight would undoubtedly be the City,

---

[432] Figuratively speaking, there need be no north represented here: for God *is* the North, as seen in Psalms 48:2.

which is of course what that prophet wrote of. But surrounding the Temple area, like jewels in a crown, there will be all these others. They will tell stories of God's lofty faithfulness, His towering strength, and His soaring glory.

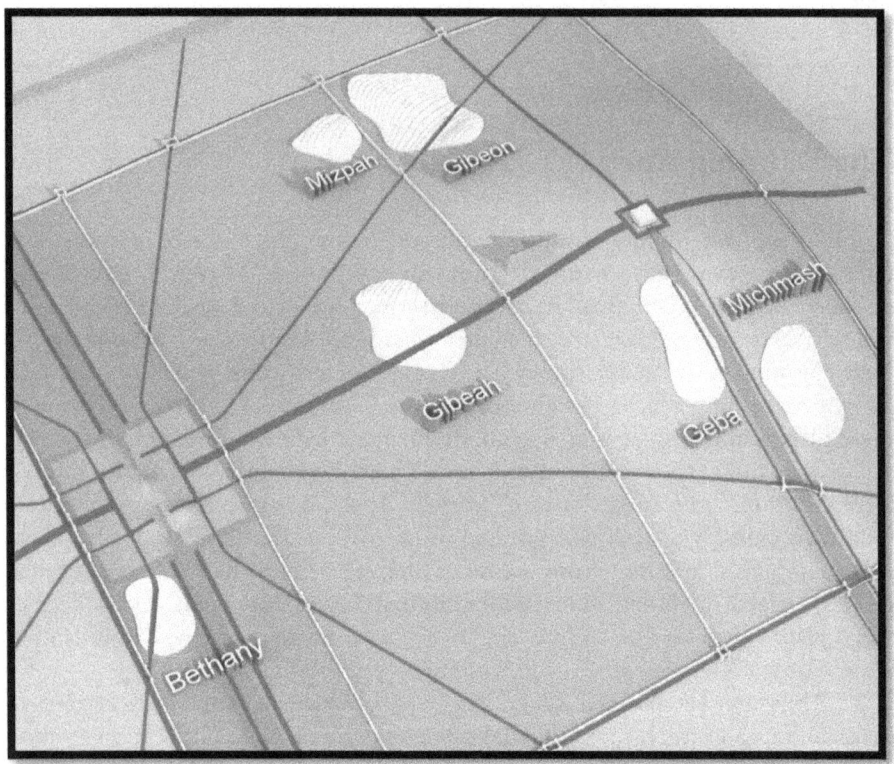

Figure 37: Key Towns of the Sacred District

In regard to such declarations, one final thought. Jesus once said that if His disciples were prevented from praising Him as the promised Messiah, the very *"stones will cry out"*[433]. And in a very meaningful sense, in a day soon to come, *these very stones will arise to do so.*

---

[433] Luke 19:40.

Chapter 9: Mountain of Joy

For the Lamb at the center of the throne will be their shepherd; he will lead them to springs of living water. And God will wipe away every tear from their eyes.
Revelation 7:17, NIV

On this mountain he will destroy the shroud that enfolds all peoples, the sheet that covers all nations; 8 he will swallow up death forever. The Sovereign LORD will wipe away the tears from all faces...
Isaiah 25:7-8a, NIV

...all nations will stream to it. Many peoples will come and say, "Come, let us go up to the mountain of the LORD..."
Isaiah 2:2b-3a, NIV

The desert and the parched land will be glad; the wilderness will rejoice and blossom. Like the crocus, it will burst into bloom; [the land] will rejoice greatly and shout for joy.
Isaiah 35:1b-2a, NIV

Focus of the World

We come at last to the spiritual and geographic focal point of the Sacred District: the apex of God's future Mountain, the most important mountaintop in any age of this planet. We have explored its surroundings and hiked its slopes several times and from many viewpoints. Now, standing once more at this high place and feeling its breezes, we will try to hear some of the marvelous stories whispered to us beforehand, and sense the Life that will soon radiate from here.

One kind of story involves perceptions, past, present, and future, about the Temple's coming location. It is a story of great contrasts. True, when Zion is made "chief of the mountains" in the sight of all nations[434], there will be great joy for the entire Earth[435]. But before then, especially in view of where it will be, this focus of attention will not always have been positive – in the ancient past, and especially in the present day. So let's take on a few of these controversies surrounding the new Temple's locale, and see how this center of world attention will change from sad or angry to joyful and grateful.

Controversies in the Past

Ezekiel's vision of the relocated Temple might have provoked some heated discussion among his original audience. For one thing, the new location is far from Jerusalem, about five miles north of where the First Temple stood. In fact, as we have seen, the coming site is back near where the *Tabernacle* last functioned! So Ezekiel's words may well have been unsettling for at least some folks, for the new Temple would not be built on the hallowed site of the one planned by David and built by Solomon, the mighty Temple that had just been destroyed[436]. It would not be a resurrected continuum of that holy facility, but an entirely new and different one.

Moreover, the new site appeared to be well within the territory of Benjamin (as its borders were defined back in the prophet's day). It would no longer be contained within the tribe of Judah, that of King David and his son Solomon. At least some people may have been quite alarmed by such a "transfer"

---

[434] Isaiah 40:5, with context.
[435] E.g., Psalms 48:2, 67:4.
[436] Ezekiel was exiled to Babylon in the same series of events in which the Temple and Jerusalem were destroyed by Nebuchadnezzar (587-6 B.C.), receiving his prophetic messages afterward.

of Temple site from one tribe to another, especially since Judah was always the "ruling" tribe from the beginning[437].

But the coming reality resolves all such ancient objections. Just as the primary place of worship was, in David's day, moved from the Tabernacle's location (Gibeon) to Jerusalem, this next relocation indicates the same idea of freshness. Rather than covering up the destruction and sadness of what came before, for all versions of the historical Temple, this new locale represents moving on to the next setting for, the nest sequential step in, God's special "cohabitation" with His human children.

As for which tribe is foremost, the coming boundaries of Israel's provinces reveal further originality to God's program. Ezekiel revealed that the City and Temple will not reside in any of the tribal provinces, but within a whole new kind of province: *the Prince's*. So instead of "belonging" to one tribe or another, the Sacred District will rest upon land literally owned by God, within property specially given for the Father's glory by the Prince-King and His people[438]. And if some remain perplexed about Judah's "ruling" status no longer being the case, even this transition was declared long ago:

> The **scepter will not depart from Judah**, *nor the ruler's staff from between his feet*, **until he comes to whom it belongs and the obedience of the nations is his.**
> Genesis 49:10, NIV

In Messiah we clearly have the "He" to whom the scepter and staff ultimately belong. So the new Temple, and even Jerusalem, will no longer reside within the borders of Judah[439], but be in the Prince's land and within the Sacred District He gives to the Father.

This striking new arrangement will be free of tribal favoritism, being equally available to all tribes of Israel. Furthermore, it will be accessible to all peoples and "tribes" of mankind, to all that come to this Mountain to honor the One True God and seek the guidance of His Son.

Conflict in the Present

If the ramifications of Ezekiel's Temple location were controversial in ancient times, they are downright explosive in our day. The coming Temple site

---

[437] Genesis 49:10, echoed in Psalms 60:7.
[438] Ezekiel 45:1-8.
[439] In another sense though, the scepter will indeed remain with Judah: for Jesus, of course, is Himself a descendent of that patriarch.

coincides with the modern town of A-Ram, an area of heated anti-Israeli conflict. There is another modern city nearby, Ramallah. This A-Ram–Ramallah region lies within the Palestinian-controlled "West Bank" region, with Ramallah being the administrative headquarters of the Palestinian National Authority[440], and the location of the tomb of Yasser Arafat. This is *not* Israel's territory today, by any stretch of the imagination.

Evidence of strife here isn't hard to come by. The comparatively small site of ancient Ramah lies near the end of a runway of Jerusalem's Atarot Airport, which was closed in 2001 because of Palestinian hostilities[441]. Nearby A-Ram lies just on the other side of the security wall separating the West Bank and Israel, and constituting a huge point of contention between the two peoples.

Clearly, the geographic position of the coming Temple is presently a politically charged place! But though the conflicts in the area run deep and vigorous now, we can know for certain that all will be resolved and healed when the Prince of Peace reigns from Jerusalem, and God Almighty's "house" stands in this very locale. For God will make this a place of worship for *all* nations[442]; and His human embodiment[443], Jesus-Yeshua, will bring true peace to *all* nations[444].

Looking forward to that time we can also know that, even before the revealing ("apocalypse") of Jesus as Prince-King, portions of "*every nation, tribe, people and language*[445]" will have gladly submitted themselves to His rulership. This means that even people from Palestine and other Arabic regions and countries will be among those raised back to life on this present Earth[446], to live peacefully and joyfully under the Lord's wisdom and sovereignty.

Today though, the situation could not be more contrasting. Yes, the area is a focal point of the world, but because of the deep fear that things could explode at any moment. This potentiality affects all peoples of the earth, and especially those living near the prophetic epicenter of Jerusalem and the coming Temple. So we see a huge gulf between what presently exists at the ancient site of Ramah and what will develop there in the future. But with this bleak landscape as the backdrop, the Lord will perform marvelous things and bring glorious works to light – to the benefit of *all* nations, and the joy of *all* peoples.

---

[440] Ramallah "currently serves as the de facto administrative capital of the Palestinian National Authority (PNA)" (Wikipedia.com, article "Ramallah," accessed 12/10/15).
[441] Specifically, the "Second Intifada," when the Palestinians revolted against Israel once again.
[442] Isaiah 56:6-7, with verse 7 quoted in Matthew 11:17.
[443] E.g., John 1:14; Colossians 2:9.
[444] E.g., Isaiah 9:6-7.
[445] Revelation 7:9, NIV.
[446] Revelation 20:4.

*'I will shake all nations, and **the desired of all nations will come**, and I will fill this house with glory,'* says the Lord Almighty.
Haggai 2:7, NIV

*Then **this city will bring me renown, joy, praise and honor before all nations on earth** that hear of all the good things I do for it; and they will be in awe and will tremble at the abundant prosperity and peace I provide for it.'*
Jeremiah 33:9, NIV

All nations will come and worship before you, for your righteous acts have been revealed.
Revelation 15:4b, NIV

O let the nations be glad and sing for joy: for thou shalt judge the people righteously, and govern the nations upon earth. *Selah.*
Psalms 67:4, KJV

In Jesus, the blessing of Israel will become a blessing to all nations[447]. Under His reign Jerusalem, and the Temple, will become the focal point of joy for the entire world.

Exaltation in the Future

Many times in our investigations we have seen that Biblical place names are marvelously significant. We have also seen that, even after thousands of years, modern names often echo their Biblical counterparts. And here, at the apex of God's Mountain, these two phenomena are very much at work. We have already seen the "exalting" names of the surrounding Biblical towns. But here at the location of the coming Temple, there is one more ancient site to explore. Its significance is also very great, but in ways much different than its neighbors.

The modern (yet old) town of A-Ram is close by the ruins of the very ancient city of *Ramah*[448]. It is easy to hear the linguistic connection: A-Ram, and

---

[447] E.g., Genesis 26:4, 18:18; Psalms 72:12; Galatians 3:8.
[448] From the ISBE, topic of "Ramah": "Eusebius... places Ramah 6 Roman miles North of Jerusalem; while Josephus (Ant, VIII, xii, 3) says it lay 40 furlongs from the city. All this points definitely to identification with er-Ram [A-Ram]. The modern village crowns a high limestone hill to the South of the road, a position of great strength." Please note however that the center of the site of ancient Ramah, as portrayed in figures here, should be considered as only approximate.

its larger and more modern neighbor Ramallah[449], have names reverberating with that of their ancient counterpart. So let's explore Ramah, and see what stories might inform the final stages of our journey.

In view of the great tensions here, and the frequent disdain for archeological concerns in the region, the site of ancient Ramah seems a forlorn place without much hope for any kind of revival. In stark contrast though, we see an astounding outcome that few residents there (or anywhere else, for that matter) can even begin to imagine. For in the Day to come, Ramah will be raised as the joyful focus of not merely "Palestine," but the entire world. Ramah will be the location of the breathtaking Temple, the mighty dwelling place of The Name[450]. The result will be a prevailing and global focus upon this very place, a centering of world attention foreseen in many passages.

> *On this mountain* **the LORD Almighty will prepare a feast of rich food for all peoples**, *a banquet of aged wine — the best of meats and the finest of wines. 7* **On this mountain he will destroy the shroud that enfolds all peoples, the sheet that covers all nations...**
> Isaiah 25:6-7, NIV

> **And foreigners who bind themselves to the LORD to serve him, to love the name of the LORD, and to worship him**, *all who keep the Sabbath without desecrating it and who hold fast to my covenant — 7* **these I will bring to my holy mountain and give them joy in my house of prayer.** *Their burnt offerings and sacrifices will be accepted on my altar; for* **my house will be called a house of prayer for all nations.**
> Isaiah 56:6-7, NIV

> *And as he [Jesus] taught them, he said, "Is it not written:* **'My house will be called a house of prayer for all nations'?"**
> Mark 11:17a, NIV

> *And many* **peoples and powerful nations will come to Jerusalem to seek the LORD Almighty** *and to entreat him.*
> Zechariah 8:22, NIV

> *In the last days* **the mountain of the LORD's temple will be established as chief among the mountains**; *it will be raised above the hills, and* **all nations will stream to it. 3 Many peoples will come and say, "Come, let us go up to the mountain of the LORD, to the**

---

[449] With the extra syllable ("al") added to "Ramah," *Ramallah* (per some sources) means "height of God."
[450] E.g., Deuteronomy 12, 14, 16.

house of the God of Jacob. He will teach us his ways, so that we may walk in his paths." The law will go out from Zion, the word of the LORD from Jerusalem.
Isaiah 2:2-3, NIV; also Micah 4:1-2

Though ignored now, peoples of the entire world will gratefully and eagerly "lift up," in their hearts, this very location. Already uplifted in a literal topographic sense, all nations will exalt in praise this coming peak of God's Mountain. The geographic feature itself will, of course, not be the thing worshipped, nor even the Temple. God will have raised this place for His glory; His Name and special Presence will dwell here. And it is He alone, God Almighty, Father, Son and Spirit, Who will be worshipped in this most unique place.

When speaking of the coming geological Mountain of God, we must also keep in mind the figurative "mountain" that has been, and will continue to be, raised by the Father: His own Son. For because of Jesus' earth-shaking work throughout the world, He is likened to this very Mountain of God.

> *...and* **the stone** *that smote the image* **became a great mountain**, *and* **filled the whole earth**... *44 And in the days of these kings shall the God of heaven set up* **a kingdom, which shall never be destroyed**: *and the kingdom shall not be left to other people, but it shall break in pieces and consume all these kingdoms, and it shall stand for ever. 45 Forasmuch as thou sawest that* **the stone was cut out of the mountain** *without hands... the great God hath made known to the king what shall come to pass hereafter: and the dream is certain, and the interpretation thereof sure.*
> *Daniel 2:35, 44-45, portions, KJV*

In a very real sense, Jesus is our Rock; and He *is* the "mountain" that will "fill the whole Earth." The arising Mountain of God therefore will, in a very dramatic and physical way, symbolize the Son of God. From ancient and desolate Ramah, the peak of this new Mountain will visibly arise, its message plain for all to see.

Source of Healing

As we conclude our expedition, here at the very top of God's coming Mountain there is one last ancient city to visit. Like those explored earlier, this town will have its own important dramas involved. We've identified it already as Ramah; and when we understand what that place symbolized, we can see that truly amazing stories will resound when it becomes the site of God's "House." If we listen closely, we can get a sense of those future stories even now.

Most Exalted Center

Ancient Ramah already lies on high ground, roughly at the same elevation as modern Jerusalem. In the time to come though, with its location corresponding with that of the Temple, it will be dramatically raised above the City[451]. So like its neighbors, Ramah will be raised in elevation. But unlike them, her location will become the highest peak by far.

Having seen that those ancient neighbor-cities "exalt" God's Mountain in their very names, we would not be surprised if Ramah did the same. And in actual fact, it does! For the word *ramah*[452] derives from *ruwm*[453], meaning "to lift up" or "to exalt." So once again, the ancient name describes not only the physical situation in past and present, but also its dramatically lofty circumstances in the future. Though surrounded by towns shouting "high!" with their similar-sounding names, Ramah will do the same, but in a completely unique way.

Drying of All Tears

Biblical stories surrounding this town are not, however, as cheerful as all that. Ramah is not mentioned many times in the Bible, and when it is, the association is generally *not* with a sense of exaltation or happiness of any kind. Instead, Ramah's Biblical memorial bears quite the opposite messages.

> *They* [the invading Assyrians] *go over the pass, and say, "We will camp overnight at Geba."* **Ramah** *trembles; Gibeah of Saul flees.*
> Isaiah 10:29, NIV

> *Sound the trumpet in Gibeah, the horn in* **Ramah**. *Raise the battle cry in Beth Aven; lead on, O Benjamin. 9 Ephraim will be laid waste on the day of reckoning. Among the tribes of Israel I proclaim what is certain. 10 Judah's leaders are like those who move boundary stones. I will pour out my wrath on them like a flood of water.*
> Hosea 5:8-10, NIV

---

[451] E.g., Ezekiel 40:2, and as discussed elsewhere.
[452] Strong's OT:7414.
[453] Strong's OT:7311.

Both passages bore painful tidings indeed for the ancient Israelites. True, that doesn't make Ramah unique, for most towns of Israel and Judah were decimated with invasions of Egyptians, Assyrians and Babylonians[454] at one time or another. But in all those examples of utter destruction by other peoples, it was Ramah that became particularly known as a place utterly stricken by sorrow.

> *This is what the LORD says:* **"A voice is heard in Ramah, mourning and great weeping, Rachel weeping for her children and refusing to be comforted, because her children are no more."**
> *Jeremiah 31:15, NIV*

We need to understand what was happening here, for this verse seems to set the stage for Ramah's coming pivotal role. Reading Jeremiah 31 from the beginning shows that overwhelming catastrophe has befallen Israel at the hand of a foreign empire, resulting in the deep and unrelenting grief of verse 15. The horrific event referred to is, in fact, the invasion of 586-7 BC when Nebuchadnezzar destroyed the Temple and Jerusalem, forcing the exile of most remaining Jews to Babylon.

Keeping that disaster in mind, there is another "target event" for prophetic fulfillment, a *second* catastrophe that occurred centuries later than the first. Jeremiah's prophecy of Ramah was also applicable to the slaughter of infants in Bethlehem and its environs by Herod, in that evil king's endeavor to slay the new-born Messiah.

> *Then what was said through the prophet Jeremiah was fulfilled:* 18 **"A voice is heard in Ramah, weeping and great mourning, Rachel weeping for her children and refusing to be comforted, because they are no more."**
> *Matthew 2:17-18, NIV*

Two events of tremendous grief, separated by almost 600 years, are given the identical description: Ramah's mourning, and Rachel's grief. We will come back to Rachel in a moment, but for now we can see that Ramah was a place directly affected by at least two hideously murderous events. Between Nebuchadnezzar and Herod, Ramah became known for weeping over her slain children; and her grief is perhaps figurative for all such calamities befalling Jacob's descendents, regardless of era.

Jeremiah 31 has, however, its most complete outworking in a time yet to come. This is easy to see in its numerous details requiring the onset of the Messianic setting. Without question, there has been foreshadowing in the deeds

---

[454] Not to mention invasions of smaller neighboring nations, e.g., the Philistines, Ammonites, Edomites, Moabites, etc.

of Nebuchadnezzar and Herod. Yet the passage clearly shows the events of "the Ramah verse" (31:15) as just prior to the "Day" of the Lord, when Messiah returns. In that time ahead, "Ramah" may again depict the same town site or area, or it may be prophetically-figuratively applied to something quite larger[455]. Either way, there is a future and third application to these sad events.

Fortunately though, the story prophesied for Ramah doesn't at all end on this painful note. If one continues to read Jeremiah's prophecy in its entirety, truly marvelous outworkings emerge in a wonderful setting that hasn't yet come about. Jeremiah 31 brings overarching hope that the Lord will indeed establish His Kingdom on Earth in the spiritual, physical, and political senses[456]. It furthermore holds forth many tangible details of Israel coming into long-promised blessings.

With that future and hopeful outworking in mind, we can extract many poignant facts from Jeremiah 31. We see that in a future time, Israel will:

- ☐ Have been scattered to the "distant coastlands" (v10)
- ☐ Have once more gone through "the desert," yet have found God's favor while doing so (v2,3)
- ☐ Be rescued from stronger, oppressive nations (v11,16)
- ☐ Be gathered "from the ends of the earth" (v8,17,23)
- ☐ Be returned to their (originally-assigned) towns (v21)
- ☐ Have forever behind them all events that might "uproot and tear down, and to overthrow, destroy and bring disaster" (v28, also 29-30)

As a result of all this, the mourning of "Ramah" (perhaps now applying to all Israel, and all God's people in Messiah) will be no more! Unlike the sad events of ancient times, Ramah's coming trials will be quickly followed by the Lord's salvation and comfort. Jeremiah elaborates on the joyful conditions to follow, for Israel will:

- ☐ Be like a joyful virgin, singing, dancing and shouting before the Lord (v4,7,12,13)

---

[455] When the third application of Jeremiah 31:15 fulfillment occurs, we should expect the disquiet to be felt not only within Israel proper, but all peoples that have joined with her in covenant relationship with God Almighty, through the Lord Jesus (e.g., Galatians 4:26; Ephesians 2:19, 3:6; Colossians 1:21-22; Hebrews 12:22).

[456] Jeremiah 31 is also quoted extensively in Hebrews 8:8-12, showing that the prophesied covenant to be made with mankind is through God's Son, Jesus the Christ (Messiah). Even so, Jeremiah did not stop with describing Jesus' redemptive acts in the first century, but proceeded to describe circumstances of His coming reign over this world.

- ☐ See agricultural prosperity throughout, in the southern region of Judah (v24) and also the northern tribal regions (v5,12)
- ☐ Desire, and be able, to come to Zion to worship the Lord, even from the far northern tribal provinces (v6)
- ☐ Be the "foremost of the nations" (v7)
- ☐ Have lands noted for "streams of water" (v9; cf v12)
- ☐ Be especially loved and protected by God (v1)
- ☐ Find fullness of rest (v2)
- ☐ Be called God's "firstborn" and "dear" son (v9,20)
- ☐ Have God as protector, "like a shepherd" (v10)
- ☐ Receive "comfort and joy instead of sorrow" (v13)
- ☐ Be rewarded with prosperity (v14,16)
- ☐ Have fully enabled and satisfied priests (v14)
- ☐ Be firmly "planted" and "built up" (v27,28)
- ☐ Participate fully in the "new covenant," one different from that of Moses (v31-32)
- ☐ Have God's Law written upon their very hearts (v33), to the extent that no rote memory via strict teaching is necessary (v34)
- ☐ Bring satisfaction to God, their sins remembered no more (v34)

In this very context Jeremiah goes on to mention several things we have already examined. When all these amazing events are brought to pass, God will also establish His "sacred mountain" (v23). The City of Jerusalem will be rebuilt, with certain of its ruins being restored (v38-39). The great City will "never again be uprooted or demolished" (v40); and in its entirety, it will be considered as "holy to the Lord" (v40). Surely an entire book could be written about Jeremiah 31!

Our purpose here though is to better understand the coming Mountain of God, and to see why ancient Ramah is associated with its very peak[457]. So as a summary, in a time yet to come, this forlorn place will be lifted up in a way like no other, becoming the peak of God's arising Mountain and the very site of God's future Temple. In utter contrast with all her times of downtrodding and woe, Ramah's experience will finally and completely match her name: *"exalted."*

---

[457] Regarding the following figure: background image ©2015 DigitalGlobe™ via GoogleEarth™, <http://www.google.com/earth/index.html>, accessed 27 October 2015. Overlaying graphics applied by author.

Chapter 9: The Healing Summit

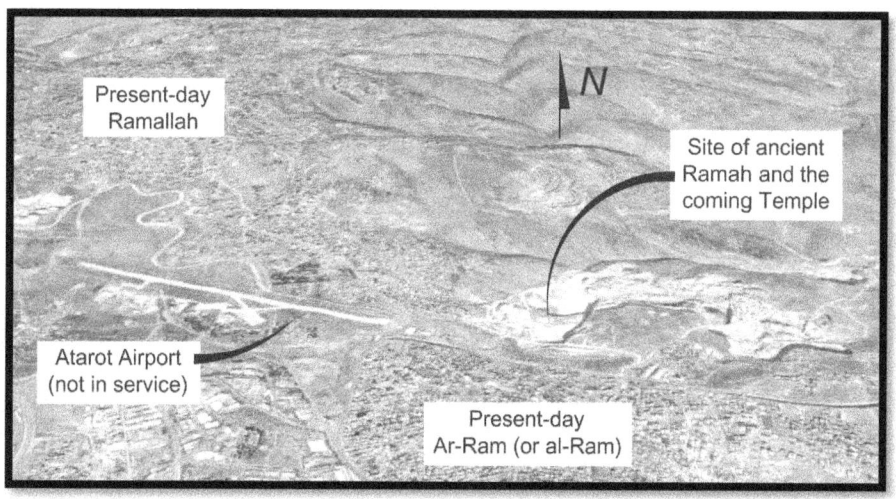

Figure 38: A-Ram / Ramah Area

Again, the town of Ramah can be seen as a metaphor for all Israel and all God's people who have undergone great suffering. Yet we can know without question that the promised Son of David, the only begotten Son of God, will return. In that day, the Prince-King will heal the sorrows of all His people, no matter how deep and ancient the wounds.

> *For **the Lamb** at the center of the throne **will be their shepherd**; he will lead them to springs of living water. **And God will wipe away every tear from their eyes.***
> *Revelation 7:17, NIV*

But the prophecies go even further. For when we look at the passage quoted in the above verse, we find this:

> *<u>**On this mountain**</u> he will destroy the shroud that enfolds all peoples, the sheet that covers all nations; 8 **he will swallow up death forever. The Sovereign LORD will wipe away the tears from all faces; he will remove the disgrace of his people from all the earth.** The LORD has spoken. 9 In that day they will say, "Surely this is our God; we trusted in him, and **he saved us.** This is the LORD, we trusted in him; let us rejoice and be glad in his salvation." 10 <u>**The hand of the LORD will rest on this mountain**</u>...*
> *Isaiah 25:7-10a, NIV*

In the day of the Prince, the tables will be turned: ultimate grief will meet ultimate comforting. And this coming healing will have a source: *"this mountain,"* the coming Mountain of God. From here, the Lord will fulfill all His promises to wounded Ramah, that is, all Israel, all His people. Pains experienced in the near past, and even in deep and ancient history, will be healed and forever forgotten.

Ramah was once the greatest symbol of deep anguish, of weeping. But Ramah will be transformed into greatest symbol and source of comfort, the *place of drying of all tears.*

Healing of Rachel

Let's return to that important verse written by Jeremiah (and quoted in Matthew 2:18).

> *This is what the LORD says:* **"A voice is heard in Ramah, mourning and great weeping, Rachel weeping for her children and refusing to be comforted, because her children are no more."**
> *Jeremiah 31:15, NIV*

What is this connection with "Rachel"? There is only one Rachel in the Bible, and she was not only the most favored wife of Jacob, but she bore two sons to him. One son, Joseph, was one of Jacob's greatest sons, becoming eventually two tribes (Manasseh and Ephraim), while Benjamin became the father of the tribe bearing his name. Such wonderful outcomes!

But, unlike what one might at first think from Jeremiah 31:15, *Rachel never saw her sons die.* So, again, why the connection with that woman? And why would she be symbolic of a mother anguishing over her children's death? The truth is that there is more than at first meets the eye here. So as we come to the end of our expedition, let's understand the mourning of this ancient matriarch. For the link between her, and God's coming mountaintop, will demonstrate further why Ramah is the chosen site for the Temple of our God.

Jacob-Israel was the father of all the tribes of Israel, and Rachel was the most beloved of his four wives. In fact, Jacob had to work for years to gain her hand in marriage[458]. From then on, the story of Rachel[459] is a colorful one, involving her lingering issues with idolatry[460]. But the bigger problem was that she was unable to bear children for Jacob – even while his other three wives did with apparent ease.

---

[458] Genesis 29.
[459] Genesis 29,30,31,33,35.
[460] Genesis 31:19 ff.

By God's intervention, however, she gave birth to Joseph[461], who remains in many ways emblematic of Messiah, the great Savior of the people. As the boy grew, Rachel observed his prophetic gifts, and that he was the favorite son of his father. Because of this, she also knew that Joseph was in danger from his older brothers[462], and that there were serious life-and-death threats ahead for him from his own family. In fact, if Rachel would have lived to a normal age, her fears would be seen as well-founded: for Joseph was tormented and sold into slavery by his half-brothers.

But Rachel did *not* live long. For in the process of giving birth to her second son, Benjamin, Rachel faced *her own* death[463].

As she lay dying, Rachel knew that the baby she was bringing into the world would face the same fraternal hatreds as Joseph. Even though God Himself had miraculously enabled her to bear children, Rachel did not know if her sons would survive the animosity of their half-brothers[464]. With the birth process that was bringing about her own death, Rachel couldn't even know if Benjamin would live at all.

After years of longing for Jacob as her husband, and many more years hoping to bear him sons, Rachel only knew one thing for sure at this point: that she would never see either son grow into manhood; that they might not survive long at all. Facing not only her own death, but also that of the children she had hoped for all her life, the woman's torment was surely indescribable.

So as Jacob-Israel's beloved left this world, perhaps we can get a dim sense of the agony she experienced. We can understand why she would name her second son Ben-Oni, meaning: "son of my trouble." And with that naming, and in that bleak moment, Rachel died.

But thank God, that is *not* the end of Rachel's story! Let's agree that this low place of misery forms an impressively dark backdrop to the Lord's brilliant love and healing touch. Indeed, we see God's comfort in this very story, as He helped heart-broken Jacob do something very profound and foretelling. For while still deeply grieving himself, the patriarch buried his beloved in a place associated with Ramah[465], building a "pillar" there to her memory. Though the

---

[461] Genesis 30:22-24.
[462] Rachel was apparently still alive to witness the violent reaction to Joseph's dream (and coat) in Genesis 37, for verse 10's reference to Rachel wouldn't make sense otherwise.
[463] Genesis 35:16-18.
[464] Genesis 37.
[465] Tradition (and a modern mosque) places Rachel's tomb near Bethlehem (south of Jerusalem), nowhere near Ramah (north of Jerusalem). However, based on the Biblical narrative, there is plenty of room for disagreeing with this traditional location. Rachel died after she and Jacob had just moved southward from Bethel, but while quite a distance from Bethlehem (Genesis 35:16), yet still "on the way to" that town (Genesis 35:19). Ramah is centered between Bethel and Bethlehem (though slightly towards Bethel), and therefore fits the Genesis description perfectly. Though the point does not

memorial is no longer evident today, it remains in Scripture, allowing us to appreciate what Jacob and Rachel went through as God used them to commence a nation for Himself.

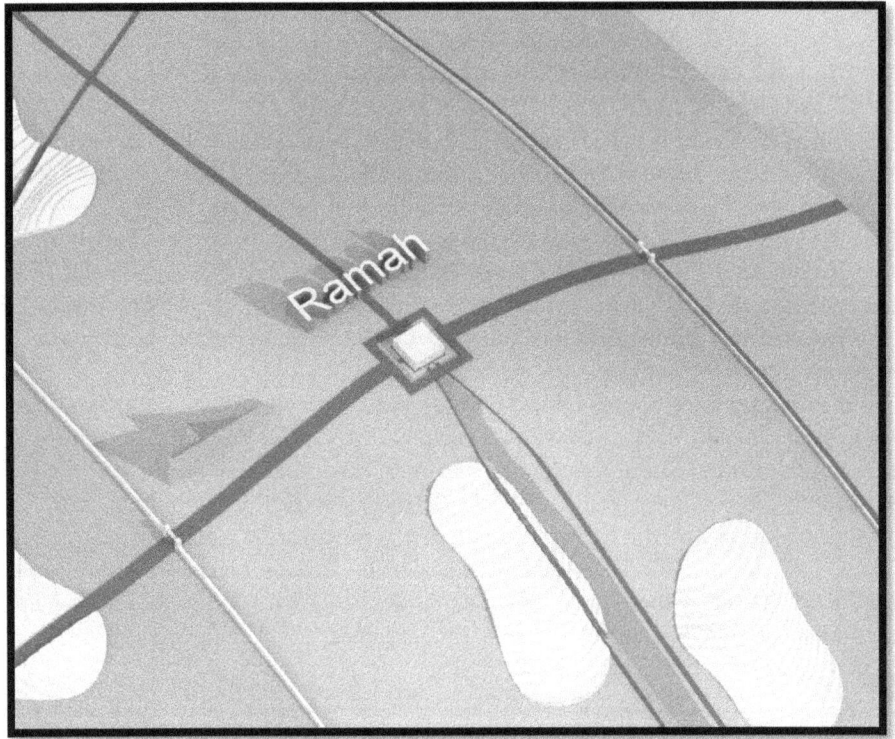

Figure 39: Ramah and the Temple Peak

While the actual stonework of Jacob has long since disappeared, perhaps it is on God's list of "ruins" to resurrect when the Son of *His* right hand, Jesus, reigns as King here. If the Lord so chooses to raise Jacob's pillar to Rachel, it may very well be near or within Ramah, and therefore near the Temple grounds.

Be that as it may, Jacob-Israel's monument foretells, in a way, of God's healing and honoring of *His* "wife[466]," that is, all His people, all Israel. He will

---

affect things greatly in our study here, Rachel's burial place may indeed have been in Ramah, adding to her significance in the story.
[466] E.g., Jeremiah 3:20; Ezekiel 16:32.

build His own eternal monument, a City that is actually called "the Bride[467];" and lofty indeed will its towering walls be, as high as they are broad[468].

Before that eternal City comes, its forerunner in *this* creation must arise: Jerusalem, residing on the southern ("right hand") slope of God's Mountain. Ezekiel described it as having twelve gates named for the twelve tribes of Israel, all arranged in the same square pattern as its eternal City-counterpart described by John[469]. For these reasons, future Jerusalem will presage God's final monument to His "bride" Israel. Perhaps this fact will remind visitors of the monument that Jacob-Israel built for his beloved Rachel; and in so doing, remind everyone of the Lord's healing of his bride, His beloved people[470].

Of course, God has long since healed the hearts of Rachel and Jacob, a loving couple that He used so mightily in His story. And now, Ramah's exaltation will be a crowning joy for them, as they and all our forerunners in faith look on from Heaven. Ramah of old corresponds with Rachel's (and all Israel's) anguish; and Ramah's exaltation will declare her complete and final healing.

Son of the Right Hand

But Rachel's story has another amazing outcome to disclose, and again it stems from what Jacob did immediately after her death. Though Rachel named her second son *Ben-Oni* as she was dying, Jacob immediately renamed him *Ben-Jamin*, which means "son of my right hand[471]." Thus, in name, the "son of tribulation" became the son of strength and dominion.

An important outworking of this prophetic renaming is seen in Messiah's Day, with Ezekiel's foretold arrangement of the tribal provinces. When someone stands upon the peak of the Mountain and faces east toward the sunrise, which of Jacob's sons has his province lying directly to the south, to the "right hand"? Is it Judah's, who was always in that position before? No, it is Benjamin's! *Benjamin, the youngest, will be the "right hand" tribe.*

This reversal of tribe positions might remind us of Jacob switching hands while blessing Ephraim and Manasseh[472]. We can also see in this a visible symbol of what Jesus foretold: that the last will be first[473].

So Rachel's second son not only survives, but receives the best position of honor – just like her first son eventually did, but now far more so. The youngest

---

[467] Revelation 19:7, 21:2.
[468] Revelation 21:16.
[469] Revelation 21:12-13.
[470] Revelation 7:17.
[471] Genesis 35:18.
[472] Genesis 48.
[473] E.g., Matthew 20:16.

son of Israel will be the most honored; and *Ben-Oni*, "son of tribulation," will literally become *Ben-Jamin*, "son of my right hand."

From her home in Heaven, Rachel will see these things and be overjoyed. In the very place associated with her crying and dying, the Lord Himself will wipe away every tear from the eyes of His children. And from this place will radiate His healing and comfort to the entire world.

Though representing the direst grief that a person might experience, Ramah will become the epicenter of God's joy. Having only experienced agony in the past, this place named for "exaltation" will find her name fulfilled at last. The Earth beneath will arise, exalting Ramah as the place of the Father's House. And the memorial to Rachel and her mourning will become the focus of celebration for all her "children," all God's people.

Pinnacle of Creation

On many occasions we have seen that the Mountain of God will be the focal point of the coming world, the "pinnacle" of glory and attention. We have also seen that it will be "exalted" not only in symbol, but in literal height as well[474]. The "chief" of all mountains is the coming centerpiece of the world, and from more than one perspective. In this last stage of our journey we will, from several of points of view, consider how "great" God's Mountain will be.

Mountains' Chief

We will first take the physical viewpoint. That is, in regard to elevation, to what degree will God's Mountain be raised? How "exalted" a peak will it be in geographic reality? One way to tackle this question is to start with Jerusalem's current elevation, and work from there.

- ☐ Jerusalem presently resides at an elevation of about 2,400ft (732M). In the Day to come it will remain in its horizontal position; but it will be raised significantly from its present height[475]. As pointed out earlier, Ramah resides at this same approximate elevation.

- ☐ Jerusalem's raising must be significant enough for God to have pointed it out to us. So for the sake of argument, let's say that a

---

[474] E.g., Isaiah 2:2; Ezekiel 40:2; Micah 4:1.
[475] Zechariah 14:10.

25% increase in elevation might satisfy this prophecy. That would be an extra 600 feet (183M), with the resultant elevation being 3,000ft (914M). *It may well be far greater*, but let's call this a reasonable minimum for discussion.

- From this hypothetical elevation of 3,000ft for the City there will be a pronounced upward slope to the Temple peak, steep enough for Ezekiel to describe the peak as "very high" relative to Jerusalem. Again, for the sake of argument, let us pick a comparatively modest slope of 1:20. This is steeper than the steepest permissible wheelchair ramp in the US (1:12), but not so steep as to require stairs.

- Over the distance involved (5.7 miles between City center and Temple center), a 1:20 slope would equate to an elevation change of 1,500 feet (467M) above Jerusalem, or 4,500 feet (1,372M) above sea level.

We will use this number of 4,500ft as a hypothetical and reasonable minimum elevation, solely for argument's sake[476].

At this height the Temple Peak would indeed rise as "chief" above its ancient mountain neighbors. This is important, in view of the Biblical conflicts with neighboring nations (along with their highest mountains, which often symbolized them). The increase in elevation from 2,400ft to 4,500ft would dramatically illustrate God's ascendency over those nations, displaying His victory over their ancient (and perhaps modern) animosities toward Him and His people. For example, Edom's Mount Seir[477] is around 3,700ft. This elevation would be easily surpassed by God's Mountain, leaving the enemy-mountain[478] symbolically and comparatively humbled.

So let's next talk about the world's mountains in general. Our hypothetical elevation is not nearly as high as Everest, or K2, or any number of the tallest peaks today. As a point of reference, Everest is about 29,000ft (8,840M). So, here's a big question: Will the coming "chief of the mountains" (as Isaiah and Micah describe it) literally rise to a higher elevation than any present-day mountain? Will the Temple area (Ramah) be raised to over ten times its current elevation? A reasonable answer would be: Not necessarily, for the basic reason that "chief" can be taken in the sense of "rulership." And since Jesus will reign

---

[476] This number is nothing more than hypothetical. The actual elevation could obviously be quite greater, especially from some texts that seem to indicate a more substantial slope than 1:20.
[477] Ancient Mount Seir is located south of the Dead Sea, in the country of Jordan.
[478] E.g., Ezekiel 35:2-3.

as King of all kings and all other earthly rulers, His Mountain will have "dominion" and "chiefdom" over theirs as well, pure and simple.

For Israel's neighbors though, there are at least two good reasons why a literal topographic ascendency is in view. First, because of the technical matters of relative elevation we just examined. Second, because of so many prophecies regarding God's coming victory over Israel's tormenting neighbors. For example, the Bible records no ancient score to settle with, say, California's Mount Whitney. But it most certainly does with Edom's Mount Seir, one that will be settled with Messiah's coming[479].

For neighbors then, there are special properties to the prophetic drama. But for all other mountains of the world, we probably would not want to say that God's mountain will be literally elevated above their present elevations. A 30,000ft elevation at Ramah would be pretty disruptive for practical reasons; one of them being that Jerusalem will be a place of broad and potentially navigable rivers[480]. That's hard to picture, if its countryside were practically vertical and its waters tending toward a frozen state.

Having said all that, the "chief mountain" title still does *not* preclude an *actual* and *comprehensive* outworking as well. So to be thorough in our exploration, we should consider how a natural elevational superiority might come about. For starters, we know already that the same terra-forming that elevates God's Mountain will drastically affect all others. Here are several clear declarations of these massive events occurring just before, or during, the Lord's return.

> *I looked at the mountains, and they were quaking; all the hills were swaying... before the Lord, before his fierce anger.*
> Jeremiah 4:24,26b, NIV

> In my zeal and fiery wrath I declare that at that time there shall be a great earthquake in the land of Israel. 20 The fish of the sea, the birds of the air, the beasts of the field, every creature that moves along the ground, and all the people on the face of the earth will tremble at my presence. **The mountains will be overturned**, the cliffs will crumble and every wall will fall to the ground.
> Ezekiel 38:19-21, NIV

> The sky receded like a scroll, rolling up, and **every mountain and island was removed from its place.**
> Revelation 6:14, NIV

---

[479] As just one example of many, see Isaiah 63:1-6, keeping in mind that Mount Seir is emblematic of Edom (Genesis 32:3, 36:8, and onward).
[480] Isaiah 33:20-21.

> *Then there came flashes of lightning, rumblings, peals of thunder and a severe earthquake.* **No earthquake like it has ever occurred since man has been on earth***, so tremendous was the quake… 20* **Every island fled away and the mountains could not be found.**
> Revelation 16:18, 20, NIV

Despite these upheavals, even in the midst of them, God will encourage His people:

> **Therefore we will not fear, though the earth give way and the mountains fall into the heart of the sea, *3* though its waters roar and foam and the mountains quake with their surging.**
> Psalms 46:2-3, NIV

These explicit prophecies point toward a singular series of events where *all* the mountains of the earth will be affected by severe quaking, with a correspondingly violent impact upon the world's oceans[481]. The results are described in terms of removal, overturning and sometimes even complete obliteration of certain mountains on both land and in the sea (that is, islands). It is therefore safe to say that a general *lowering* of the Earth's mountains will be the norm, and God tells us why:

> *The Lord Almighty has a day in store for all the proud and lofty, for all that is exalted (and they will be humbled)…14 for* **all the towering mountains and all the high hills*…* 17b the Lord alone will be exalted in that day***…*
> Isaiah 2:12,14, 17b NIV

Of course, that is the point: *"the Lord alone will be exalted in that day."* Creation itself, and as a whole, will bow to its Creator – mountains and all. Though His Mountain may likely not be the highest ever, we can say that it *will* be literally elevated above *many* high places as measured even today. And since today's peaks will be *greatly* lowered, the physical superiority of the "Chief Mountain" may well be far more pervasive than we might first think.

Let's apply all this to one example: Mount Hermon, residing on the present border between Israel, Syria and Lebanon. It is actually a cluster of peaks, one of them being the highest within modern Israel[482]. The uppermost of all

---

[481] Recall Jesus' declaration, describing events just before His return: "*… nations will be in anguish and perplexity at the roaring and tossing of the sea*" (Luke 21:25b, NIV).

[482] From Wikipedia.org, topic of Mount Hermon (accessed 12/2/15): "A peak in this area rising to 2,236 m (7,336 ft) is the highest elevation in Israeli-controlled territory."

Hermon's peaks is 9,230ft (2,814M)[483], over twice the conservative estimation for the coming Mountain of God (given earlier) of 4,500ft (1,372M). This area marked the northernmost point of Israel's original conquest[484], when they took Hermon from the Amorites[485]. But that people (and their idolatrous practices) remained an ongoing dilemma for Israel[486], with difficulties to follow with the ancient Sidonians, Lebanese, Assyrians, and all others who took ownership of that mountain. Fast-forwarding to today, it goes without saying that modern Syria and Lebanon, having claims to portions of Hermon, present contemporary conflicts for Israel as well. So Hermon remains a pretty solid candidate for prophesied geographic humbling.

In short, Mount Hermon's current 9,230ft high point will most likely be greatly lowered. At the same time, God's Mountain will be greatly raised. As a reminder, the coming Mountain may easily be raised far higher than what has been conjectured. One way or another then, God's Mountain will rise above this high place where Israel meets her ancient neighbors to the north. And what is the present-day name of Mount Hermon, in Arabic? *Jabal Ash Shaykh*, or *"mountain of the chief"* [487]! Even so, a coming Mountain on the horizon will "subdue" Mount Hermon, and arise as "Chief" over even this towering mountain. And that is just one mountain-story-example.

When the ascending of God's Mountain takes place, will the result be natural obliteration? With the revealing ("apocalypse") of our Lord, when the earth quakes, the seas roar, islands disappear and land elevations are radically altered, will what follows be chaos and darkness? No, just the opposite!

> *This is what the Lord Almighty says: 'In a little while* **I will once more shake the heavens and the earth, the sea and the dry land. 7 I will shake all nations, and the desired of all nations will come, and I will fill this house with glory,'** *says the Lord Almighty. 8 'The silver is mine and the gold is mine,' declares the Lord Almighty.* **9 'The glory of this present house will be greater than the glory of the former house,'** *says the Lord Almighty. '***And in this place I will grant peace,'** *declares the Lord Almighty.*
> Haggai 2:6, NIV

God has long ago declared that the "shaking" will be absolutely necessary. Yet the same prophecies show that, afterward, He will usher in the healing era of

---

[483] From <http://www.newworldencyclopedia.org/entry/Mount_Hermon>, accessed 12/2/15.
[484] Deuteronomy 3:8.
[485] Deuteronomy 3:8.
[486] E.g., Judges 1ff.
[487] Encylopedia.com, topic of "Hermon, Mount" (accessed 12/2/15).

His Son's brilliant kingdom. The arising Mountain, the place of the Father's "House," will radiate His glory and receive the world's willing and heartfelt praise. It will stand visibly high for all to see, loudly declaring the Lord's ascendency over His creation and His wise dominion over all of it.

Nature's Zenith

Another way to describe the coming Mountain's greatness is in regards to physical well-being. From here, and through His Son, Father-God will bring healing at so many levels: to the nations in general, to His "first-born" nation Israel, and to individuals that truly seek Him. Scriptures abound with hopeful details on these matters; and because of the focused nature of our expedition, we have addressed only a few aspects. Whatever the area of need though, this place will be the center and apex of all true avenues of remedy and health.

But there remains another form of healing we must touch upon more. It relates to a sphere of life that existed before mankind came on the scene, yet it has suffered greatly because of human occupation ever since man's original sin. This injured realm is Creation itself. Though God's job for our earliest ancestor was to work the garden and take care of it[488], and though this objective has never been recalled, the natural realm has been tremendously wounded from the Curse, then the Flood, and ever since. Without question, a vast amount of curative intervention is needed at every natural level, all the more so after the prophesied events preceding Messiah's appearing [489]. And here, in the story of God's Mountain, we also have the story of Creation's coming healing as well.

When the holy Presence radiates from His Mountain, it will be with the same glory and power that brought nature into being. When the Creator-Son resides as King over this world, He will personify the same Wisdom that designed all forms of life. Absorbing all this divine light first hand, nature will accordingly resonate. Creation will thrive in a manner unlike anything witnessed since Adam and Eve.

Speaking of our initial forebears, let's try to appreciate the abject hobbling of creation that directly resulted from their sin, via the great Curse levied in consequence.

> *To Adam he said, "Because you listened to your wife and ate from the tree about which I commanded you, 'You must not eat of it,'* **Cursed is the ground** *because of you; through* **painful toil you will eat of it all the days of your life.** *18* **It will produce thorns and thistles for you**, *and you will eat the plants of the field. 19* **By the sweat of your brow you will eat your food.**

---

[488] Genesis 2:15.
[489] Revelation 6-19, and the numerous prophecies in the First Testament describing "the Day of the Lord."

Genesis 3:17-19a, NIV

Prior to that time things had been easy in the food department, for Adam and Eve were vegetarian [490], and fruit, grain and vegetables grew prolifically without much intervention on their part. But ever since, the environment itself has been cursed. Creation was greatly wounded then, brought low from its intended and initial conditions. And to this day it anticipates the time when the curse is removed and the children of God reign with His Son.

> *The **creation waits in eager expectation for the sons of God to be revealed**. 20 For the **creation was subjected to frustration**, not by its own choice, but by the will of the one who subjected it, in hope 21 that the **creation itself will be liberated from its bondage to decay** and **brought into the glorious freedom of the children of God**. 22 We know that the whole **creation has been groaning as in the pains of childbirth right up to the present time**.*
> *Romans 8:19-22, NIV*

These verses really explain the story: that all botanic life, including grasses, bushes, shrubs, vines, flowers, succulents, trees, everything, was subjected to the overarching curse upon this natural realm. This will only be lifted when God's children, walking and breathing people like you and me, are revealed with Messiah, when He comes. And a "revelation" it will indeed be: for the same word *apokalupsis*[491] is used for the revealing to this world of the "sons of God" as well as of Jesus[492]. The "apocalypse," the *real* one, is what Creation is longing for.

So we can say for a fact that the removal of the curse and curing of creation will start when the Creator comes to govern it, bringing His healed people to reign with Him[493]. During His rule the wonderful results will continue to grow and be increasingly evident, for:

> ***For he must reign until he has put all his enemies under his feet.***
> *26 The last enemy to be destroyed is death.*
> *1 Corinthians 15:25-26, NIV*

The final eradication of death – affecting all "kingdoms" of nature – comes after the conclusive Millennial "day" is concluded, when Death – right

---

[490] Interestingly, only after the Flood were people permitted by God to eat animals in addition to plants (Genesis 9:2-3).
[491] Strong's NT:602.
[492] In Revelation 1:1, where *apokalupsis* refers to our Lord, and His revealing to this world.
[493] E.g., Revelation 20:6.

after Satan – is itself sentenced to eternal death[494]. Beforehand though, creation will have been "liberated from its bondage to decay" when Yeshua and His people are revealed on this earth, in glory, and in charge.

How awesome will it be when the soil is no longer impaired, but instead promotes botanic life in a manner not seen since Adam and Eve? How amazing will the crops be, when no longer fettered by the mysterious inhibitors of the curse (and also our chemicals in the soil, water and atmosphere), and simply explode with fruit, grain, and vegetables? How fun will it be to gather those crops when there are no weeds or thorns or poisons anywhere? How helpful will it be when the food is available without overly strenuous effort in tilling, planting, watering, or harvesting, and at all times of the year? And how astounding will it be to discover and partake of entirely new kinds of plant-based foods that haven't existed since Adam and Eve left Eden?

But beyond food, and food-producing grasses and vines and shrubs and other plants, let's talk about the biggest item: trees. We have already seen proof of an entirely new species of tree growing to the north and south of the river flowing from the Temple, and that these trees will have spectacular features.

> ***Fruit trees of all kinds*** *will grow on both banks of the river.* ***Their leaves will not wither, nor will their fruit fail. Every month they will bear,*** *because the water from the sanctuary flows to them.* ***Their fruit will serve for food and their leaves for healing.***
> *Ezekiel 47:12, NIV*

We can learn a lot from this example of the coming biosphere. These trees will grow leaves having tremendous medicinal value, far more so than natural remedies of today. Because of the leaves (vs. needles), the trees appear to be deciduous. But not exactly, because "deciduous" means to shed annually, as leaves are shed – unlike these leaves, which "will not wither." Though evergreens bear nuts sometimes, these trees bear fruit. Not only that, but fruit of various kinds; and not just in the regular growing seasons we know, but all year long, incessantly! These facts all point to a new product of nature: a form of evergreen-deciduous fruit tree, which also has miraculously healing leaves.

God's glory is clearly affecting the agriculture here! In fact, we are told that this miraculous tree-vitality goes beyond the effects of even the foretold natural rejuvenation in general. These particular trees will have a very special water source that explains their uniqueness: "*because the water from the sanctuary flows to them.*" Unlike all rejuvenated tree species on the horizon, these growing beside the Temple River will exude life and health in a unique and exquisite manner befitting their proximity to, and source from, the Presence of God Almighty. All of this, of course, reminds us of Eden's Tree of Life.

---

[494] Revelation 20:24.

But will the miracle of creation's emancipation stop there, at the shores of the Temple River? No! When all nature is *"liberated from its bondage to decay and brought into the glorious freedom of the children of God,"* we can expect to see the impact all over. We might expect to see evidence in God's Word of pervasive natural healing – which we do!

> *In that day the Branch of the Lord will be beautiful and glorious, and* **the fruit of the land will be the pride and glory of the survivors in Israel.**
> Isaiah 4:2, NIV

> *The* **desert** *and the* **parched land** *will be glad; the* **wilderness** *will rejoice and* **blossom.** *Like the crocus, 2 it will* **burst into bloom***; it will* **rejoice greatly** *and* **shout for joy.** *The* **glory of Lebanon** *will be given to it, the* **splendor of Carmel and Sharon***; they will see the glory of the Lord, the splendor of our God... 4b he will come with vengeance; with divine retribution he will come to save you... 6b* **Water will gush forth in the wilderness** *and* **streams in the desert.** *7 The* **burning sand** *will become a* **pool***, the* **thirsty ground bubbling springs.** *In the haunts where jackals once lay,* **grass** *and* **reeds** *and* **papyrus** *will grow.*
> Isaiah 35:1-7, portions, NIV

This is astounding! Within Israel (at the least), areas presently characterized by desert, parchedness, wilderness, burning and thirst will be entirely reworked in their fundamental ecology. In the Day of our Lord they will be known instead for gladness and rejoicing of natural splendor, including flowers blossoming and "bursting" everywhere.

As a kind of exclamation mark in this prophecy, the foliage of the Nile is deliberately brought up: *"reeds and papyrus."* Even these aquatic plants, clear reminders of Israel's "nativity" out of Egyptian captivity, will grow where historically desert regions still lie. Let that sink in: plants that can only grow where their roots are perpetually immersed will have that opportunity within dry wilderness regions of the Holy Land. And each of these little plants will loudly declare God's faithfulness to His people and His own Word.

Enabling this foretold aquatic foliage, we have seen that springs of water will gush forth in these same barren realms, resulting in frequent pools, streams and rivers. The presence of this pervasive water is a key factor in the prophesied botanical transformation, an "impossible" (and miraculous) phenomenon that is often remarked upon in prophecy.

> **You care for the land and water it; you enrich it abundantly. The streams of God are filled with water to provide the people with grain, for so you have ordained it.**
> Psalms 65:9, NIV

> ... *streams of water will flow on every high mountain and every lofty hill.*
> Isaiah 30:25b, NIV

> **There the Lord will be our Mighty One.** *It will be like* **a place of broad rivers and streams.**
> Isaiah 33:21, NIV

> *See, I am doing a* **new thing!** **Now it springs up;** *do you not perceive it? I am making a way in the desert and* **streams in the wasteland.** *20 The wild animals honor me, the jackals and the owls, because* **I provide water in the desert and streams in the wasteland...**
> Isaiah 43:19-20a, NIV

> **I will lead them beside streams of water** *on a level path where they will not stumble, because I am Israel's father, and Ephraim is my firstborn son.*
> Jeremiah 31:9b, NIV

This "new thing" is just that: <u>new</u>, in all the geological history of the Middle East. Water, useful and pleasing, and not in a destructive manner, will absolutely *permeate* the Holy Land in the coming Day. Why would God do this? One reason is that His Creation will be intended, with unrestrained vitality, to reflect and symbolize His own nurturing Life.

> *For* **I will pour water on the thirsty land,** *and* **streams on the dry ground; I will pour out my Spirit on your offspring,** *and my blessing on your descendants. 4* **They will spring up like grass in a meadow, like poplar trees by flowing streams.**
> Isaiah 44:3-4, NIV

So while physical water is being poured upon His Land, God will pour out His Spirit upon His people. They will shine and prosper in His life; and creation's enveloping health will effectively signify this abundance. The overarching declaration, every way one turns, will be unmistakable:

> *He is like a tree planted by streams of water, which yields its fruit in season and whose leaf does not wither. Whatever he does prospers.*
> Psalms 1:3, NIV

Here again we see the motif of "unwithering leaf," the same kind growing from trees planted beside the Temple River. When someone holds one of those leaves in his or her hand, they will be holding Psalm 1:3 in a marvelous personal way, seeing in its perpetual moisture the lesson that *all* life flows from God. When someone drinks tea made from those leaves, they will find healing in their body; and when they consume fruit from one of those trees, they will sense spiritual nourishment as well as physical. When drinking from the Temple River, there will be a sensation reminiscent of God's Spirit. And when someone walks beside any of Israel's other rivers and experiences the gardens flourishing all around, it will seem as if God's life-blessing is being poured out everywhere in a beautiful, colorful, and tactile expression.

Here on God's Mountain, the mighty trees of the Temple River will lead the way for all creation; from this Mountain the Temple River will flow, eventually touching all waters of the Earth. From the Creator, restoration and rejuvenation will proceed throughout His Creation. The curse will be eradicated, its effects overcome. And once more, all will be as it first was: *Good.*[495]

Eden's Answer

When all this natural exuberance breaks out, it will be as though nature, in all its "kingdoms," is celebrating. In fact, that is the case. When Messiah walks this Earth again, the Creator will be doing so as well: for that is Who He is[496]. Furthermore, Jesus is the final "Adam," the progenitor of God's eternal life in any of us[497]. Adam was the first ruler of all animate life on Earth[498]; Jesus has that authority as well, and far more. In regards to nature, He is therefore both Creator and Ruler. When Jesus comes, all Creation will therefore sense it; and when Jesus frees it from the Curse, the entire natural realm will celebrate in Him!

In short, what is coming to this world is a "garden" that surpasses its original counterpart, Eden. So as we explore God's Mountain, we must also touch upon this sub-plot of God's Garden.

At the start of this Earth's story came the Garden of Eden; at the end of that story, during Earth's final 1,000 years, will be the garden of God's Mountain. There are many connections between the two, and we can briefly cite a few here. In the original garden, food was plentiful, varied, and always available[499]. Botany was not invaded by weeds and other destructive influences [500]. Water was

---

[495] Genesis 1:31.
[496] E.g., John 1:1-3; Ephesians 3:9.
[497] 1 Corinthians 15:22, 45-47.
[498] Genesis 1:28.
[499] Genesis 1:29-30.
[500] Genesis 3:17-19.

abundant, with springs of water everywhere emerging from the ground[501] and Eden's main river being the headwaters of the major rivers of its day[502]. God, in person, walked with His first people here[503], in the garden He had Himself designed and planted[504]. So the point here is this: that we have seen all of these same attributes describing the coming Mountain.

When the superior Garden arrives, these connections will be unmistakable. When the Lord walks here with His people, Eden of old will be far eclipsed; yet it will have been the prophetic precursor. The awesome message will be plain: God indicated at the very beginning what He was going to do; He has been in sovereign control ever since; and He has shown His faithfulness through *all* episodes of the human story.

With all that as motivation, let's look at additional evidence for the coming Mountain being the final "Eden." For if this world is to once again witness those original conditions of creation, we would expect to see one more key aspect, related to big differences with the animal realm of today.

In Adam's time, animals were not naturally fearful of man. In fact, that kind of fear only came after the Flood[505]. Before then, not only were people herbivorous[506], but all animals were as well[507]. So if Eden returns, we should expect evidence that animals will again be friendly to each other and to humans, and not be trying to eat each other. And that is *exactly* what is prophesied!

> ***The wolf also shall dwell with the lamb***, *and **the leopard shall lie down with the kid;*** *and **the calf and the young lion and the fatling together;*** *and **a little child shall lead them.*** *7 And **the cow and the bear shall feed;*** *their young ones shall lie down together: and the **lion shall <u>eat straw</u> like the ox.*** *8 And the sucking **child shall play on the hole of the asp**, and the weaned **child shall put his hand on the cockatrice'*** [viper or adder] ***den.*** *9 They shall not hurt nor destroy **<u>in all my holy mountain</u>:*** *for the earth shall be full of the knowledge of the Lord, as the waters cover the sea. 10 And in that day there shall be a root of Jesse, which shall*

---

[501] Genesis 2:6.
[502] Genesis 2:10-14.
[503] Genesis 3:8.
[504] Genesis 2:8.
[505] Genesis 9:2-3. This was also when God first permitted mankind to eat meat.
[506] Or, at least, supposed to be. The wickedness before the flood was of every form, and most likely included eating animals – against God's permission. Without any natural fear of man, many species were perhaps on the verge of being wiped out.
[507] As demonstrated in the cooperation with Adam (in the naming story) and Noah (in the ark story). In both stories, animals of every kind were in close proximity and cooperative, never trying to eat one another. The new carnivorous factor of Genesis 9:3 appears to have affected animals as well as people.

stand for an ensign of the people; to it shall the Gentiles seek: and his rest shall be glorious.
Isaiah 11:6-10, KJV

No *lion will be there* [on the Lord's Highway], **nor will any ferocious beast get up on it**; *they will not be found there. But only the redeemed will walk there...*
Isaiah 35:9, NIV

The wolf and the lamb shall feed together, *and* **the lion shall <u>eat straw</u> like the bullock**: *and dust shall be the serpent's meat. They shall not hurt nor destroy* **<u>in all my holy mountain</u>**, *saith the Lord.*
Isaiah 65:23, KJV

It is really hard to conceive of lions routinely eating grass or straw. It is hard to imagine any sane person allowing their toddler to play with venomous snakes. It is almost impossible to consider one's self (let alone a small child) playing with a *wild* [508] wolf, leopard or lion, leading them from one place to another, with friendly cooperation on the animals' part. It is equally difficult to picture any major carnivore lying next to a vulnerable herbivore (of any size), and the two getting a peaceful night's sleep.

We are so used to reading these verses that maybe we should consider different animals with the same phenomenon. For the carnivore side, think of a hyena, cobra or grizzly bear. Coming up next to one of these and taking a nap, picture a baby llama, a poodle pup, or a bunny. Would the nap be quick, with the carnivore having an easy snack? No! For the rule is a general one: *"They shall not hurt nor destroy in all my holy mountain, saith the Lord."* So here in the animal kingdom, we see this additional and massive sign of Eden's return.

True, this phenomenon is mainly declared for the Lord's Mountain (and His royal highways leading to it). This is as it should be, for it glories the Creator. When this calming effect in the animal kingdom comes, it is only fitting that it reaches its crescendo in the Garden of God. Furthermore, in addition to all the other wonders to come, this will assist mankind's attention on this most holy region and provide even more motivation for the annual pilgrimages[509].

But it does not stop there, for the entire world will be touched by the coming "Eden effect." We have already seen that other kinds of creation's healing will echo throughout Israel, and reverberate throughout the world. Especially in the animal kingdom, we can expect the healing to be global. For it was not in Eden that the animals were made to fear man, but as they exited the

---

[508] The implication of these prophecies is that the animals in view have not been tamed, but are living freely, in the open, yet exhibiting new behavioral norms.
[509] Zechariah 14:16-19.

ark on Mount Ararat. It was a separation experienced by the entire world, and to our present day; and it is another wound that only Jesus can and will heal[510]. When this antagonism is done away with, the resultant restoration of the animal kingdom to its original form will be seen by all.

In all these natural aspects, the overlaying idea is that of a very special place: a Mountain-Garden standing out as the marvelous apex of a creation now freed and rejuvenated. As such, it will be the earthly counterpart of the Garden of God in Heaven. Yet here, on this Earth, our Lord will walk with His people and enjoy once again "the cool of the day,"[511] and the wonders of His creation, with them.

In the coming garden, we can expect pools, rivers, lakes, streams, waterfalls, fountains; forests, flower gardens, meadows, orchards, natural vistas of many kinds. We are told of some of these wonders, but the rest we can only imagine. For people to enjoy them, whether in large gatherings or in small groups, we can expect "level paths" of various widths; bridges, plazas, overlooks with parapets, and special landscaping[512]; and grand ramps or staircases leading up to the Temple.

Countless and wonderful details such as these remain to be disclosed to us; yet the Artist-King knows all their intricacies. The matter remains His wonderful surprise for His "bride," all people in covenant with Him.

> *No eye has seen, no ear has heard, no mind has conceived what God has prepared for those who love him.*
> *1 Corinthians 2:9b, NIV*

Whatever these coming wonders may be, they will find their epicenter in the Holy Mountain.

The Shining Peak

We have explored many things on the Lord's Mountain, and have seen through Scripture's binoculars numerous jaw-dropping wonders awaiting those who live in the next age of this world. But before we pack up and go home, as it were, there is one last aspect of the Mountain to examine, and it deserves this honored place in our expedition's conclusion.

---

[510] I John 3:8, with Romans 8:19-22.
[511] Genesis 3:8.
[512] Genesis 2:15. After all, this is the new Eden; and the Lord will have many willing people available to tend His garden, perhaps having roles echoing Adam's original one.

Once more, this additional feature relates to Eden, both primordial and prophesied. But while we have discussed animals, plants, water, and even the soil in this regard, our final subject relates to the very atmosphere.

In the Genesis account, we see that there was the "firmament" consisting of the air and nearer atmosphere, where birds fly. This is simply the visible sky we are familiar with, but in our time populated not only by birds but also planes, fireworks, and the occasional drone. But before the flood, we are informed of something additional that we are *not* familiar with. We are told that above that earlier sky was another layer of "water"[513] which evidently collapsed in the events of Noah's flood[514].

To this day the subject of the antediluvian "canopy" provides fuel for debate. We don't need to get into the arguments here; but we *can* acknowledge that something was going on with Eden's skies. Its atmosphere was clearly different from what we are familiar with, involving far more suspension of moisture and perhaps more reflection of certain solar rays.

If Eden's conditions return, we might expect to see clues in Scripture. We might anticipate hints that something special will be happening in the sky over God's Mountain. And once again, this is precisely the case!

> *In that day the Branch of the Lord will be beautiful and glorious... 5 ...***over all the glory will be a canopy. 6 It will be a shelter and shade from the heat of the day, and a refuge and hiding place from the storm and rain.**
> *Isaiah 4:2a, 5b-6, NIV*

It is clearly explained here that some kind of "canopy" in the sky will once again be a permanent natural feature. We are not told of its specific physical composition, only of the impact of its presence. For over God's Mountain, this amazing atmospheric feature will provide:

- ☐ Shade – diminishing uncomfortably bright sunshine
- ☐ Coolness – reducing the heat from the sun's rays
- ☐ Barrier – preventing rain and other forms of precipitation

This canopy will not be something out in space, or in upper atmospheric levels. It will be much closer, like an umbrella for the rain falling from above it, clearly making it a lower-atmosphere phenomenon. Just as in Eden's mysterious atmospheric makeup, the coming phenomenon will prevent rainfall – at least in any damaging or unpleasant amount, and at least in the vicinity of the Sacred

---

[513] Genesis 1:6-8, 20.
[514] The "floodgates of Heaven were opened" (Genesis 7:11). There had been no rain until this event (Genesis 2:5-6), indicating a massive atmospheric alteration.

District. So whatever form of canopy was held above or within Eden's skies, the coming version will be near in altitude, that is, lower than any rain clouds potentially forming above the high peak of the coming Mountain.

Beyond natural characteristics, the new "canopy" will miraculously declare additional important messages. The first message harkens back to the story of mankind's redemptive emergence, in the *Exodus*. Referring to the Mountain of God to come, here is the complete version of a verse just cited:

> **Then the Lord will create over all of Mount Zion** and over those who assemble there **a cloud of smoke by day and a glow of flaming fire by night; over all the glory will be a canopy.**
> Isaiah 4:5, NIV

So over God's Mountain there will not only be something special in the natural atmosphere, but also a *supernatural* phenomenon in the sky beneath it: fire by night and smoke by day, just as the original Israelites experienced!

> *And* **the Lord went before them by day in a pillar of a cloud, to lead them the way; and by night in a pillar of fire, to give them light; to go by day and night.** 22 He took not away **the pillar of the cloud by day, nor the pillar of fire by night,** *from before the people.*
> Exodus 13:21-22, KJV

What a spectacularly encouraging testimony to God's faithfulness this will be to all citizens of Israel and all people coming to this Mountain year after year. For not only will there be a "canopy" over the new "Eden," there will be a factual return of the smoke and fire witnessed in the Exodus. The potency of these two signs will be easily felt by all who witness them.

The fire and smoke will be directly over the peak of God's Mountain, directly above the Temple from which His brilliant glory will emanate. Does all this have precedent? Yes indeed, for this relationship between atmospheric fire and Divine glory is seen with the original "pillar of fire" and the Tabernacle:

> *And it came to pass,* **as Moses entered into the tabernacle, the cloudy pillar descended, and stood at the door of the tabernacle, and the Lord talked with Moses. 10 And all the people saw the cloudy pillar stand at the tabernacle door: and all the people rose up and worshipped, every man in his tent door.**
> Exodus 33:9-10, KJV

It may well be that the coming "cloudy" pillar of fire and smoke will, like its predecessor, descend closer to the courts of the Temple when our High

Priest[515], Jesus, comes before His Father's Presence. Either way, there is clearly an explicit relationship between the Exodus pillar of fire and smoke and the coming Millennial version. During the Exodus, promises of God's glorious protection were displayed through these signs. In the coming reign of Messiah, those promises will be fulfilled; yet the signs will be repeated, making the connection easy to see for everyone.

One more point about protection. We have seen that the atmospheric canopy will comprise a protective shield against unwanted precipitation and radiant energy, just as Isaiah wrote. But, with the pillar of fire and smoke, it will also shield God's people against the final "storm" of military conflict at the very end of the Millennium. God Almighty will protect Jerusalem when the Enemy and his followers make one last assault[516]; and as with the Exodus story, Isaiah has told us that His fiery pillar will be involved.

Now, another point about "shade." One might first think that this rain-preventing and shade-providing marvel would result in darkness over the Temple area. But not so! Since the canopy will be "above all the glory," it will reside above the supernatural atmospheric fire of the pillar and reflect that same luminescence back upon the Temple area and the Mountain in general. We understand "sky glow" when clouds reflect artificial illumination from the ground today. But what an utterly spectacular nighttime sight it will be, when above-ground supernatural illumination is involved!

But there is another source of light beneath the canopy: the glory of God Himself. Ezekiel, our prophetic guide through the Sacred District, is also the greatest seer of God's glory that will come to the new Temple. The prophet carefully portrayed the arrangement of God's glorious "chariot," having fiery wheels, Cherubim, a luminous "expanse" above them, and His "sapphire" throne above all[517]. This was the "glory" that departed from Solomon's Temple long ago[518]. But this *same glorious arrangement* will return to the coming Temple, when it stands upon God's arising Mountain. Within that explicit future context, Ezekiel gives us, for *our* day, these amazing foresights.

> ***I saw the glory of the God of Israel coming from the east.*** *His voice was like the roar of rushing waters, and the land was radiant with his glory. 3 The vision I saw was like the vision I had seen when he came to destroy the city and like the visions I had seen by the Kebar River, and I fell facedown. 4* ***The glory of the Lord entered the temple*** *through the gate facing east. 5 Then the Spirit lifted me up and brought me into the inner court, and* ***the glory of the Lord filled***

---

[515] Hebrews chapters 7 through 9.
[516] Revelation 20:9.
[517] Ezekiel 1 and 10.
[518] Ezekiel 10:18-19, with 11:22-23.

> *the temple... 44:4 ...I looked and saw* **the glory of the Lord filling the temple of the Lord**, *and I fell facedown.*
> Ezekiel 43:2-5, 44:4b, NIV

These things will take place in a time not too far ahead, on what will become the peak of the Mountain of God. Exceeding the marvels of Eden's canopy in the sky, surpassing the wonders of the fire and smoke pillar witnessed by Moses and the Israelites, there will be the awe-striking fact of God's very real, very beautiful, and very dangerous[519] glory on this earth. The Father's Presence will again be felt in this creation, not just for a prophet to witness, or occurring when a historical high priest entered the Most Holy Place. God's glory will be evident to all that come near His Mountain, and its effects will be experienced throughout the Earth. Even the ancient words of the Cherubim can be heard as prophetic here:

> *... and one cried unto another, and said, Holy, holy, holy, is the Lord of hosts:* **the whole earth is full of his glory.**
> Isaiah 6:3, KJV

Portions of God's glory will presumably "escape" the Temple, for no architecture can possibly contain it[520]. The Temple-glory will therefore merge with the luminescence of the smoke-fire pillar, producing the combined brilliance of what the canopy will reflect back downward. Both these sources will be forms of God's glory, radiating from the Source of all power and life. Even if only partially understood, the effect will be plain for those seeing it. For all will felt compelled to do as Ezekiel did: to fall facedown, worship the glorious Lord Almighty, and in their own small way reflect His light back upon Him.

Such is the Glory that will radiate from His Temple, by night and day. By night, the fire will accompany the glory, just as in the Exodus drama. By day, a cloud of smoke will accompany the glory, even as it does God's throne in Heaven right now[521]. And "above **all** the glory," natural and divine, will be this amazing and mysterious feature in the skies over new Eden: the canopy. We don't know exactly what this returning or augmented feature of nature will be. But whatever its physical-chemical composition, it will shield God's people and reflect God's brilliance in a display everyone will see.

The coming canopy will perform an additional function, one that goes even beyond all we have discussed. The Millennial-era brightness over God's Mountain, though astounding, will point toward something far greater: His

---

[519] E.g., Exodus 33:20.
[520] 1 Kings 8:27; 2 Chronicles 2:6, 6:18.
[521] E.g., Isaiah 6:4.

ongoing physical glory, providing illumination for eternal City and Earth forever, far more than even the sun might do:

> *The city does not need the sun or the moon to shine on it, for* **the glory of God gives it light, and the Lamb is its lamp.** *24 The nations will walk by its light, and the kings of the earth will bring their splendor into it.*
> Revelation 21:23-25, NIV

In the coming and conclusive age of this creation, glorious things will signal that *final* age and *eternal* creation in which God's Glory is *the* light, at all levels and in all senses. The Name of our God will reside in the mighty Temple; and His Son, David's "glorious Branch[522]," will reign over all the earth as Father's Prince and our King.

These events won't be within the ultimate eternal setting, but will rather announce it. In doing so, they will form the amazing conclusion to this present realm, in its closing and seventh Day[523] of rest long ago presaged in the Genesis story. The soon-arising Mountain of God, with the City on its southern slope, will also be the final symbol in this present creation of the Mountain and City in Heaven, the one that will last forever:

> *You have not come to a mountain that can be touched and that is burning with fire; to darkness, gloom and storm... 22* **But you have come to Mount Zion, to the heavenly Jerusalem, the city of the living God.** *You have come to thousands upon thousands of angels in joyful assembly, 23 to the church of the firstborn, whose names are written in heaven. You have come to God, the judge of all men, to the spirits of righteous men made perfect, 24 to Jesus the mediator of a new covenant, and to the sprinkled blood that speaks a better word than the blood of Abel.*
> Hebrews 12:18, 22-24, NIV

That eternal Mountain and City will blend with the completely new creation, lasting for all eternity. But they will have had their final overture here, in creation's healing and restoration in the near future. The arising Mountain will be a mighty prelude to the eternal age, and trumpet its message for a thousand years. Yet it will signal the fulfillment of so much in this age, and is therefore something we should greatly look forward to. Indeed, in a time soon to come, on *this* Earth and in this *restored* creation,

> *The moon will be abashed, the sun ashamed; for* **the Lord Almighty will reign on Mount Zion and in Jerusalem, and before its elders, gloriously.**
> *Isaiah 24:23, NIV*

---

[522] Isaiah 4:2.
[523] Combining the idea of the Day of the Lord, the seventh day of rest, and the fact that a day to the Lord is one thousand years (Psalms 90:4; 2 Peter 3:8).

Once again we are told that God's coming Mountain will be illuminated by His sheer glory. Once more we are reminded that, by day or by night, His Presence is the awesome light for His people; and visibly so, here on His Mountain where He is the Source of great brilliance at its apex. From Temple and Pillar, the canopy will reflect His glory back onto the Mountain, causing all to glow by His own Persona. Pilgrims such as you or I, whether arriving by day or by night, will observe this awesome brilliance; from far off, they will see God's glorious Mountain.

This, then, is the shining peak on our horizon, the luminous summit of God's soon-arising Mountain. It reminds us of the original mountain in Eden[524]; it reflects the holy mountaintop presently in Heaven; and it points toward the new and eternal creation where all will have been completed. This is the gleaming height to which our expedition has brought us.

I hope that this journey has encouraged your personal expedition, as you maintain your grip on Jesus' hand and keep your eyes upon the Father's Word. Between now and the Mountain's arising, I hope that, whatever happens in your own journey, you abide in trust of the Lord's leading, knowing that He will surely complete the weaving of your own wonderful story, and the planting of your unique garden.

---

[524] Evident in that Eden's single river formed the headwaters of the four major rivers in the world of that time.

Selected Bibliography

Beitzel, Barry J. <u>The Moody Atlas of Bible Lands</u>.
Chicago, IL: Moody Publishers, Inc., 2000.

Gundry, Robert H. <u>The Church and the Tribulation: A Biblical Examination of Posttribulationism</u>.
Grand Rapids, MI: Zondervan Publishing House, 1973.

Howard, Kevin and Rosenthal, Marvin. <u>The Feasts of the Lord: God's Prophetic Calendar From Calvary to the Kingdom</u>.
Nashville, TN: Thomas Nelson, Inc., 1994.

Ladd, George Eldon. <u>A Commentary on the Revelation of John</u>.
Grand Rapids, MI: Eerdmans Publishing Company, 1972.

Orr, James, ed. <u>International Standard Bible Encyclopedia</u> (ISBE).
Grand Rapids, MI: Eerdmans Publishing Company, 1939.

Jennings, Clifford A. <u>The Approaching Country</u>.
Highland, MD: CubitHound Publishing, 2014.

<u>PC Study Bible</u>
Seattle, WA: Biblesoft.

About the Author

Cliff Jennings lives near Baltimore, Maryland with his wife Linda. They are the proud parents of Rebecca, Hunter, Leah and Bethany. Cliff is a mechanical design-engineer who enjoys studies in Biblical prophecy, particularly from a technical perspective.

If you would like to learn more about further work in this book series, or give feedback on what you've read here, please visit our website: www.EarthAwaits.com.

www.ingramcontent.com/pod-product-compliance
Lightning Source LLC
Chambersburg PA
CBHW022110040426
42450CB00006B/653